PAUL V. McNUTT

PORTRAIT
OF A
HOOSIER STATESMAN

Paul V. McNutt:

PORTRAIT OF A
HOOSIER STATESMAN

By

I. GEORGE BLAKE

Professor of History-Political Science
Chairman, Division of Social Sciences
FRANKLIN COLLEGE

Central Publishing Company, Inc.

Indianapolis, Indiana

1966

TO OUR GRANDCHILDREN

SHERRY LYNN

DAVID BLAKE

LESLIE CAROL

HOBBS

DESCENDANTS OF HOOSIER PIONEERS

TABLE OF CONTENTS

Introduction By Governor Roger D. Branigin

Preface

Illustrations Follow Page 192.
Unless otherwise indicated, all were furnished to the author
by Mrs. Roy Garrett Watson.

From the INTRODUCTION

By Governor Roger D. Branigin

Indiana's 34th Governor Paul Vories McNutt, took the oath of office on January 9, 1933, ending sixteen consecutive years of Republican leadership. He came to the office from the campus, not from the legislature nor the courts as had most of his predecessors.

"Both the lineage and the certain sire" as Edmund Spenser phrased it, were good. He grew to be a handsome man, of strong body and excellent mind. His family was not of great wealth but they were able to give him unusual educational opportunities at Indiana University and the Harvard Law School. His scholastic record in literature and the law was superior.

After little more than a year at the Morgan County bar, he joined the law faculty at Indiana University and, until he became governor fifteen years later, he was by choice and by chance teacher, soldier, loyal Legionnaire.

Along the way Paul made fast friends among students, the faculty, the army, the American Legion. He was aggressive and ambitious; his critics even thought him arrogant and snobbish. He made enemies, but they were not so effective as the small, intensely loyal band of Hoosier Democrats who had great plans for their man of high talent.

They guided his steps through the Indiana Department of the Legion to the post of Commander and a little later to the high office of National Commander of the American Legion at the famed San Antonio Convention.

Finally, with the 1932 election coming on and with the depression auguring well for a change in state and national administrations, Paul V. McNutt and his skilled advisers led by Frank M. McHale, made the fateful decision. Paul would seek the highest office in Indiana—the governorship.

[xi]

What is past is prologue. "Paul V." is ready in the wings, handsomely equipped in voice and in heart. He steps upon the stage, young, attractive, and vigorous. By the skilled hand of Dr. George Blake, all of the excitement of those days, now three decades old, are preserved within these covers. You can feel the very presence of the Governor, cheer his successes, discount his failures, sympathize with his sorrows according to your estimate of the man. Well, here he is—"tall, tan and terrific" as he really was—from student to statesman. No higher tribute can be paid to his biographer.

Roger D. Branigin

Roger D. Branigin
Governor of Indiana

November 12, 1966
State House
Indianapolis

PREFACE

In the Foreword of Charles N. Thompson's *Sons of the Wilderness* (Indiana Historical Society Publications, vol. 12, 1937), Professor John C. Parish of the University of California is quoted: "Historical understanding is perhaps advanced as much by the biographies of secondary individuals as by the reiterated accounts and appraisals of the lives of the truly great." To better understand and appreciate the services of one of the leading Hoosiers of this century has been the reason for the preparation of this book.

To write a biography of a man as contemporary as Paul V. McNutt has not been easy. Only a little more than a decade has elapsed since his death. Many people are still living who knew him well, and as with all men of political significance he has his fervid admirers and avid enemies.

As an historian I have endeavored to be objective in my presentation and conclusions, although I am sure some will accuse me of political partisanship. But when one works closely over the years with certain materials he may be forgiven somewhat if he comes to have some slight affinity toward his subject, even though he may be of the opposite political persuasion.

Paul V. McNutt was no common man. He became a distinguished Hoosier who rose from a small county-seat town to within grasp of the highest honor which the American people could bestow. From the youngest dean of a major law school to the Ambassadorship to the young Republic of the Philippines, McNutt's life was a succession of outstanding achievements in the field of public service.

In the collection of material for this biography I have been assisted by a great number of individuals to whom I wish to acknowledge my indebtedness. First of all I am grateful to Franklin College for the grant of a Sabbatical from my teaching duties in order to do the necessary research. Mrs. Roy

Garrett Watson (the former Mrs. Paul V. McNutt) and her daughter Miss Louise McNutt have been most generous in supplying me with materials, and have assisted me in various personal ways which I deeply appreciate. Mr. Henry A. Dudley of Washington, D. C., and Mr. Frank A. Celentano of New York City, former law partners of McNutt, were most helpful in making my research easier. Mr. G. Bowdoin Craighill of Washington gave me valuable assistance at the start of the project. The staffs of the Library of Congress, the National Archives, and the New York Public Library placed their McNutt holdings at my disposal. I am especially indebted to Miss Elizabeth Drewry, Director of the Franklin D. Roosevelt Memorial Library at Hyde Park, and her associates, for their interest and cooperation. Much important material was obtained from the Lilly Library of Indiana University. For their assistance I wish to thank Dr. David A. Randall, Librarian, Mrs. Doris M. Reed, Curator of Manuscripts, and Dr. Elfrieda Lang of the Lilly staff. The Indiana State Library at Indianapolis likewise aided me in my research. Special thanks are due Mrs. Hazel Hopper and Miss Dorothy Riker. I am also indebted to Mr. Rand Burnette who allowed me the use of his Master's thesis on a phase of McNutt's political career.

The pictures in the book were supplied by Mrs. Watson, Miss Grace Woody, Miss Margaret Paddock, and Miss Thelma Sines, to whom I wish to express my thanks. Permission to quote brief passages from the books listed in the Bibliography has been granted by the various publishers. Numerous others have helped me in many ways, but it would be impossible to list them all. To those who are not mentioned my appreciation is no less sincere. Special thanks, however, must be given to Mr. Frank McHale, former National Democratic Committeeman from Indiana, for his many courtesies and words of encouragement. Mr. Harold Feightner, newspaper writer and political reporter during McNutt's governorship, has read the entire manuscript and has offered many suggestions for the proper interpretation of various aspects of politics during the depression years. I am happy to acknowledge the valuable advice and assistance of Colonel Robert L. Moorhead, who also read the entire manuscript and made important suggestions.

To my personal friend, the Honorable Roger D. Branigin, Governor of Indiana, I am most grateful for his willingness to write the "Introduction" to this book. Mrs. Vernice V. Irish has labored in typing the manuscript from the hand-written copy. She has also done much of the proofreading. Without her expert skill my work would have been infinitely more difficult. And finally, special gratitude is given to my wife, who has been a real help every step of the long journey.

I. George Blake

Franklin, Indiana
December 1, 1966

CHAPTER I

Laying the Foundation

"I see for thee a great future, and thou art poring over books of great size wherein are written words of law. And it shall be that thou shalt write for thyself a great name in the annals of the world."

With uncanny accuracy, the prophecy of the Martinsville High School senior class of 1909 foretold the career of Paul Vories McNutt, whose wheedling and argument with the school trustees finally won their reluctant permission to print a yearbook, which was appropriately named *The Nuisance*. McNutt became its editor. Beneath his name in the class roll are the flippant remarks, "a villain, a liar, a mean horsethief. All these and more make an editor-in-chief."[1]

Such remarks were common in the juvenile publications of the day, and merely emphasized the respect which the students had for their peers. But reading between the lines, one can detect the beginnings of envy and jealousy toward one of their number who was already displaying signs of leadership and superiority. For this willowy high-school boy, still showing the physical effects of serious childhood illnesses, was to grow into a commanding six-foot-two-inch giant of 195 pounds.

He was to develop a magnetic personality that swayed men, and was to acquire a tanned, handsome face and prematurely white hair that overwhelmed women instantly. His was to be an active and successful life as a soldier, educator, state governor, political leader, director of gigantic federal government enterprises, ambassador, and corporation lawyer. He was to become the personal friend of presidents, and might have won the highest office in the land for himself, had he chosen to fight for the nomination. But his loyalty to his chief was greater than his own personal aspirations.

Paul Vories McNutt, whose middle name was given by his father in tribute to a family friend, was born on July 19, 1891, in the Johnson County seat town of Franklin, Indiana. The family could trace their ancestry back to the MacNaughts of Kilguharity, County of Kircudbright, Scotland, in the fifteenth century. When they came to America in the eighteenth century, they adopted the simplified spelling of the name. After leaving Scotland they first settled in Northern Ireland, but not finding that region any more to their liking, they continued on to America.[2]

According to one account, the family spent considerable time in northern Ireland before coming to America. It is uncertain just where they first settled in America. In a brief biographical sketch written by Paul McNutt in 1939 it is stated that the family migrated to Indiana from North Carolina by way of Tennessee and Kentucky,[3] although in the same year Paul's father wrote that the family came to Indiana from Ohio.[4]

At any rate, Paul's father, John Crittenden McNutt, was born in Hensley Township, Johnson County, Indiana, on May 25, 1863. He was the son of James and Mahala Hensley Mc-Nutt, whose parents had been among the first settlers in the township. Paul's ancestry on the maternal side went back to a Daniel Prosser who served as a Virginia private in the American Revolutionary War. Paul's grandfather, Jacob M. Neely, was described as "an unrelenting, unchangeable Republican" during the American Civil War. He was a circuit court clerk in Morgan County, Indiana, in his later years. His daughter Ruth was born near Bean Blossom, Brown County, on April 22, 1865. She and John C. McNutt were married at Morgantown on July 7, 1886. Five years later, Paul, their only child, was born.[5]

John C. McNutt was serving as prosecutor of Johnson and Shelby counties when Paul was born, but the following year on the expiration of his term he accepted an appointment as librarian of the Indiana State Supreme Court Library. Consequently the family moved to Indianapolis and took rooms in a boarding house in the vicinity of 12th Street and College Avenue.[6]

Almost from the time that he could walk Paul was a constant companion of his father, and a close friendship developed between them. As a boy Paul was not very strong, and his mother had to keep a close watch on him. But with his toy garden rake and his popgun he would play around the house, or accompany his father to the law library where he was fascinated by the huge legal tomes. He attended the first grade of an Indianapolis school on Ashland Avenue. Apparently he was a normal boy. The story is told by one of his contemporaries that he was severely reprimanded on one occasion by his mother when he refused to eat his soup because "it was too damned hot."[7]

In 1889 the elder McNutt gave up his library position and moved to Martinsville, where he established a law practice which he continued almost until his death. His uncle, Cyrus Finley McNutt, had also practiced there before going to Bloomington as professor in the Indiana University law school.

When the legislature refused to appropriate money for the law school, Cyrus moved to Terre Haute where he practiced law for many years, and was judge of the superior court there. Paul's father studied law in Cyrus' office in 1883.[8]

It was in Martinsville that Paul received all of his elementary and secondary education, with the exception of the brief period in Indianapolis. But it wasn't easy at first for the city-bred boy to make the adjustment to the ways of the boys of this small resort and farming community. At the end of his first day in the second grade at Bucktown school, at the north end of the town, he was thrown into the creek as a baptism for his courtly manners and his Little Lord Fauntleroy appearance, with its ruffles and lace.[9]

This experience was the very thing which was needed to induct Paul into the fellowship of the gang. His mother had always taught him not to fight, but one day the boys chased him home from school and he demanded that he be allowed to fight for his rights. His mother finally gave her consent. His "city-boy clothes" were packed away in deference to "the crowd." The next day he came home with torn clothes and a broken umbrella. He had tried to whip the entire class, and had succeeded in winning a place for himself among his Bucktown oppressors.[10]

From then on for the rest of his school days in Martinsville, Paul was one of the gang, and a leader in their various activities, from harmless pranks to more serious types of mischief. He did his share of Halloween tick-tackings and tying cows to doorknobs and shuffling books in school desks on nightly prowls. But at the same time he was a leader in worthwhile extra-curricular activities. Besides being president of his senior class, he organized a drama club and played a lead role in the class play, *A Cricket on the Hearth*. From this there developed an interest in the theatre which remained with him throughout his life. He also excelled in scholarship, being highest in his class.[11] One of his teachers declared that he was the most nearly perfect pupil she ever had. In debates he would toss his head emphatically in arguments as much as to say "I've investigated and I know." He made friends easily among both sexes in school.[12]

Things didn't always go well with Paul, however. His mother was a strict disciplinarian, and she often interfered with his plans. Once he wanted to go to the circus, but he had neglected to do some of his household chores beforehand. When he returned home he had to clean the stairs and hallway five times. They were never neglected again. Once his mother found a pipe and tobacco he had been smoking while tending the furnace, and she disposed of them. This was the last time Paul ever smoked in the basement.

Paul became a freshman at Indiana University in the fall of 1909. Although his great-uncle Cyrus McNutt had been dean of the law school in the 1870's, and Cyrus' son had been professor there at one time, the decision to enter the state university was made by Paul without such consideration. He soon became affiliated with Beta Theta Pi fraternity, yet he made many friends in other groups as well. He dominated campus and fraternity meetings. He had a cool and calculating manner of knowing what to do and when was the best time to do it. He won the high approbation of his professors for his scholastic accomplishments, and finally won election to Phi Beta Kappa.[13]

While McNutt was winning honors in the classroom, he also took an active part in various campus extra-curricular activities. He played first base on the freshman baseball team, and he found time to throw himself vigorously into campus politics and elections, which gave him an excellent training in organization. He headed Strut and Fret, one of the leading dramatic organizations of the university. He boasted that his own presidency of the organization had given the university a "new regime." He claimed that under his leadership "Strut and Fret had adopted a broader policy, and a larger field of endeavor was entered in a single year than in all subsequent years of activity." He took pride in the fact that the membership had been increased to fifty, and declared that its motto "under the *new regime* has become to produce the best for Indiana."

McNutt was not without his political enemies, however, even at this early date. Campus wits lampooned his dramatic club in the 1913 *Arbutus*, the university yearbook. They called it a "political organization with dramatics as a side issue." They charged that it was composed chiefly of a couple of officers, an *Arbutus* picture, and a mass of student publicity." They criticised the realism which "is cherished sacredly by the management. A youth of 17 in the first act grows a full beard and long hair; but becomes bald and toothless by the time the curtain falls," they scoffed.

McNutt was the stage director of Strut and Fret, and played the leading role in *Quality Street,* by J. M. Barrie, and was the king of France in *Babette,* a seventeenth-century drama. His interest in the theatre which began in high school was continued through college.

The embryonic political generalship of McNutt was displayed when he was elected president of the senior class. Wendell L. Willkie, who was later to be his political rival in the national political arena, was at that time president of the Jackson Club, a campus organization based on the principles of the Democratic party. The two men were then very good friends, and Willkie worked hard for Paul's election. McNutt was also president of the student union and editor of *The Student,* the campus newspaper. His other activities included

[6]

the student council, the board of student marshals, executive committee of the Jackson Club, secretary of the YMCA cabinet, and membership in the Sphinx Club, Writers' Club, and English Club.

The academic program always came first with McNutt. He was a member of other scholastic fraternities besides Phi Beta Kappa, such as Phi Delta Phi and the Order of the Coif.

"Produce the best for Indiana," is the exact wording with which the university yearbook, the *Arbutus*, records for 1913 the thoughts and actions of the youthful McNutt. In all his campus activities he was continually urging his fellow students to produce the best for Indiana.

Shortly after his graduation from the university in 1913, Paul McNutt became a student at Harvard University Law School, where he continued his high academic achievements. His outstanding scholarship won him the presidency of the Harvard Legal Aid Union. Again he found time for many extra-curricular activities. He worked as a Harvard and Boston correspondent for the United Press, and his knowledge of baseball gave him the opportunity to cover the World Series of 1914, 1915, and 1916, when the Boston Braves and the Boston Red Sox fought for the championship.

When he graduated from Harvard in 1916 McNutt returned to Martinsville and went into a law partnership with his father. He had been admitted to the Indiana bar in 1914. At this time the elder McNutt was busy in politics and was serving by appointment as judge on the Indiana Appellate Court. Many of the legal affairs of the office were left in the hands of the junior partner. During this time Paul ran for prosecuting attorney of Morgan County, but was defeated by five votes.[14]

Paul McNutt was not to remain in Martinsville long. In the fall of 1917 Indiana University Law School's dean became ill, and a professor was sought to teach his classes. McNutt was offered the job as assistant professor, and he accepted. When he discussed the offer with his family, he reasoned:

"We'll be going to war soon and I'll go. This will be good experience when I come back."[15]

He enlisted in the army on November 27, 1917, and was sent to Camp Travis, near San Antonio, Texas, where he became a captain in the field artillery.

While attending a dance the following Christmas Eve, McNutt met Kathleen Timolat of San Antonio. She was the only child of H. N. Timolat, a chemist, who had established a wax mill near Bustamente, Mexico, some years before. When the mill was destroyed by bandits during the Mexican Revolution, Timolat returned to the United States and established his residence at San Antonio.

Kathleen and Paul were married on April 20, 1918, in the Episcopal Church at Fort Sam Houston, near San Antonio. Their honeymoon was brief, for the next day Captain McNutt was transferred to the Headquarters Field Artillery Replacement Depot at Camp Jackson, Columbia, South Carolina. On April 29 he changed the beneficiary of his $10,000 War Risk Insurance from his parents to his wife. Her address was given as 1115 W. Agarita Avenue, San Antonio. The document was dated from Martinsville. Kathleen apparently remained in Texas for the time being after he was transferred to South Carolina.[16]

On August 22, 1918, McNutt was appointed a major in the field artillery, and he held this rank for the duration of the war. He was never sent overseas, but spent the rest of the war period in a training program and writing instruction booklets. Had the war continued a few weeks longer he would have been promoted to the rank of lieutenant colonel, according to a document signed by R. M. Danford, Brigadier General, and dated January 3, 1919, from the War Department, Office of Chief of Staff, Washington. Danford considered McNutt "one of the very best reserve officers in the command, and his name was to have been submitted early in December as recommended for promotion to the grade of Lieutenant Colonel."[17]

Danford wrote McNutt a personal letter on the same day, saying he was sorry to hear that he had decided to leave the service, but added:

"Perhaps, however, it is just as well, for I realize how uncertain things are to any officer who is contemplating taking a commission in the Regular Army. If we are fortunate to get from Congress a safe and sound military policy involving universal training, you who have done so well in the business will doubtless have the opportunity to come back. In fact, if I am in a position where I can, I shall write to all of you whom I would like to have and urge you to join."[18]

After McNutt had retired to civilian life, Danford, now a lieutenant colonel at the United States Military Academy at West Point, wrote another letter of recommendation, dated October 15, 1919, to which he attached a certificate signed by Colonel Phillip W. Booker which set forth the various duties which had been assigned to McNutt. It stated that "in each instance this officer was the man picked to command the next higher unit. Seniority did not enter into the selection. The service of this officer was of an unusually high order."[19]

On March 11, 1919, Major McNutt signed a document in which he asserted that he did not desire an appointment to a commission in the regular army. He requested instead that he be given a commission in the Officers' Reserve Corps, in the Field Artillery Section, and asked that he be discharged from his present commission March 14, 1919. This request was endorsed by Colonel Booker, who stated that McNutt "would make a valuable man for the regular army."[20]

Many high tributes were paid to McNutt when he returned to civilian life. The one from Lieutenant Colonel C. P. Parker, Jr., Camp Adjutant, dated Headquarters, Camp Jackson, South Carolina, March 14, 1919, is typical:

"I cannot let you leave the Military Service without expressing to you my great appreciation and high regard for your splendid work as an Officer in the United States Army. It is with deep regret that I see you leave the Army, as I feel that we have lost the services of a very capable officer, services which will be very hard, if not impossible to replace. Your work has been under my close observation for the past seven months and during all that time it deserves much praise. You have performed all duties willingly and in an excellent manner, and produced fine results. I have written many letters of commendation on the services of officers but have never written one with as much pleasure, or one more deserving, than this one. I earnestly hope that if you ever return to the Service that I will have the pleasure of serving with you."[21]

In the meantime McNutt's application for a commission in the Field Artillery, Officers' Reserve Corps, had been received, but on April 15, 1919, in a letter from P. P. Bishop, Brigadier General, General Staff, Chief, Personnel Branch, Operations Division, he was informed that under the law then in effect no man could be commissioned in any grade higher than that of major, except in the Medical Corps, and therefore he could not be given the grade for which he had been recommended at the time of his discharge. He was, however, offered a commission as major. It was hoped "that you will accept this in order that your services may be retained pending the passage of the new Reserve Corps legislation. You will be considered for a higher grade when such is authorized." This appointment was dated April 22, and was effective April 18. Subsequently the law was amended, and on August 21 of that year McNutt was appointed to the rank of lieutenant colonel, effective August 18. He was advanced to full colonel January 8, 1923.[22]

His discharge from active service did not lessen McNutt's active interest and participation in military affairs. From 1924 to 1937 he was commanding officer of the 326th Field Artillery Reserves. As a reservist he helped organize and was elected first president of the Reserve Officers Association of Indiana, serving as vice president of the national organization in 1928.[23]

In 1927 and 1928 he was civilian aide for Indiana to the Secretary of War, and a member of the Army's Fifth Corps Area Advisory Board, 1927 to 1934. At the same time, however, he held membership in the American Peace Society.[24]

During this entire period McNutt took a keen interest in the affairs of the reserve corps. On April 7, 1921, he wrote a long letter to Major A. C. Sandeford, Office of Chief of Staff, War Department, Washington, in which he set forth his views on future policies and activities of the organization. He deplored the limitations of the National Defense Act, which, he said, was a compromise between the regular army and the national guard. Because the reserve corps could not maintain such a lobby as the national guard, he felt that the regular army must protect the interests of the reserve corps if it were to flourish.

McNutt promised to do everything in his power to see the reserve corps live and prosper. He felt that it must be made attractive, but not by pampering and catering to its members. He claimed that "during the piping times of peace it is futile to rely on pure patriotism to sustain an interest in affairs military. During a national emergency it is easy. Afterwards it is not," he said. He had addressed the Indiana University corps twice, "in an effort to induce the members to seek reserve commissions. . . . But the farther we are from a national emergency the harder it is to build a good corps on patriotism."

McNutt continued:

"The youth who will become eligible for the reserve corps will soon be asking 'What is there in it for me?' The question is that of a materialist but the most of us are materialists. What will the answer to the question be? It will be necessary to reply—'You will be held up to the same standards of efficiency as officers of the regular army and national guard. You will be prepared and equipped, at your own expense, at all times. You will be paid only when on active duty. Your pay will not buy your uniforms. All the money available goes to the pay of national guard officers because they drill once a week. Yet you are supposed to know as much as they do. You will be judged by the same standards when called to active service.'"

According to McNutt's reasoning the reserve officer "bears his burden of taxes along with everyone else. There is no reason why he should bear an additional tax simply because he is willing to work to be ready to serve his country in time of need. As the matter now stands a commission in the reserve corps is like saying 'We will use you when we want you and kick you out when we see fit. You will look like part of the army but you are not except in times of emergency'." McNutt concluded the letter with another plea to make the reserve corps attractive.[25]

Soon after his discharge from active military service in 1919 McNutt resumed his teaching in the law school of Indiana University. At the end of the school year President William Lowe Bryan re-appointed him for the year 1920-21 as full professor with an increase in salary from $4,000 to $4,200.[26] On June 11, 1921, his salary was increased to $4,700.[27] He also taught in the summer session. During this period he began to build up his personal library.[28]

McNutt had also branched out into a business enterprise known as the Cantol Wax Company, which had been established by his father-in-law in San Antonio. This business had been reorganized and moved to Bloomington, Indiana, in 1920. Timolat was the president of the company, and McNutt was treasurer. Many of McNutt's friends were induced to buy shares of stock in the business, including Thomas Taggart, the leader of the Democratic party in Indiana, who invested $2,000 on January 17, 1921.[29]

The company apparently experienced considerable financial difficulty in its early years in Indiana. Attached to a tax statement for 1922 is a statement which declares:

"The expense of moving was heavy and this was assumed and paid by the company. The company bought a factory building which had to be repaired and greatly improved. The expenses of organization had to be paid and the company spent considerable in the way of advertising and trying to get the business started in the new location. In consequence the company has sustained considerable loss up to July 1, 1921. Owing to general business situation the business of the company has not been what was expected. We hope that another year will tell a different story."[30]

During this early period Professor McNutt was approached by several law schools with offers to join their faculties, but apparently the offers were not attractive enough to wean him away from the Hoosier institution. One of these overtures was made by E. H. Lindley, chancellor of the University of Kansas at Lawrence, who, in a letter dated June 25, 1921, offered him the deanship of the law school at a salary of $5,600 to $5,800, in addition to remuneration for summer teaching.[31]

Domestic developments, however, precluded McNutt's immediate acceptance of the offer. Mrs. McNutt had been ill following the birth of their daughter Louise, and this together with other complicating factors made it impossible for McNutt to assume new responsibilities at that time. Lindley wrote McNutt on August 21:

"I fully appreciate the difficulties which lay in the way of an affirmative decision. It is possible, however, that we may complete our roster and proceed for a time on the committee basis as last year. I should be glad to have you let me know if you could contemplate coming later in the year, say the second semester. A reply within a few weeks would be satisfactory."[32]

The next day Lindley sent the following telegram to McNutt from Estes Park, Colorado:

"Can you give decision this week service to begin second semester salary six thousand please wire collect address below."

But McNutt finally made his decision not to identify himself with Kansas, and so informed Lindley by letter on September 5. On September 20 Lindley wrote him a letter in which he expressed his regrets "that you will not find it possible to cast your lot with us. I appreciate the many ties which bind you to dear old Indiana. We shall go forward this year on the Committee basis . . . and hope by next year to secure the sort of dean that we have in mind."[33]

Western Reserve University in Cleveland also was interested in McNutt's services during this early period, although not as dean. They were looking for a fifth resident teacher to be added to the law faculty. On February 13, 1922, A. H. Throckmorton wrote him:

"I have been reluctant to approach you in regard to the matter, both because of your local ties at Indiana and also because I should be sorry to take you away from Mr. Hepburn [dean of the Indiana law school], but I know of no one whom I should so gladly welcome to our Faculty as yourself."

The salary would depend very much upon the man chosen, Throckmorton said, but he understood that "it may be as high as $4,500."

Obviously this salary did not appeal to McNutt, although Throckmorton painted a glowing picture of the conditions at Western Reserve. He indicated that the character of the work would be very much the same as at Indiana, the other members of the faculty were congenial, and "Cleveland is an exceptionally attractive place in which to live." The school, he said, was on a graduate basis, and had an attendance of two hundred. He declared they had "every reason to expect a steady development, and it is hoped that the salaries may eventually be advanced to $7,500."[34] Such temptations were not strong enough to lure McNutt away from Indiana.

Besides his duties in the classroom McNutt was extremely active in the field of public relations for the university. During the summer and fall of 1922 he and Mrs. McNutt spent considerable time in New York City and Washington, as well as Chicago, conducting an intensive campaign for the million-dollar Indiana Unversity Memorial Union Fund. In this he was very successful, although apparently there was some criticism of his heavy expenditures. However, the university administration seemed to be generally satisfied, as a letter, dated October 3, 1922, from W. A. Alexander, executive secretary, seems to indicate:

"I fully approve of everything you have done, and am much pleased that you are on the job there. It seems that we need someone who can take the bit in their teeth and go to it, and I can see that you have done that very thing. . . . I feel sure that you will be sent a check for $500.00 as an honorarium for your work. . . . You need not worry about your expenses being excessive in New York. We know that you will proceed as economically as possible, and whatever the bill is, I am sure that it will be taken care of most willingly. Dean Hepburn has secured Hugh E. Willis of the University of North Dakota to do your work, and told me that he was much pleased with him and considered us fortunate in getting him.

. . . I am glad that Mrs. McNutt is with you and is able to render such valuable assistance."[35]

McNutt's services in behalf of the Memorial Fund were also recognized by President Bryan, who wrote him on October 13, 1922:

"I realize what a heartbreaking task you have had and all the more I feel that the thanks of the University are due you for your splendid work. I am profoundly convinced that the thing we are now doing is the most important enterprise that the University has ever had in hand. We must convert the alumni to a new I. U. of sacrifice. Those who like yourself are giving of themselves as well as of their money are doing more than anyone else to make this a new I. U."[36]

The following year was the tenth reunion of the Class of 1913, and Professor McNutt was one of the leaders responsible for its success. Letters were sent to all the class alumni, and the response was gratifying. An alumnus who was later to become famous in Republican circles wrote him from Akron, Ohio, on May 3, 1923:

"My dear Paul: Your letter of invitation to the ten year reunion of the class of 1913 received. If at all possible, I will be present. With kindest personal regards, I am, Very truly yours, Wendell L. Willkie."[37]

Professor McNutt continued to serve his university in many ways. One of his outstanding contributions was as president of the Alumni Association, to which office he was elected in the summer of 1923. The selection was a very popular one, and met with universal approval among the alumni. Letters and telegrams of congratulation were received from all over the country. One, dated August 24, 1923, signed by Ralph V. Sollitt, chairman of the United States Shipping Board, Washington, was typical:

"My dear Paul: . . . I was more than delighted that you were elected President of the Alumni Association. You have done a magnificent piece of work for the University, and have been brought in contact in a truly remarkable way with all of the alumni. It cannot help but do a lot of good later on; and I believe, from a selfish point of view, will be worth the sacrifice that I know you are constantly making."[38]

After the conclusion of his term as president McNutt continued as a member of the Alumni Council from 1924 to 1927, and was generally recognized as one of the most valuable workers in the interest of the university. He had much to do with the planning of various physical aspects of the campus, which were a part of the over-all development program resulting from the Memorial Fund campaign. On October 31, 1923, J. C. Bollenbacker, of the architect firm of Lowe and Bollenbacker, Chicago, wrote him:

"We are about ready for the final decision on the form the Memorial Feature will take in the Women's Memorial Residence Hall. We have our recommendations, and would like to present these to you so that you can get a decision from your committee."[39]

During these early years McNutt was very busy on the campus in many extra-curricular activities. He was a member of the Faculty Committee on Promotion of University Interests. He served as chairman of the Activities Fees Committee, and was also chairman of the Faculty Athletic Committee, in which capacity he had much to do with the entire athletic program, especially intercollegiate sports. The scheduling of football and other games came under his jurisdiction. It was not always easy to satisfy the administration, the faculty, the students, the coaching staff, and the alumni. But other colleges welcomed Indiana as a rival, and sought to be included in its athletics schedules. Even West Point Military Academy sought to be included on Indiana's 1924 schedule.[40]

McNutt was also in great demand by several publishers who requested him to write articles and textbooks on various phases of law. The *Illinois Law Quarterly* asked him to submit a paper "of interest to the practicing lawyer or law teacher."[41] The Marquette University Law School also asked him for a manuscript,[42] and he was requested to contribute an article for the *Columbia University Law Review*.[43]

The West Publishing Company of St. Paul, Minnesota, wrote McNutt on October 26, 1923:

"You are now back on the job as a law teacher and perhaps you will have some leisure time to devote to gathering material for your proposed casebook on Taxation. We are interested in this subject, as you know, and wish to cover it with a casebook in our American Casebook Series before very long."

They asked McNutt if he were in a position to prepare such a casebook to cover both state and federal taxation, and suggested that terms be discussed.[44]

McNutt replied on the 30th that he would be willing to prepare such a casebook, providing the terms were satisfactory. In a letter on November 9, the company wrote that they had prepared a contract providing for a book of about 700 pages, and offered to pay McNutt $500 in cash at the time of publication and a like amount when a thousand copies were sold. The contract provided that the manuscript be in the hands of the company by January 1, 1925, but an extension would be granted if necessary.[45]

These terms, however, were not favorable to McNutt. He asked for a reconsideration of the contract, in view of the fact that he would have some stenographic expense in connection with the manuscript. He further said that a payment of $500 on publication would barely cover the actual outlay in the preparation of the casebook. Consequently on November 23 the publishers wrote him that in view of this fact they would agree to pay him $1,000 on publication "in full of your right, title and interest to the manuscript, thus assuming all the risk of the enterprise instead of sharing it with you." A new contract incorporating these changes was then sent to McNutt.

On February 23, 1924, William L. West, secretary of the publishing company, wrote Professor McNutt, stating that there was no good recent work on the general principles of taxation. Because McNutt had taught the subject for years, and was already at work on a casebook and therefore was pretty familiar with the subject, West asked if he would be willing to consider the preparation of a comprehensive treatise on the subject which would be adaptable to all states.[46]

Five days later West wrote that if McNutt would undertake to prepare such a comprehensive treatise, the company would be willing to extend until July 1, 1925, the date upon which the manuscript for the casebook on taxation was to be completed. However, on March 26, West wrote that the Callaghan Company had just announced a new edition of *Cooley on Taxation,* in four volumes, edited by Nichols, to be published about May 1. West assured McNutt, however, that the publication of this work "would not preclude our contracting with you for a treatise on taxation if, after examining the new edition of Cooley, you were of the opinion that you could produce a much superior treatise."[47]

In the meantime McNutt was anxious to do further graduate work in law at Harvard University, and some of his friends there urged him to seek appointment to the Ezra Ripley Thayer Teaching Fellowship. Dean Roscoe Pound had a very high regard for him, and personally wished to see him return to Cambridge. Apparently McNutt had no difficulty securing the appointment. In a letter from Cambridge dated September 1, 1923, addressed to "My dear MacNutt [sic]." Calvert Magruder wrote him:

"Pound has just written to tell you that the Thayer Teaching Fellowship is yours for 1924-1925. If he sees your wife no doubt he'll give her a scholarship too. So you have no excuse now for not coming."[48]

McNutt subsequently requested a leave of absence from Indiana for the following year. Dean Charles M. Hepburn of the Indiana University Law School had previously been alerted to this possibility, and he and McNutt had several conversations about it. On November 7 Hepburn wrote McNutt that he had discussed the situation with President Bryan, who said he would "be glad to talk with Professor McNutt . . . and shall be glad to have the matter fully presented to the Trustees at their coming meeting." Hepburn suggested that it might be well "to have a conversation with President Bryan sometime soon," before the Board meeting later in the month.[49]

Formal request for a leave of absence was not made immediately, although Pound wrote to McNutt on December 8 confirming his letter to Magruder the previous summer in which he had recommended McNutt. He stated that he was still reserving the Thayer Fellowship for McNutt for the next year, and if he wanted it, "you have only to say so and I will have the appointment made at the proper time."[50]

Professor McNutt wrote to President Bryan on December 27, 1923, formally requesting the leave, "for the purpose of engaging in research and completing my work for the degree of Doctor of Juridical Science, provided such leave is granted on full pay in consideration of my agreeing to teach a total of thirty-six weeks in summer sessions without pay." McNutt stated that the director of the summer session was willing to enter into such an agreement, with the thirty-six weeks of teaching to be spread over a five-year period.

In reply to this request President Bryan wrote on December 29 that he would refer the matter to the trustees at the first opportunity. He suggested that in the meantime, Mc-Nutt and Dean Smith, director of the summer session, exchange letters, "copies being filed with me," making sufficiently definite the arrangements regarding the summer school work. This request was finally granted by the trustees on February 4, 1924. On May 8 McNutt accepted appointment to the full summer session at a salary of $1,065.33.

Dean Pound wrote McNutt on January 24 informing him that "at a meeting of the Faculty of Law . . . you were unanimously recommended for appointment as Thayer Teaching Fellow next year. The nomination has gone to the Corporation and the appointment will be made in due course. You may treat this as an assured fact." On January 28 an official letter was sent to McNutt by F. W. Hunnewell, secretary, Office of the President and Fellows of Harvard College, formally announcing the appointment.

As soon as the appointment was made public, letters and telegrams of congratulations from his friends and associates began to flood McNutt's mail, especially from members of his fraternity. One of these, dated February 18, 1924, from Akron, Ohio, on stationery of the Goodyear Tire and Rubber Company, was addressed "Dear Mac." Referring to the appointment, the letter called it a "well merited distinction . . . and Hubert Hanna, Wendell Willkie and I all send to you our best wishes." The letter closed with the usual fraternity greeting "Kai," and was signed "Pied" [C. M. Piper]. Another letter, from Henry W. Nuckols, 60 Broadway, New York City, February 18, was addressed to "My dear Colonel McNutt," and forecast the future with "Indiana certainly hopes for big things for you."

McNutt immediately attempted to locate a suitable apartment in Cambridge, but his search was unsuccessful, in spite of the efforts of his friends. The type of accommodations he wished were too expensive, and available quarters were undesirable. His personal assets were rather limited, and the move to Cambridge would create a considerable strain on his resources. As a matter of fact, a schedule of his personal property in 1924 revealed that he owned no real estate, and had only $252 on deposit in a bank. He owed notes valued at $900. His personal property, which included a 1923 light six Studebaker sedan, diamonds and other jewelry, firearms (3), watches, two typewriters, books, and household goods, were valued at only $1,236.

Other complications entered into the picture which made it extremely difficult for McNutt to carry through with his aspirations. Shortly after summer school began he requested permission to be absent from his classes for fifteen days on active duty for training at the 326th Field Artillery Headquarters at Camp Knox, Kentucky, from July 6 to 20. On June 18, H. L. Smith, director of the summer session wrote him that his request was granted, but that it was understood that during his absence his classes would be taken care of by other members of the law school faculty "or by men from the outside equally competent in the particular lines." This proved an added burden for McNutt.

As the time neared for McNutt to leave for Cambridge he still had not been able to locate an apartment, but personal family misfortune prevented his leaving Bloomington anyway. He immediately notified Dean Pound, who sent him a telegram from New Portland, Maine, on September 15:

"Will find someone else at once sorry to lose you sympathize in your misfortunes."

This was followed by a handwritten letter from Strong, Maine, September 18, 1924:

"Your message of the 15th was telephoned to me here and I got enough of its purport to wire you an answer. Now the message itself comes by mail. Of course I could do nothing but release you under the circumstances. I am sorry to lose you and sorry that you have had to give up your year with us. When you are able to come notify me not later than January or early in February, and you shall have the place again."

Pound followed this by another letter on October 10. He said he quite understood the circumstances which made it unreasonable to hold McNutt to his appointment that year. He was quite happy, however, that he "was able to find a very respectable substitute at the last minute. You may have the Fellowship for next year if you desire," he informed McNutt, "and I will hold the matter open until the first of February for you, if you like."

On December 19 McNutt wrote another letter to Pound advising him that he had made application for a leave of absence for the scholastic year 1925-26, and that he had assurances that the request would be granted. Therefore he wished to take advantage of the offer contained in Pound's letter of October 10 and to make formal application for appointment as Thayer Fellow for that year.

The same day McNutt wrote to President Bryan requesting such a leave, on the same terms on which the grant had been made the previous year. On December 12 Bryan wrote McNutt that he would refer his request to the trustees of the university at their next meeting. This request was thus granted on March 30, 1925. In the meantime Pound assured McNutt on December 23 that he would see to it that he was appointed to the Fellowship, and on March 9, 1925, the formal appointment was made, effective September 1, 1925.

Greater opportunities soon presented themselves to Professor McNutt, however. The beloved dean of the Indiana University law school, who had served so long and so well, was growing old and tired, and now asked to be relieved of his administrative responsibilities, so that he could devote his full time to the study of torts. During the second semester of the academic year 1924-25 McNutt assumed many of these duties and was to all intents and purposes the acting dean. He entered into his new responsibilities with enthusiasm.

McNutt submitted to the university trustees on March 17, 1925, a lengthy report on certain facts and possible solutions to the problems which had arisen in connection with the law school. Asserting that only a school of the highest rank was a fitting part of the university, he claimed that its elements must have certain qualities. Its faculty, he said, "must consist of able teachers of the law and have a degree of permanence." Its library must be adequate and the school "must attract the best students in the territory which it is supposed to serve," he insisted.

As to the law school faculty itself, McNutt agreed that it "has had, from time to time, some of the ablest teachers of the law in this country." But the tenure of most of them had been short, according to McNutt, with scarcely a year passing without some change in the personnel of the faculty. "Our school has been merely a stepping stone," he said. "No law school can attain the first rank with a constantly changing faculty. Our budget . . . does not permit the retention of a good man, or the filling of his place with a man of desired ability," he insisted. The law library, he charged, was pitifully inadequate, and the law school itself did not attract the best law students in the state of Indiana.

McNutt was of the opinion that many of the reasons for the present state of affairs in the school were to be found in the current budget, which totaled only $29,286. Of this amount, $25,050 went to pay the salaries of the resident faculty members, $1,700 for the library, $936 for a secretary,

[24]

$720 for special lecturers, $500 for departmental expenses, $300 for a curator, and $80 for assistant librarians.

Acting on the assumption that the members of the Board felt that there could be little or no increase in the budget during the next biennium, McNutt submitted various suggestions as a means of removing some of the difficulties and solving some of the problems of the law school. He requested that additions be made to the library if at all possible, and that the unexpended balance of any fund such as that for departmental expenses be transferred to the library fund. These suggestions involved cutting the number of faculty members to five for the next two years, yet McNutt insisted that the minimum for a law school such as Indiana was six members. However, he felt it was better to keep a faculty of five desirable men during a period of stress than to fill vacancies with less desirable men. These suggestions also involved a much-needed revision of the curriculum.

According to the acting dean, the proposed salary scale was $500 less than the minimum for such positions, but was so placed in recognition of the necessary limitations on the university's program for the next two years, and with the understanding that at least the minimum would be adopted as soon as the legislature and governor granted relief.

As to his own salary, McNutt felt that the dean should receive at least $1,000 more than that of a major professor, with half of it for his administrative duties and half for expenses necessarily incident to the position. He pointed out, however, that the proposed salary for the next two years included nothing for administrative duties. In this connection he invited the attention of the Board to the fact that he had refused a definite offer of $6,000 a year to become dean of a law school of a nearby state four years previously.[51]

Continuing, McNutt referred to the fact that the proposed

salary scale for resident faculty members contained a tentative scale for 1927-28. He felt that if the legislature made adequate appropriation for the university during its next session, such a scale could be met. "If it does not," he wrote, "I am willing to agree to take a leave of absence for that year for the purpose of doing graduate or research work, thus relieving the Board from any embarrassment arising from an increased salary roll."

The other perplexing question which McNutt discussed in his report was whether the editing and publishing of a law journal should be added to the duties of the law faculty. The views of a majority of the faculty had been set forth in a resolution which expressed their anxiety to promote better relations between the active bar and the law school. They promised to cooperate to the fullest extent in this or any other movement leading to better relations. It was their feeling, McNutt said, that such a journal might perform a valuable service to the bar by making available for the practitioner articles discussing problems in the law within its jurisdiction. But the faculty was of the opinion that no such publication ought to be established unless it could be maintained on an equality with the law journals published by other law schools of the same class as Indiana. Anything less than this, they believed, would result in an actual loss of reputation and prestige of the Indiana law school.

In view of the objections contained in the faculty resolution, McNutt was of the opinion that the publication of such a journal seemed inadvisable at that time. The limited faculty would be called upon to extend itself too much in effecting a reorganization and in inaugurating a new curriculum. Also, a managing editor would have to be selected. McNutt further pointed out that each of the major professors had already declined at least six invitations to write articles for the leading law journals of the country during the current academic year on account of the pressure of work.

McNutt concluded his report with the statement that if the reorganization of the law school were complete, and a full faculty were in residence, then the work of publishing a law journal might be undertaken with some hope of success. But he felt it was not likely that such conditions would be satisfied until the academic year 1927-28. In view of these facts, therefore, he thought it seemed advisable to postpone such publication until that time. But if the Board agreed to meet certain conditions, then McNutt himself would be willing to attempt to manage such a publication, provided the bar gave assurances of cooperation. He made the offer, he said, "not as a matter of choice but as a means of saving the situation."[52]

President Bryan replied to this letter on March 30. He informed McNutt that "in view of the prospective income of the university for the next two years, we shall meet almost insuperable difficulty in maintaining the morale and quality of the university as a whole and of its major departments and schools. Solving the problem for one department or school, so far from solving the problem as a whole, may make the problem for the university as a whole immeasurably worse."

Bryan continued:

"You know that men (and their wives) are concerned not alone with the amount of their salaries but with the relative amount of the salaries. Men (and wives) who will endure heroically with others will if they think others inequitably preferred turn to feelings quite other than heroic—feelings which kill morale with all the attendant evil consequences. While giving searching consideration to the interests of the law school and its faculty," Bryan said, "we must no less consider the interests of other men and other faculties and must (without money) find a fair solution of the whole problem in peril of injury to the university as a whole as grave as that which confronts the Law School."

The president admitted that McNutt knew all this as well as he did, "but it may not have come home to you with a force so overwhelming as it does to me." The problem of the law school was tied up with the problem of the university as a whole, he wrote. "It is because of this fact that the Trustees find it impossible to adopt the proposal for the Law School submitted by you," he concluded.[53]

In the meantime, Professor Hepburn requested that he be relieved entirely of his administrative duties as dean of the law school. Consequently President Bryan informed him on May 5, 1925, that the trustees had elected him Research Professor of Law "with the privilege of devoting to research and writing the time which you now must spend at executive work." The trustees, he wrote, were sure that under such an arrangement he "would render service of the utmost importance to the University and to legal education." President Bryan said that he was glad to learn "that this action is very agreeable to you."[54]

On the same day Bryan sent a letter to Professor McNutt, informing him that "the Trustees have elected you as Dean of the School of Law for the year beginning August 1, 1925, at a salary of forty-nine hundred dollars ($4,900.00)."[55] Thus, at the age of thirty-four, McNutt had the honor and distinction of being the youngest dean of an accredited law school in the country. The Thayer Fellowship was sacrificed. Harvard University lost a scholar, but Indiana gained a law school dean.

McNutt received many letters of congratulation from well-wishers throughout the country. One wrote he thought "the college is entitled to congratulation in having the good judgment to recognize your worth and to make the promotion. I hope that you will have a long and successful career and that you will never become emeritus dean, if there is such a thing, but before that time arrives you become President [of the university]."[56]

Another wrote:

"Your opportunity is large and I know you will really fill the job as the leader of legal education in Indiana. If you will remain as Dean ten years, Indiana's standing in legal education will be notably higher. Also the leadership of the university in legal training will have a marked effect upon the bar of the state."[57]

One of Dean McNutt's fraternity brothers wrote him that he was "well-qualified for this position and under your administration the Law School of Indiana should rise to be among the foremost Law Schools in the Middle West."[58] Lawrence B. Davis, president of the Indianapolis Bar Association, expressed the hope that the new dean "will put the . . . [law school] in the first rank of American university law schools."[59]

A letter from W. Earl Kaiser, a recent law graduate, expressed the general feeling of the younger alumni in regard to the appointment. He wrote:

"Three years ago at a large 'borass' in front of the Law School a group of us were discussing the possible successor to Dean Hepburn and you were unanimously elected. Two years ago the same thing happened and last spring just before final exams you were again elected by acclamation and I am glad to see that our Trustees had the foresight to agree with undergraduate opinion. . . . I have always considered you as more than a 'prof' but as one of my friends that I could go to in case of need . . . you are so rich in . . . friends among the undergraduates."[60]

Judge John Rabb Emison of the Superior Court of Knox County, Vincennes, Indiana, wrote Dean McNutt:

"You can't keep a good man down."[61]

Another considered the appointment "a progressive step for Indiana. You have gained this honor early in life and I hope you may gain many more and greater ones."[62]

Dean Pound of the Harvard Law School wrote that he was sorry McNutt would not be with them the following year, "but I congratulate you and the University of Indiana. I am sure your appointment will mean great things, not only for the Law School of the University of Indiana, but for the law of that Commonwealth."[63]

John S. Hastings wrote from Washington, Indiana, on May 9, 1925:

"It was with genuine pleasure and satisfaction that I read of your appointment. . . . My wish is that our School of Law will respond to your enthusiasm and direction, and my conviction is that such will be the case."[64]

Another wrote from the George Washington Law School:

"I see a future ahead for the Law School now such as I had despaired of in times past."[65]

Another wrote:

"The accomplishment of such things as this seldom comes except as the result of honest, unselfish service and this kind of service must of necessity be conceded by the action of the Board of Trustees."[66]

One of McNutt's American Legion friends sent his congratulations and declared that there would be much more "kick" in the law school in the future. He felt that the appointment was "the best thing that ever happened . . . [for a] Greater Indiana."[67]

Others also looked forward to the time when Indiana's president would be Paul V. McNutt.[68] This same sentiment was voiced by another fraternity brother, C. M. Piper of Akron, Ohio, who considered the appointment "simply another advancement toward the post as President of the University."[69]

Wendell L. Willkie also wrote from Akron:

"You know I predicted when you first made your professional connection with the University that it was but a question of time until you would be its president."[70]

Val Nolan, an Evansville attorney, expressed the hope that McNutt's new position "marks a step to your future advancement in official life in the university."[71] Perhaps the letter which McNutt received from V. M. "Skitz" Simmons of Bluffton summarizes rather succinctly the general reaction to his appointment:

"This was a very fine recognition of your service and ability. From our past acquaintance and association I know of your very great interest in Indiana University, and especially in the School of Law. I also know that you are fully informed concerning the things that are needed, and feel that under your direction, our Law School in a short time will compare favorably with and enjoy the reputation of Chicago and Michigan. . . . We have always had fine gentlemen on the faculty . . . but in some instances at least they have not been as progressive and active as they should have been. . . . I feel sure that you will be able to correct conditions and put the Law School on a sound basis and high standing."[72]

Notes for Chapter 1

[1] Scrapbook in possession of Mrs. L. M. Robertson (Jean L. Allen), Greenwood, Indiana. Lent to author.

[2] Letter from R. W. Terhune, M. D., Martinsville, Indiana, January 29, 1943, to Mrs. Hazel Franklin (Mrs. C. E.) Lewis. Lent by Mrs. Lewis.

[3] Biographical sketch in McNutt Collection, Lilly Library—letter of Paul V. McNutt to Miss Elizabeth McNutt, Charleston, Illinois, September 22, 1939.

[4] Letter from John C. McNutt to Mrs. Lewis, August 5, 1939. Lent by Mrs. Lewis.

[5] See also letter from James C. McNutt, M. D., Bloomington, Illinois, August 13, 1939, to Mrs. Lewis. Lent by Mrs. Lewis.

[6] See (3) above. See also Indianapolis *Star*, March 25, 1955, and Bloomington, Indiana, *Star-Courier*, January 10, 1947. Clippings in Indiana State Library.

[7] Told to author by Mrs. Forrest Ragsdale, September 11, 1963.

[8] Letter from John C. McNutt to Mrs. Lewis, August 5, 1939. Lent by Mrs. Lewis.

[9] Clippings in Indiana State Library.

[10] *Ibid.*

11 Report cards from Martinsville, Indiana, High School, 1905-1909, show outstanding grades. McNutt Collection, Lilly Library.

12 Clippings in Indiana State Library.

13 See report cards in McNutt Collection, Lilly Library. Unless otherwise indicated, the following material has been taken from the McNutt Collection in the Lilly Library.

14 Henry F. Pringle, "McNutt is Willing" in *The Forum*, vol. 312, June 1940. Cited by Rand W. Burnett, "Paul V. McNutt: A Study of Machine Politics, 1928-1937," an unpublished Master of Science thesis, University of Wisconsin, p. 4. Lent to author.

15 Mrs. Robertson's scrapbook.

16 McNutt Collection, Lilly Library.

17 *Ibid.*

18 *Ibid.*

19 *Ibid.*

20 *Ibid.*

21 *Ibid.*

22 *Ibid.*

23 *Ibid.*

24 Indianapolis *Star*, March 25, 1955.

25 McNutt Collection.

26 Letter from W. L. Bryan to Paul V. McNutt, June 11, 1920, McNutt Collection.

27 *Ibid*, June 11, 1921.

28 McNutt Collection.

29 Letter from Tom Taggart to Paul V. McNutt. McNutt Collection.

30 McNutt Collection.

31 *Ibid.*

32 *Ibid.*

33 *Ibid.*

34 *Ibid.*

35 *Ibid.*

36 *Ibid.*

37 *Ibid.*

38 *Ibid.*

39 *Ibid.*

40 *Ibid.*

41 September 10, 1923. McNutt Collection.

42 May 28, 1924. McNutt Collection.

43 July 21, 1924. McNutt Collection.

44 McNutt Collection.

45 *Ibid.*

46 *Ibid.*

47 *Ibid.*

48 *Ibid.*

49 *Ibid.*

[50] *Ibid.*

[51] *Ibid.*

[52] *Ibid.*

[53] *Ibid.*

[54] *Ibid.*

[55] *Ibid.*

[56] Letter to McNutt from John H. Kiplinger, Rushville, Indiana, May 6, 1925.

[57] Letter from Col. Robert L. Moorhead, May 6, 1925.

[58] Letter signed "in-Kai," "Pete" [Walter Lieber], May 6, 1925.

[59] May 7, 1925.

[60] W. Earl Kaiser to Paul V. McNutt, May 7, 1925.

[61] John Robert Emison, Vincennes, Indiana, May 7, 1925.

[62] Emil W. McCoy, special agent, Aetna Life Insurance Company, Indianapolis, May 8, 1925.

[63] Dean Roscoe Pound to McNutt, May 8, 1925.

[64] John S. Hastings, Washington, Indiana, to McNutt, May 9, 1925.

[65] Walter L. Moll, Washington, D. C., May 9, 1925.

[66] Ira L. Rupley, San Antonio, Texas, May 9, 1925.

[67] Elmer F. Straub, Indianapolis, May 10, 1925.

[68] Posey T. Kime and James H. Meyer, lawyers of Evansville, to McNutt, May 9, 1925.

[69] C. M. Piper, Akron, Ohio, May 18, 1925.

[70] Wendell L. Willkie to McNutt, May 16, 1925.

[71] Val Nolan to McNutt, May 19, 1925.

[72] V. M. "Skitz" Simmons, Bluffton, Indiana, May 15, 1925.

CHAPTER II

Early Achievements

Dean McNutt plunged enthusiastically into his new responsibilities as head of the Indiana University Law School, and as a result the hopes and aspirations of the alumni for a more fully respected law school were greatly stimulated. There is very little in his official papers to indicate that he had any extensive extra-curricular interests beyond the campus during his first year in office. The task of improving the academic reputation of the law school apparently demanded much of his time and energy, although he engaged vigorously in many activities connected with other phases of the university program. On July 4, 1925, H. L. Smith, Director of the Summer Session, appointed McNutt to the faculty Summer Session Committee, of which Dean Herman B Wells, later president of the university, was chairman.[1]

During his first year in the law deanship, however, McNutt was being pressured from many sources to take an active interest in politics, although it appears that he felt that his obligations, at least for the time being, were to the university first. While there is no definite proof that he had any political ambitions at this early date, yet he must have realized that such would be a probability in due time. As early as September 28, 1925, Meredith Nicholson, a prominent Hoosier author, urged him "to keep going in politics. There's a place to work and God knows the laborers are few. We've got to lift the tone of our politics—get away from blind partisanship, and persuade young men of the best sort—the very best— to take a hand, or some day something very unpleasant will happen to this proud union of commonwealths."

Nicholson continued:

"It sometimes seems to me that the moral courage has gone out of us. Everybody's afraid of somebody else. We're going to need a Grover Cleveland awful bad in a few years, and you, son, are the boy I've picked to stand for things as he stood for them."[2]

Yet McNutt's time to enter politics was still several years away. He had much other work to do first.

One of McNutt's major extra-curricular interests during this early period was his attempt to thwart what he considered un-American activities. During the decade of the Twenties many organizations were preaching the doctrine of pacifism and anti-militarism. Such theories were unpatriotic and therefore dangerous in the eyes of certain groups in which veterans of the recent world war had played a prominent role, especially the American Legion. McNutt seized the opportunity to denounce these unpopular doctrines which he felt were a menace to the welfare and security of the country.

McNutt was especially vehement in his denunciation of Frederick J. Libby, who had been lecturing throughout the country in favor of pacifism and other such theories and doctrines. Reports began to come to McNutt's attention indicating that Libby was carrying on various subversive activities, although it was extremely difficult to prove anything very definite against him. Apparently he was very clever, and while those who were aware of his activities had fixed opinions about his bad tendencies, it was hard to pin anything on him.

About the worst that investigation revealed about him was that contained in a dossier circulated by the American Defense Society. According to this pamphlet he was a Congregational minister until some time in 1918 when the age limit for the draft was lifted to forty-six years, at which time Libby became a Quaker.[3] He was considered by one of McNutt's investigators "quite smooth and clever, a very intelligent man and a good speaker. He certainly uses the Bible and Christianity for all it is worth in preaching disarmament." Yet he was too smooth to say anything in public or in print that was definitely subversive, and therefore nothing could be proved against him. He had powerful friends, and McNutt was warned not to say anything he could not prove, no matter how thoroughly he believed it.[4]

According to this reporter, Libby "was one of the most dangerous men abroad in the country and the very cleverness and smoothness with which he does his work is what makes him so dangerous, as well as difficult to attack. . . . The only thing you can do is watch his statements closely and then ask him questions which will bring out his real attitude."

McNutt was advised to use caution in dealing with Libby: "I do not know how far you want to go personally in getting into this fight and perhaps get yourself into difficulty, but I think if you and some of your associates listen closely to what he has to say, you will find enough statements that will permit you to tear his speech to pieces and spoil his affect [sic] on his audience."[5]

On one occasion Libby spoke to a large body of students and townspeople on the campus of Purdue University, and his visit aroused keen interest. He was faced by "quite a numerous body of military students, well prepared, who gave him a warm reception."[6] But Libby had many honest defenders throughout the state, and McNutt was criticized for his attacks on him. Mr. Frank Streightoff, representing the Indiana Council on International Relations, asked McNutt to send him "a correct statement" of the charges which the dean had made against Libby in a speech in Indianapolis, together with the evidence on which they were based.[7]

In a long reply McNutt chided Streightoff for not seeing fit to attend the meeting himself, because "hearsay evidence is never reliable. The legal profession learned that centuries ago," he said. He pointed out that he had been discussing the subject of character education and had sought to point out the necessity of teaching children to accept responsibilities. One of these is the responsibility for the welfare and protection of this nation. He had then stated that "certain groups of individuals, some of them honest and well-meaning, some not, were attempting to bring about the abolition of military training in our schools and colleges; that some were going so far as to attempt to exact a pledge from the youths of this land never to serve the nation in time of war."[8]

McNutt then quoted from his speech:

"Those who oppose military training fall into two groups. One group consists of those who are honestly and really 'conscientious objectors.' I have no abuse for those who are honest and well-meaning. I respect but disagree with their ideas. The other group consists of 'Reds,' of varying shades, some representative of the International. These should be unceremoniously pitched out on their heads," he declared.[9]

Reference was then made to the "charge" which Streightoff had mentioned. McNutt quoted it as follows:

"Those who are seeking to abolish military training in the schools and colleges are striking at the very heart of our national defense. We are now facing the result of such an agitation. I refer to the recent visit of one Frederick J. Libby and to the proposed visit of Thomas Que Harrison, agitator of the 'fellowship of youth for peace.' In this connection I am opposed to Mr. Libby and the organization which he represents. I believe it to be the duty of every American citizen to serve this nation in time of war and that military training in the schools and colleges is an essential and proper part of an adequate national defense. I propose to strenuously oppose these gentlemen or any others who would seek to impair that defense."

This was the complete context of his remarks concerning Libby, McNutt said.[10]

A representative of the American Association of University Women also wrote McNutt in criticism of some of the charges which he had made about Libby and his association with various groups in the state, and demanded at once a substantiation of the charges made. In a letter to McNutt, Mrs. Frank D. Hatfield declared that his admonition to the American Association of University Women was out of place, as the Association "bears a high community respect, and is only one of eighteen national organizations of repute now on the National Council for the Prevention of War." She also demanded proof of McNutt's charges against Libby, who had spoken in the state at several meetings under the auspices of the AAUW, the Indianapolis Department Club, and the League of Women Voters.[11]

Opposition to Libby was apparently not confined to McNutt and Indiana. A copy of a letter from Colonel C. L. Townsend, Infantry (D O L) Chief of Staff, to Major General R. L. Bullard, president of the National Security League, New York City, was sent to McNutt. The letter expressed concern over Libby's speaking in the various colleges and before women's societies and elsewhere "presumably on the subject of the World Court . . . but it seems probable that the main aim is action against the R. O. T. C." The letter further charged that Libby's "history is bad, that he has spent some time in Soviet Russia and is possibly in the employ of Moscow."[12]

Colonel Townsend was apparently quite correct in believing that Libby's chief target was the R. O. T. C. program in the schools and colleges. As a result of his activities and speeches around the state, considerable agitation was felt on the campuses, and minor demonstrations occurred in several places, such as at Indiana and Purdue universities, where a limited number of students had revolted against military service. The National Judge Advocate of the American Legion, Robert A. Adams, wrote McNutt that the best thing that could happen to such students, "although they could never appreciate it themselves, would be to put them all in the Regular Army under an old-time corporal. If any youth needs discipline, that sort certainly does. . . . I hope that there will be an early stopping of this spirit in Indiana University."[13]

In his reply to Adams, McNutt wrote that he had "received some brickbats ealong with the bouquets" on account of his views. He declared that "these sentimental pacifists rant about freedom of speech and then assert that they have been 'attacked' whenever the name of one of them is mentioned." He felt that the whole situation "is more serious than most of us realize. I am thoroughly aroused and intend to wield the cudgel whenever the opportunity presents itself. I am not afraid of the situation here but the people of the state are entitled to know the persons who are sowing the seeds of discontent."[14]

It seems that the question of compulsory or optional training in the R. O. T. C. was the basis of the controversy, as far as the Indiana University campus was concerned. According to the student publication, the fight had become quite animated. McNutt received a carbon copy of a letter addressed to Colonel Nelson H. Kellogg, president of the Department of Indiana, R. O. T. C. Purdue University, from Fred B. Ryons, who was secretary of the Reserve Officers Association of the United States, in which it was charged that a certain element was trying "to undermine our national defense and they have taken as their point of attack the R. O. T. C. Their first objective is to remove the compulsory feature and later to eliminate the R. O. T. C. in toto." Such a result, it was felt, "would destroy our main source of procurement, destroy the Reserve, destroy our plans for national defense as set forth under the National Defense Act, in other words, it would destroy our plans for a citizen Army and then require the maintenance of a very large Regular Army at a tremendous expense to the Government."[15]

In his reply to Colonel Ryons, McNutt pledged that he would "give Colonel Kellogg any assistance he calls for. I am in the midst of a fight and am in close touch with the situation." There was no immediate danger, he wrote, as Indiana University President William Lowe Bryan had issued a statement that he shared the view held by a vast majority of the people of the state and the United States "that we still require police and army and navy and that the R. O. T. C. in the universities is a wise part of the national defense." President Bryan believed that "for the vigorous and effective maintenance of the R. O. T. C. the work should be required . . . of all freshmen and sophomores except those excused for justifiable cause." McNutt asserted that President Bryan "is supported by all administrative officers and an overwhelming majority of the faculty."[16]

McNutt quite agreed with Ryons that certain pacifist forces were seeking to destroy the country's national defense and had selected the R. O. T. C. as the first point of attack.

This was the claim that he had made in his recent speeches when he referred to the activities of Libby. According to McNutt's letter to Ryons, the Indianapolis *News* had carried an editorial intimating that Libby was advocating a program of "non-resistance," but Libby had replied in a signed statement to the effect that the National Council for the Prevention of War did not advocate such a program, although a letter made public by President Coolidge on the Council's attitude and influence relative to National Defense Day would indicate the contrary.[17]

Continuing, McNutt claimed that Libby "very carefully refrained from making any statement of his own attitude on this matter," and stated that he had "nothing to do with the situation at Indiana University." McNutt denied, however, that the agitation had started within the university, but asserted that it was "a direct result from propaganda . . . sent out by eastern pacifist organizations." He charged that the movement had been helped "by a pacifist Y. M. C. A. secretary who is now on campus," and that Libby's protestations were "camaphlage" [sic]. Libby, he said, "seems to appear unexpectedly whenever a drive is on against national defense. The circumstantial evidence against him is very strong." He further wrote:

"These pacifists prate about freedom of speech but the instant you mention one of their names they cry out that they have been attacked. . . . If that is the way Libby's friends feel about it I will try to live up to their expectations and go after the gentlemen hammer and tongs."[18]

In the meantime McNutt's reputation as an administrator was receiving wide acclaim not only in Indiana but throughout the country as well. Several colleges considered him for their presidency. He was suggested by at least one person as a possible successor to President McIntosh of Wabash College.[19] Herbert S. Hadley, chancellor of Washington University, St. Louis, carried on an extensive correspondence with him over a considerable period regarding the possibility of his acceptance of the deanship of their law school.[20] But McNutt finally wrote to Hadley that he would be interested in the position upon two conditions, "first, that the directors of the corporation decide to make the law school a national institution of the first rank and adopt a program looking to that end; and second, that they offer compensation in keeping with such an understanding."[21]

McNutt felt that the possibility of building such an institution at St. Louis was one of the chief determining factors which forced him to even consider making such a change, although he declared that his relations at Indiana University were most pleasant, and he was beginning to see the fruition of his efforts to build up the Hoosier law school. He concluded, therefore, that a larger opportunity together with a corresponding increase in financial return were the only things which would tempt him to leave Bloomington.[22]

After McNutt had a personal interview with Hadley at St. Louis, the chancellor wrote that he felt the directors were disposed to pursue a very liberal policy towards the law school, although it would take time to build it up. He mentioned these matters, he said, "not to indicate any lack of willingness on our part to comply with the conditions you name, but to emphasize necessary limitations and to ask that you specify rather more concretely what you mean and what you would expect by such an assurance in this regard as you request."[23]

Hadley asked McNutt to advise him as to what compensation he would expect if he went to St. Louis. He also stated that he would want some assurance that if McNutt were to make the move, he would "stay long enough to accomplish something worth while." This he felt could not be done in one or two years, but if McNutt were offered the presidency of Indiana University at the end of the first year or two, "it would seem that the interests of education, which are always the major consideration, would require your acceptance."[24]

In answer to Hadley's request for a suggested salary, McNutt wrote:

"Judging from what other institutions have been willing to pay for my services, I feel that they are worth $10,000 a year. I know that I am able to contribute that much to the institution which I serve. I am unwilling to make a change for less than that."

As to the question of his tenure at Washington University, he said he would stay "until I had completed the task of building a first rate law school and perhaps longer. . . . The possibility of becoming president of Indiana University," he wrote, "is not of immediate importance." For one thing, he did not expect "a change in administration here for five or ten years." Furthermore, he admitted he had "no assurance that the place will be offered to me when the vacancy occurs."[25]

Apparently McNutt was confident that a firm offer would be made to him by Hadley with the salary which he had suggested. He wrote his father for advice on the matter. In his answer the elder McNutt said it was very hard to make up his mind what to advise him, although he agreed "that $10,000 a year for nine months of work is certainly very attractive, and you will have to do less work, in all probability, than you would do if you stayed at Indiana, and I am anxious that you be relieved of some of the work you have been doing for several years."[26]

At the same time McNutt wrote to his friend David Jennings of "my possible acceptance of a very tempting offer," although no firm offer had yet been made to him. He said he really wanted to stay at Indiana "and feel that I can be of more value to this institution than to any other, but it is very hard to refuse a salary which is more than twice as large as the one I receive here." McNutt confided to Jennings that Chancellor Hadley "intends to build a national law school of high distinction, and he wants me to undertake the work. In many respects it is a wonderful opportunity and demands serious consideration."[27]

Finally, however, Chancellor Hadley wrote that, although McNutt had presented an attractive and ambitious program, yet "it involved such a radical change, financial and educational, in the policy of the Law School that I would not feel warranted in committing the University to it without opportunity for further consultation than I have had or could have at this time." He therefore had decided to appoint an acting dean and wait a year before appointing a permanent one.[28]

It was about this time that McNutt began to be seriously considered for the office of state commander of the American Legion. He was a charter member of the Burton Woolery Post at Bloomington, and in 1921 he had been post commander. During his year in that office the membership of the local group had been increased from 92 to 502, largely through McNutt's personal efforts, and the whole tone of Legion affairs had been improved during the succeeding years, mostly through McNutt's leadership. It was not surprising, therefore, that his name was mentioned seriously for the state office. He was backed by Frank McHale and Bowman "Bo" Elder, who saw in him the qualities of a great leader.

Yet McNutt publicly was reluctant to have his candidacy advanced. Even his personal correspondence would indicate that he preferred some spontaneous decision at the state convention. He wrote to a friend that he had "no intention of entering a general scramble for election. . . . I was approached on this matter several weeks ago and said that if the members of the Legion wanted me that I was willing to serve. I have a feeling that this office should seek the man rather than the man seek the office."[29]

No such "approach" letter has been found in McNutt's correspondence, although there are many letters from McNutt indicating that such an "approach" had been made to him several times. McNutt agreed that the selection of the state commander would be made by the convention, but he suggested that the work of friends in various parts of the state should be most useful in creating a friendly atmosphere toward his possible candidacy. The Legion, of course, was traditionally a non-political organization and frowned upon anyone using it as a steppingstone for some political favor. Therefore McNutt, being a Democrat, persuaded three Republican friends to back him for the state post.[30]

The eighth annual state convention of the American Legion was held at Marion on August 29-31. There was a lively contest between McNutt and Eugene O'Shaughnessy of Lawrenceburg, but McNutt won the election on the 9th ballot by a vote of 206 to 176.[31] His election was then made unanimous, following which McNutt declared:

"Nothing within the gift of the people of Indiana is a higher honor than to lead the American Legion. The heart of the Legion is in the local posts.[32]

Immediately letters of congratulation began to pour in on McNutt. Hugh A. Barnhart of Rochester wrote him:

"I certainly am pleased that the right man is in the right office. . . . I like your platform, of going after pacifism, as I think this is our greatest danger now that the 'reds' are a thing of the past. Our national indifference to being ready when danger does come, really is discouraging and it is only by constant hammering of the fellows, who can see it and know it, that will eventually wake up the people—and let us hope it will be in good time." [33]

Others thought the next honor coming to McNutt would be the presidency of Indiana University.[34]

After McNutt's election to the Legion post the question was immediately raised as to his availability for possible participation in the fall political campaigns, although he was not scheduled to take office until the following January. The Legion's policy had been to refrain from any active participation in partisan politices, but some of its members were urging McNutt to make political speeches throughout the state in support of the Democratic candidates. It was felt that he could do the ticket "an enormous amount of good."[35]

McNutt delayed making a decision in this matter until he could talk with some party leaders, especially the state chairman and his father. He was of the opinion, however, that he should represent the entire Legion in all public appearances, not just the adherents to one or the other political faith. He also had a feeling that "any political speeches from me would do more harm than good because of the strenuous effort the Legion has made to keep partisan politics out of the Legion affairs." He thought that any political speeches made by him "might serve to alienate some strong Legion men who otherwise would support the Democratic party."[36]

Early in October, however, McNutt had a conference with R. Earl Peters, chairman of the Democratic state central committee, who at first thought it would do no harm for him to go on the stump, but he later changed his opinion. McNutt's father also thought it would be unwise both from the standpoint of the party and the Legion. The decision was made, therefore, that he would refrain from any public speech-making. But McNutt was deeply interested in the success of the entire Democratic ticket, and he promised "to do all that I can in a quiet way."[37]

During the year 1927 when McNutt was state commander of the Legion, he spent a considerable amount of time on the affairs of the organization. The state membership was increased from 18,336 to 25,505. The commander traveled widely not only throughout Indiana in the interests of the Legion, but he spoke in 18 other states as well. He was also engaged at the same time in raising funds for the Harvard Law School. He was forced to use the airplane to make connections, although this was an innovation in the 1920's. He continued to teach his classes at Bloomington and to carry on the duties of the deanship as well. He also remained a member of his father's law firm, and devoted much time to private legal work.

McNutt was in great demand as a high school commencement speaker during this period, for which his usual fee was $50 and expenses. Often, however, when the schools were informed of his regular fee, they cancelled the invitation. One such school official wrote that, due to McNutt's charge for his services, "it will be impossible for us to use you. We were very sorry to have to turn you down, but the school felt that the price was too high."[38]

Yet McNutt insisted that "the making of such addresses is a 'labor of love' and I have never made any fixed charge for such work, realizing that some schools could pay more than others. . . . A commencement address requires the better part of two days for a trip, to say nothing of the time spent in preparation." Furthermore, he said, "the school usually gets what it pays for."[39] On at least one occasion McNutt accepted a check for $15 in payment for a commencement address.[40]

[47]

Certainly it is doubtful if McNutt were becoming wealthy as a result of his extra-curricular activities during this period. In a schedule of his personal property for the year 1926, it was found that he had only $929 in cash and on deposit, with notes amounting to $1,400, and personal property worth less than $800.[41] This included a Studebaker '23 sedan valued at $350. The schedule for 1927 was approximately the same, although he now had a 1926 Chrysler coach valued at $800.[42]

Actually, McNutt was finding that his duties as state commander of the Legion were costing him considerable which was not reimbursed by the organization. He complained that the practice of the Legion in regard to traveling expenses was far from satisfactory. He was given an allowance of $1,800 a year for his expenses, but after only three months in office he had exceeded this amount by almost $500, he claimed, and "at the present rate the year will cost me some place between $1500 and $2000."[43]

A schedule of McNutt's speaking engagements for the month of May, 1927, is typical of the tremendous pressure under which he worked. He made twenty-three speeches during the thirty-one-day period. Many were made in Indiana, but he spoke also at Neenah and Menasha, Wisconsin, Cleveland and Toledo, Ohio, and Washington, D. C. His schedule for June was somewhat lighter, with only eleven speeches listed, all within the state.[44] In July and early August, however, his engagements included speeches in Minnesota and Tennessee.

At least one of his friends advised McNutt to "cut out some of this speech-making and . . . give yourself a little rest and a little recreation." He invited him to visit him at Akron, Ohio, "and you can make a speech here if you want to. If you just feel a speech coming on, I can get you some kind of an audience, I assure you. Quit trying to build up those Democratic political fences of yours and push back your grey hairs, sit down in an easy chair and enjoy yourself. We will be patting you in the face with a shovel if you don't slow up anyway."[45]

One of the highlights of McNutt's year as state commander was his participation in the ceremonies centering around the laying of the cornerstone of the Indiana World War Memorial Building on July 4, 1927, in Indianapolis. The principal speaker on this occasion was General John J. Pershing, a close personal friend.

Along with his speaking engagements and his regular classroom teaching, McNutt was invited to serve on a study commission created by the Indiana General Assembly to make a survey concerning corporation laws of Indiana and to report to the Assembly in the 1929 session as to the findings of the commission. Frederick E. Schortemeier, Indiana's secretary of state, was directed to appoint members of the commission and to proceed with the survey. In writing McNutt to ask him to serve as a member of the commission, he said he hoped very much "that you can give of your experience and ability in the performance of this public cause." McNutt accepted the appointment on June 3.[46]

During this period, various contacts were made with McNutt to determine his possible interest in the presidency of certain educational institutions. One such gesture was made by L. W. MacKinnon, vice president of the University of Toledo, who suggested that "if there is the slightest possibility that one might be able to interest you in such an undertaking, will you please indicate where and at what time you would be willing to listen to something about us?"[47]

On July 11 McNutt replied to MacKinnon that he had "refused all offers to leave Indiana University because I desired to complete certain tasks here. Some of these undertakings have not been finished and I do not wish to avoid the responsibilities which they entail. Of course anything which offers a wider opportunity interests me and I shall be glad to talk to you concerning the matter."[48] Although a conference between the two men took place at Indianapolis later in the month, no commitments were ever made, and the matter was finally dropped.

Meanwhile McNutt's term as Indiana commander of the Legion had been highly successful. In his annual report he reviewed his year of progress and achievement. His program for 1927 had set out certain definite objectives, the first of which was an increase in membership, and as a result Indiana was the first department to exceed its previous year's membership. For the first time since 1921 Indiana had regained its place among the ten largest departments of the country.[49]

The second objective of the state commander was the improvement of the organization internally. The establishment of county organizations and the strengthening of district organizations contributed largely to the success of the 1927 program. The third objective was to improve the quality of the service to disabled veterans and to the needy and homeless children of ex-service men. McNutt believed that such service was the Legion's most important duty and privilege. The department's vigorous support of a program of national defense had attracted wide attention and gratifying public support. The fact that the state of Indiana had passed its quota for the Citizens' Military Training program for the first time was further substantial evidence of the effectiveness of McNutt's work.

Community service and the education of the people in the duties of citizenship were also leading accomplishments of McNutt's term of office. A successful legislative program culminated in the victorious fight for the adequate support of the Knightstown home for the children of soldiers and sailors. One outstanding achievement of the year was the establishment of the *Hoosier Legionnaire,* an unpretentious news medium which contributed greatly to the successful completion of the year's program.[50]

During his year as state commander McNutt had corresponded with practically every state Legion organization, and his reputation as an orator brought him speaking engagements throughout Indiana and other parts of the country. It is not surprising, therefore, that he should be elected a member of the Legion national executive committee at the South Bend convention on July 25-26, 1927.

Toward the end of his term as commander, McNutt and his wife attended the annual Federation Interalliee Des Ancient Combattants (F I D A C) convention in Paris. They sailed on the *Celtic* on August 13, and returned on the *Leviathan* on October 11.[51] Shortly after his return he was appointed Civilian Aide to the Secretary of War for the state of Indiana for the next four years. His chief duty in this post was to perfect the civilian organization for the Citizens' Military Training Program.

But the governorship of the state of Indiana was also beckoning to McNutt at this time, and he had to make a decision whether or not to become an active candidate for the nomination in 1928. This would be the year when Indiana would elect a new governor, and many of McNutt's friends were pressuring him to become a candidate on the Democratic ticket. There was some feeling that the time was right for a housecleaning in Indiana, and many believed that with McNutt at the head of the ticket it could be done.[52] One correspondent wrote that he shared McNutt's opinion that 1928 "is a great opportunity for the Democratic Party" and would naturally like to see him make the race. He admitted, however, "under our present primary law it takes a millionaire to stand the pace, but I feel you are in a most excellent position to make the race with less expense than anyone else I know."[53]

Yet McNutt secretly was not sure that 1928 would be a Democratic year in Indiana. The Democrats had been in the minority in the state since 1916. Samuel M. Ralston had been the last Democratic governor, elected in 1912. But in the 1920's, the Republican Party had been weakened by the Ku Klux Klan episode. D. C. Stephenson, head of the Klan, had boasted that he was the law in Indiana. The Democrats, however, were not entirely free from connection with the Klan, although the Republican governor, Ed Jackson, seemed to have the support of Stephenson. But the Democrats had been gradually losing their strength in the state. Tom Taggart, their long-time leader, was no longer as powerful as he had been previously, and when he died in 1929 his son, Tom Jr., who succeeded him as the head of the party, did not have his father's political acumen. The party thus suffered through inadequate leadership.

Frank Dailey of Indianapolis appeared to be the strongest contender for the Democratic nomination for governor, in spite of McNutt's popularity in certain quarters, but the sentiment was not at all unanimous that Dailey could be elected if nominated. Much depended on the party's choice for president. McNutt's father wrote him in September, 1927, that "a bunch of western democrats got together the other day in Utah and undertook to boost Al Smith for president, but there was considerable opposition to their plan. I have no doubt that the boosters out there are working under the direction of one of Smith's eastern friends. I look upon his nomination as impossible if we are to have any hope of success. His nomination would make it next to impossible to elect a governor in

Indiana as I see it." The elder McNutt believed that if there were a separate ticket for president, Smith's nomination would not hurt the Indiana ticket, but this was, of course, out of the question. He was convinced that "if the Democrats ever get in power in Indiana they should pass a law providing for a separate ticket."[54]

Apparently McNutt concluded, therefore, that 1928 would not be a good year for any Democratic candidate for the Indiana governorship, so the decision was made to seek instead the office of national commander of the American Legion at the annual convention to be held in San Antonio, Texas, in the fall of 1928. He continued to write to his many Legion friends in Indiana and elsewhere, sounding out what support he might expect from various quarters.[55]

Many of his friends promised to back him after the favorite sons of their states had dropped out of the running. But McNutt was primarily concerned with the backing of his own and neighboring states. The Wisconsin department commander had readily given his support,[56] yet McNutt was not sure of Ohio and a few other strategic states.

In reply to a letter from a friend in Michigan City, McNutt declared that he was perfectly willing "to abide by the wishes of the majority of Hoosier Legionnaires but I must confess that an attempt on the part of some one outside of the state to meddle with our internal affairs goes against the grain. It looks as if the Campbell letter was a deliberate attempt to create some dissension within our own rank."[57] This was in reference to a letter which had been received from Milton Campbell, a businessman from Cincinnati and a leader in the Ohio Legion. In this letter, Campbell had urged the election of General Lee R. Gignilliat, head of Culver Military Academy.[58] Campbell did not believe McNutt could get the majority support in Indiana,[59] although he was reluctant to in-

terfere with affairs in his sister state.[60] Campbell admitted
that his own state commander was in favor of McNutt.[61]

McNutt wrote to Frank McHale, who had succeeded him
as state Legion commander, that "some one ought to enlighten
Milt Campbell that we will select our own candidate without
the aid of anyone outside."[62] But Campbell persisted. In
March he wrote McNutt directly, and again admitted that
Gignilliat could not be nominated or elected unless Indiana
were back of him. He knew that McNutt was a potential
candidate, but he asked him to give his confidential opinion
of the general's chances and if he would have any real opposition in the state "outside of yourself, and would you be
willing to step aside for the General if he does have a real
chance in the State of Indiana?"[63]

By this time, however, McNutt had no intention of stepping aside for Gignilliat or anyone else, although he wrote
to a friend that he feared Campbell's actions would cause
dissension in the ranks resulting in the defeat of any
Hoosier.[64] McNutt began to work furiously to line up support for himself throughout the state. Letters went out to all
district commanders, urging endorsement of his candidacy.
Such tactics produced favorable results immediately, and it
began to appear that he had nothing to fear from the Campbell opposition.

John Wheeler, who now became head of the McNutt-for-
Commander Committee, wrote to Howard P. Robinson, commander of the fourth district at Franklin, that McNutt
"should come away from San Antonio the National Commander. . . . Where could we find Paul's equal? . . . Paul has
endless ability and through faultless power of speech can display it. His diplomacy is of high rank and he can when called
upon, assume dignity that is genuine. . . . There may be
others in the state who aspire, or whose friends aspire for

them . . . but for services rendered and ability to carry on, it seems to me that McNutt is the man who deserves the honor and the easiest man to win with."[65]

McNutt himself wrote to one of his friends that he had been led to believe "that I will receive the endorsement of the state convention . . . and I have already received the assurance of support from several other states. I am in no sense a candidate against General Gignilliat and I do not feel that he is a candidate against me. The question, if there is a question, as to whose name should be presented from Indiana should be decided by the state convention and I am perfectly willing to abide by the decision of the majority."[66]

In the meantime other McNutt friends were writing him favorably on his candidacy. They deplored the situation caused by Campbell's support of Gignilliat. R. E. Snoberger of Goshen, Indiana, felt that "the present representatives of Legion thought can be depended upon to see that the American Legion as a whole is not yet in a condition where it can afford to honor any man, regardless of how deserving he may be, simply because it chooses to honor. We need now perhaps more than ever before, a man with ability and a will to work, to lead the Legion to its rightful place in both power and public opinion. We are not yet ready to give the helm to some Grand Old Man who is not in physical shape to conduct his administration with vigor."[67]

Another friend who had received Campbell's letter endorsing Gignilliat wrote McNutt:

"Nothing would please me more than to see you go to the top in anything that you desired. . . . I have no binding ties on the National Commandership, and if you want it, I will go the limit to assist you in any way to reach the goal."[63]

During the next two weeks McNutt had become confident of his nomination and he wrote Campbell on March 21, 1928, informing him that "without any solicitation on my part" various districts had already passed resolutions unanimously endorsing him, and "naturally I cannot disregard such an expression of confidence."[69] But Campbell replied that "the call [for Gignilliat] is not coming from Indiana but outside of Indiana and this being the case you should step down and wait your turn at a later date.[70]

Of course not every leader in the state was in favor of McNutt's candidacy. Tom McConnell of *The Benton Review* wrote him:

"I might as well be frank. I do not think this is a McNutt year for National Commander. . . . I have never been very enthusiastic over either your candidacy or that of the General this year. I do not believe that the Department should give any endorsement at the convention and would work against it if I thought I had any influence there. . . . It has not been a personal grudge or anything of that kind against you that has kept me opposed to your candidacy for National Commander. It has been my honest opinion in the interests of the Legion as I see them."[71]

McConnell further contended that there were many men in the Legion throughout the country who were more entitled to the commandership "long before any man I know in Indiana." When the time was right he thought McNutt could have the office without any opposition, but "to go out demanding it this year or even next year, to me brings many Legionnaires to the idea that you want it for personal rather than for Legion enthusiasm."[72]

However, many districts throughout the state now began to jump on the McNutt bandwagon. Flattering resolutions were passed endorsing his candidacy. The Henry Ray Post No. 65, Richmond, declared that McNutt had "conducted himself honorably and with great merit from his birth . . . even through his years . . . as a soldier in the World War. . . .

His judgment, patriotic interest and executive ability . . . was so recognized during the war. . . . His devotion to the patriotic interests of his country have won further recognition in National Defense Councils by his appointment as one of the Key Men of America, and as a past president of the Reserve Officers Association of Indiana. . . . He has displayed to the membership of the American Legion a keen conception of the organization's opportunities and responsibilities, to the objectives of the Legion has given tirelessly of his time and energies, . . . and upon whom all scholastic degrees and public honor rest modestly." The Post therefore did "unanimously and unreservedly recommend and urge . . . earnest consideration . . . confident his election will assure the conservation of the good name and traditions of our organization and that his matured judgment and youthful energies will add new lustre and achievements."[73]

Other resolutions and endorsements from many posts throughout the state followed in rapid succession, so that when the state Legion convention met at Lafayette August 26-28, McNutt became Indiana's favorite son for nomination at San Antonio. Congratulations came from all over the state. Frank A. White, state publicity officer for the American Legion, wrote:

"I have been all over the state and am happy to find that you have made many friends for yourself and for the Legion wherever you stopped. Assuring you that from first to last I believe in your sincerity, integrity and honesty, and that I am hoping that you may have every success at San Antonio and in the Legion in years to come."[74]

Frank M. McHale, state commander, sent a form letter to the Legionnaires in September, in which he praised McNutt's vigorous and wise leadership, and reviewed his Legion record and his services to the civic welfare of his community and state. He declared:

"No man is better qualified for leadership. His record as a soldier, a citizen and a Legionnaire is an unblemished record of unselfish constructive service. It is with pride and confidence that we offer him to the national organization for National Commander and solicit your active support."[75]

Many endorsements now began to arrive from various states, and McNutt was spurred on to more vigorous activity. He spoke at Legion gatherings from Wisconsin to Florida, and from New York to California, and won overwhelming support for his candidacy.

The national convention of The American Legion was held at San Antonio, Texas, in October, 1928. This city held pleasant memories for McNutt, as it was here that Mrs. McNutt had lived before they were married. He was therefore in friendly territory, which helped him with the press.

The strategy of Frank M. McHale, chosen as McNutt's national campaign manager, was most effective in finally securing the election for McNutt. McHale realized that McNutt would not be among the first two or three candidates on the first ballot, but he contacted all the Legion delegates and arranged to have the states, as their candidates dropped out of the running, cast their votes for McNutt. Finally, on October 10, all eight candidates lost ground and McNutt won the election unanimously on the third ballot. Incidentally, this was the same strategy that McHale and his followers employed later when McNutt was a candidate for the Vice Presidency of the United States; and had McNutt not withdrawn, he would have been nominated on the third ballot, if not the second.[76]

Telegrams and letters of congratulation began to flood the McNutt headquarters following his election as National Commander of the Legion. President William Lowe Bryan of Indiana University and President Edward C. Elliott of Purdue were among the first to send him greetings. A letter from Dwight Davis, Secretary of War, was especially significant. He wrote that he desired to "place at your disposition my personal services and the facilities of the War Department. Your record of fine leadership in the Organized Reserves attests your familiarity with measures for national defense and many of the problems of the War Department. That you bring such attributes to your new office gives us keen gratification, for we recognize that The American Legion constitutes a very important element in the formulation of policies with reference to national defense."[77]

McNutt's year as national commander of the Legion was a memorable experience. He and Mrs. McNutt traveled widely throughout the United States, but the highlight of the year was their trip to Europe to attend the F I D A C congress and to participate in the dedication of the Paris headquarters of The American Legion on August 7, 1929. McNutt gave one of the addresses on this occasion, and General John J. Pershing gave the response. M. Paul Painlevé, French minister of war, also spoke. A banquet was tendered in honor of McNutt on the same day. The McNutts were out of the United States from July 27 until September 1. During this period they toured the leading European capitals, and McNutt was received by Mussolini and the Pope, as well as by other leaders.

At the end of his year in office McNutt submitted to the Legion a statement of his mileage on official business. From October 13, 1928, to September 27, 1929, he had traveled 7,204 miles by steamship, 5,180 by plane, 61,740 by rail, 14,785 by auto, and 5,500 by taxi, for a grand total of 94,409 miles.[78]

After McNutt relinquished the duties of his office at the 11th annual Legion convention at Louisville September 30 to October 3, 1929, Harry H. Woodring, commander of the Kansas department, wrote him, expressing the sentiment of thousands of Legionnaires throughout the country. He predicted that "as a guide for excellency, prestige, real service, and leadership unsurpassed, future Commanders and administrations will tear from Legion history the page marked '1929–Paul V. McNutt, Commander.' With no thought of flattery, but true sincerity, Paul, the year has been outstanding in the leadership you have given us. To me, your great contribution and outstanding service has been through your speeches before the citizenry of the nation other than the Legionnaires, because of the prestige you have brought to our organization in giving the résumé of the ideals, the aims, purposes, and accomplishments of The American Legion to the general public. To me, this has been your greatest contribution. You have given much when you raised the prestige of our organization in the minds and opinion of the citizenry of the nation."[79]

An interesting pesonal reference to McNutt's activities as head of the Legion has been furnished by John T. Winterich, who was at that time editor of *The American Legion Monthly*. This periodical was a New York corporation owned outright by The American Legion, and the national commander was ex-officio president of the corporation. As such, he had to attend the annual meeting, which was a pro-forma affair designed only to fulfill the corporation's legal obligations. The only time McNutt was ever in the *Monthly* office (then at 520 Fifth Avenue) was for this purpose.

Winterich relates the following incident which occurred on this occasion:

[60]

"I greeted him [McNutt] and assigned him an office in which he could make himself at home. His first act was to lift a briefcase to the desk-top and open it. 'Technically,' he said, 'I am violating the laws of your state.' He reached into the briefcase and extracted a large Colt revolver. 'I spoke to the Legionnaires of Hartford, Connecticut, last night,' he explained, 'and they gave me this.' He signed whatever papers he was required to sign and was soon on his way."[80]

McNutt's handling of Legion affairs was quite typical of the man. Winterich reports that "the personnel of Legion national headquarters at Indianapolis and, to a lesser extent, the staff of the magazine were in a dither every time a new national commander was elected. Over the years a good many national commanders, on election, appeared to act on the idea that all of their predecessors had done everything wrong but now things were going to be different. In practice, a new commander soon found himself caught up in such a tough schedule of speaking dates that he forgot all about his plan to lop off a few heads at Indianapolis or to tell the editor how to run the magazine, though he might occasionally pop into the magazine office and lay down some commands which he promptly forgot all about."[81]

"Not so McNutt," according to Winterich. "His appearance at the annual corporation meeting that fell during his commandership was the full extent of his 'interference' with the conduct of the magazine. You may be sure that endeared him to me. I have good second-hand evidence that his 'interference' with the operation of national headquarters was no more extensive. The national adjutant of the Legion at the time of McNutt's election was James F. Barton. Barton later told me that on McNutt's first visit to national headquarters as commander, he said to Barton:

'Jim, you stay here and run things and I'll go out and put on the medicine show.' "[82]

Whether his activities could be called a "medicine show" or something else, McNutt spent a good deal of his time during the year as national commander in denouncing the peace-by-disarmament propagandists who were working throughout the country. These agents were vigorously condemned by the American Legion at its state and national conventions, and McNutt was determined to weaken or destroy their effectiveness. As early as 1926 he had stated that the people had to choose between the Legion's program of "a sound national defense system and the pacifist plea that this country shall disarm and hope that the rest of the world will follow."[83] Yet some in Indiana and elsewhere criticized him for his attacks on "those he pleases to brand as pacifists."[84] Others called him "one of the world's most consistent, if not the most effective peace advocates," whose thoughts "on the subject of war, or of guarding against war, deserve consideration by every citizen in this country who is capable of thinking."[85]

McNutt impressed many thinking citizens as having one of the most effective plans for insuring peace, that of being prepared for war to such a degree that this country could not be safely attacked by any other on any pretext, or for any reason. He did not want war, but he was certainly no pacifist. He would not incite another country to violence against the United States, of course, nor would he want his country to remain in a weakened condition which would be a handicap should it be forced into war. His influence did much to bring added support to the national defense program.

While McNutt was national commander there was considerable debate following the failure of the Geneva Conference of 1927, which had sought a formula among the leading world powers to limit lesser naval craft, especially destroyers, cruisers, and submarines. In Novembner, 1927, the so-called Butler Cruiser bill was introduced in Congress, providing for the construction of twenty-five cruisers, five aircraft carriers, and other craft at a cost of $725 million. Some members of Congress attacked the bill as a step toward immediate and inevitable war, and this view was supported by Quakers and many other groups, with the result that the bill was finally withdrawn in favor of a substitute providing for fewer craft at about a third of the cost.

This new Navy Cruiser bill passed the House in March, 1928, but the Senate did not consider it until February, 1929. President Hoover, who took office in March, now urged complete naval parity between England and the United States. Meanwhile McNutt, representing the American Legion, was advocating the passage of the cruiser bill. He protested the curtailing of cruiser building, and sent a telegram to President Hoover insisting that the lost naval parity must be regained.[86]

In his reply, President Hoover commended the Legion for its support of parity, which he described as a first step toward reduction of excessive world naval armament. It seemed to him that it was far better to have parity than disparity, which "creates burdensome expenditure, a constant stream of suspicion, ill-will and misunderstandings." Moreover, he felt that "by constant expansion of naval strength we cannot fail to stimulate fear and ill-will throughout the world toward both of us [the United States and Great Britain] and thus defeat the very purposes which you have so well expressed as being the object of the Legion, when you say, 'The Legion stands uniformly for movements which will make permanent peace more certain and assure better understanding between nations.' "[87]

President Hoover expressed his confidence that the American Legion "will be sympathetic with the principles of parity by negotiation and of reduction and limitation instead of competitive building, with its continuous expansion and all its train of world dangers." He was further confident that the Legion "will join with me in endeavoring to establish and cooperate with others in an atmosphere of good-will and sincerity within which to find such a solution." He declared that the United States and other nations had entered into a solemn covenant "that we shall seek to settle disputes by pacific means . . . and every effort should be made to establish confidence in our intentions and to hold our preparedness programs solely within the area of efficient defense." Hoover was certain that "these policies are consonant with the many declarations of the American Legion and the sentiment of the American people."[88]

The cruiser and parity issues continued to be debated throughout the rest of McNutt's term as national commander. In his annual report to the 11th annual Legion convention at Louisville, he strongly urged that the United States continue to build cruisers until parity was reached.[89] Apparently the position of the Legion was accepted generally, because the principle was recognized at the London Naval Conference which opened on January 21, 1930. As a result, the London Naval Treaty of April 22, 1930, provided essentially for parity with Great Britain, with an "escape" clause, which allowed any signatory nation to build above treaty limits if some other power, not bound by the London agreement, engaged in a construction program that might threaten the safety of the signatory power. This was fundamentally McNutt's position, although some experts warned that the treaty might prevent the American navy from satisfactorily defending the United States and its positions. Nevertheless the treaty was approved by the Senate on July 21 by a vote of 58 to 9.[90]

Notes for Chapter 2

[1] McNutt Collection.

[2] *Ibid.*

[3] Letter to McNutt from William M. Mumm, Columbus, Ohio, February 20, 1926.

[4] McNutt Collection

[5] February 26, 1926.

[6] Letter from L. J. McNair, Major F. A. (Dol) P. M. S. & T., Purdue University, March 5, 1926.

[7] McNutt Collection. Letter from Frank Streightoff, Indiana Council on International Relations, 3343 North New Jersey Street, Indianapolis, on letterhead of National Council for Prevention of War, Washington, D. C., date March 6, 1926.

[8] McNutt to Streightoff, March 8, 1926.

[9] McNutt Collection

[10] McNutt Collection.

[11] Letter to McNutt from Mrs. Frank D. (Mary N.) Hatfield, 3858 North New Jersey Street, Indianapolis, March 7, 1926.

[12] Copy of letter to Major General R. L. Bullard, President, National Security League, New York City, from C. L. Townsend, Corporal, Infantry (DOL) Chief of Staff, March 10, 1926. Copy sent to McNutt.

[13] Robert A. Adams, National Judge Advocate, The American Legion, Indianapolis, March 8, 1926.

[14] McNutt to Robert A. Adams, March 10, 1926.

[15] Carbon copy of letter to Nelson H. Kellogg, President, Department of Indiana R. O. T. C., Purdue University, Lafayette, from Fred B. Ryons, Lt. Col., Engr. Res., Sec. R. O. A. of United States.

[16] McNutt to Col. Fred B. Ryons, Washington, D. C., March 15, 1926.

[17] McNutt Collection.

[18] McNutt Collection.

[19] Letter to McNutt from B. F. Ristine, Indianapolis, March 15, 1926.

[20] Herbert S. Hadley to McNutt, May 28, June 2, June 19, June 20, June 23, June 28, 1926.

[21] McNutt to Hadley, July 14, 1926.

[22] McNutt Collection.

[23] Hadley to McNutt, July 20, 1926.

[24] McNutt Collection.

[25] McNutt to Hadley, July 23, 1926.

[26] John C. McNutt to Paul McNutt, July 23, 1926.

[27] McNutt to David Jennings, July 28, 1926.

[28] Hadley to McNutt, August 3, 1926.

[29] McNutt to Freal H. McIntosh, Indianapolis, August 2, 1926.

[30] Jack Alexander, "It Would be Kind of Nice to be President, Wouldn't It?" in *Life* N. V.:71, January 29, 1940.

[31] Frank M. McHale to author.

[32] *Vincennes Commercial,* September 1, 1926.

[33] Hugh A. Barnhart to McNutt, September 1, 1926. McNutt Collection.

[34] W. M. Louden, Commandant, Indiana State Soldiers Home, to McNutt, September 16, 1926.

[35] Carl M. Gray, Petersburg, Indiana, to McNutt, September 10, 1926.

[36] McNutt to Gray, October 6, 1926.

[37] McNutt Collection.

[38] Edith Wright, Fairmount, Indiana, to McNutt, February 12, 1927.

[39] McNutt to J. H. Eilar, Supt. of Schools, Henry County, New Castle, Indiana, February 28, 1927.

[40] From Unionville High School, Unionville, Indiana, April 28, 1927.

[41] McNutt Collection.

[42] *Ibid.*

[43] McNutt to Ray H. Weisbrood, Commander Harry Ray Post No. 65, The American Legion, Federal Building, Indianapolis, March 5, 1927.

[44] McNutt Collection.

[45] C. M. Piper, Akron, Ohio, to McNutt, May 2, 1927.

[46] Letter to McNutt from Frederick E. Shortemeier, Indiana Secretary of State, June 2, 1927.

[47] L. W. MacKinnon to McNutt, July 6, 1927.

[48] McNutt to MacKinnon, July 11, 1927.

[49] Annual Report of the Department Commander for 1927. McNutt Collection.

[50] McNutt Collection.

[51] McNutt to Frank H. Henley, D. F. C. O. Dept. of Indiana, Indianapolis, May 2, 1927. Telegram to McNutt from W. M. Louden, Lafayette, Indiana, July 24, 1927. Also letter to McNutt from Charles R. Metzger, Indianapolis, August 10, 1927. Letter to McNutt from A. B. Bowman, Johnson City, Tennessee, August 11, 1927. Letter to McNutt from William Hyland, Commander, Funkhouser Post #8, Evansville, August 13, 1927. Sent to McNutt at Grand Hotel Place de L'Opera, Paris. McNutt Collection.

[52] Letter to McNutt from Ralph W. Smith, LaPorte, Indiana, September 15, 1927. McNutt Collection.

[53] Letter from J. M. Stephenson, Publisher of the South Bend *News-Times,* September 15, 1927. McNutt Collection.

[54] John C. McNutt to Paul V. McNutt, September 27, 1927.

[55] See 51 above.

[56] Letter to D. J. Kenny, March 10, 1928.

[57] Letter to Richard J. Kruse, Michigan City, Indiana, February 24, 1928. McNutt Collection.

[58] Milton D. Campbell to Richard J. Kruse, Chief of Police, Michigan City, Indiana, February 22, 1928.

[59] Campbell to Kruse, February 28, 1928.

[60] Campbell to Frank M. McHale, February 28, 1928.

[61] McNutt Collection.

[62] McNutt to McHale, February 28, 1928.

[63] Campbell to McNutt, March 13, 1928.

[64] McNutt to John W. Wheeler, March 2, 1928.

[65] John Wheeler to Howard P. Robinson, March 16, 1928.

[66] McNutt to Jackiel W. Joseph, March 10, 1928.

[67] R. E. Snoberger to McNutt, Goshen, Indiana, March 3, 1928.

[68] Pleas E. Greenlee Shelbyville, to McNutt, March 16, 1928.

[69] McNutt to Campbell, March 21, 1928.

[70] Campbell to McNutt, March 22, 1928.

[71] Tom McConnell, *Benton Review,* Fowler, to McNutt, July 24, 1928.

[72] McNutt Collection.

[73] Resolution of the Harry Ray Post No. 65, The American Legion, Richmond, Indiana, March 26, 1928.

[74] Frank A. White to McNutt, August 28, 1928.

[75] From letter from Frank McHale, Commander, Dept. of Indiana American Legion, September, 1928.

[76] McHale to author.

[77] Dwight Davis, Secretary of War, to McNutt, October 15, 1928.

[78] McNutt Collection.

[79] McNutt from Harry H. Woodring, Neodesha, Kansas, October 15, 1929.

[80] Letter to author from John T. Winterich, Brayton Park, Ossining, New York, March 24, 1963.

[81] *Ibid.*

[82] *Ibid.*

[83] Editorial, Indianapolis *News,* November 16, 1926.

[84] Editorial, Kokomo, Indiana, *Dispatch,* December 3, 1926.

[85] Editorial, Bloomington *Star* (no date)

[86] New York *Sun,* January 23, 1929; New York *Times,* July 15, 1929.

[87] Letter from President Herbert Hoover, Washington, D. C., to McNutt, July 30, 1929. McNutt Collection.

[88] McNutt Collection.

[89] Louisville *Herald Post,* September 30, 1929.

[90] Oscar Theodore Barck, Jr. and Nelson Manfred Blake, *Since 1900* (Third Edition) Macmillan, New York, 1959, pp. 426-429.

CHAPTER III

Political Stirrings

Although McNutt chose the national commandership of the American Legion instead of the possible governorship of Indiana in 1928, his interest in partisan politics was by no means curtailed or even reduced during the year. It was merely not so publicly apparent. He continued to carry on an extensive correspondence with his friends in the Democratic party throughout the state and other parts of the country regarding issues and candidates of both political parties.

This correspondence reveals some interesting side lights on the general political situation which prevailed in 1928. There was much speculation, of course, as to the identity of the person whom the Republicans would choose to head the national ticket, and also his possible running mate. The decision, naturally, would affect the outcome of the gubernatorial race in Indiana. Senator James E. Watson was being mentioned for the presidential nomination by some Hoosiers, although the situation in Indiana seemed very confused. It was felt by some that if the Republicans were to nominate somebody like Watson, or even Charles Curtis, the Democrats would have an excellent chance of a victory.[1]

As for the Democrats, the nomination of Governor Alfred E. Smith of New York seemed inevitable, although even the Democrats were not sure that he could win the election if Herbert Hoover were his opponent. George Ade, prominent Hoosier humorist, thought the Republicans started with a big edge "because they have reduced taxes for those influential citizens everywhere who provide campaign funds and know how to mold public sentiment by indirect methods." In his opinion Hoover was "a most useful citizen but I do not think he will ever be a popular figure. I think he is too clammy and autocratic." Ade thought the Republican party had "treated the farmers of the middle west with extreme contempt. It is bad enough to starve to death without being scolded about it," he wrote.[2]

Ade was vitriolic in his comments. He thought the Republicans "deserve defeat for their absolute cowardice and hypocrisy regarding prohibition and the Volstead Act. The national and state legislators and the delegates to all of the conventions sit in their rooms and drink anything that comes out of a bottle and has an alcoholic content and then march over to the convention hall, stepping high, and vote for 'rigid enforcement.' They do not believe in it and if enforcement ever became rigid they would suffer greatly but they continue to enact the sickening farce because they are afraid of the Anti-Saloon League, the Baptists, the Methodists and the W.C.T.U."[3]

As for the Democrats, Ade thought that the party was "certainly a medley, an olio, a crazy quilt and an assortment of odds and ends." He felt that Smith was a good candidate, but doubted if he could be elected in 1928. "Sooner or later," he wrote, "we should elect a Catholic to the Presidency just to prove that we are living in the 20th Century instead of the 18th and that witch-burning and religious persecutions are no longer the pastime of a free and intelligent people." He believed that Al Smith "is entitled to all the praise in the world for his courage and sincerity in telling the truth about the Eighteenth Amendment and the Volstead Act. He said what ten thousand politicians in the Republican party knew to be true but were afraid to say out loud. He will develop great strength in the east and in the cities and will be ambushed by all of the Protestants and fanatics and bigots who have dark minds and are narrow between the eyes."[4]

After checking up on the opposition to Governor Smith, Ade wrote that he was tempted to vote for him "because I do not wish, at any time, to be found in the same camp with the mental dwarfs and perverts who are raging against him. I think he would be a much pleasanter room-mate than Herbert Hoover. Al knows how to sing a song and to him the world is an alluring spectacle." As for Hoover, Ade admitted that he "has been a real humanitarian, but he does not sing. He has filled many a stomach but probably never made a heart beat any faster. If he is elected our beloved country will continue to be run on a factory system of scientific management and prosperity will continue. If it continues much longer in the present direction, we who have invested our money in farm lands will be playing checkers in the large red-brick poor-houses which dot the middle west."[5]

Governor Smith, of course, was nominated for the presidency at the Democratic convention at Houston. But many of McNutt's friends were bitterly disappointed in the nomination. One wrote that "Tammany had the convention under its paw from the beginning. The opposition was not only steam-rollered, but gagged. One way to get harmony is with a sandbag and the Smith crowd were very efficient in this method. . . . Never before have I felt it necessary for a Democrat to think about a national election. However, I am thinking harder than I ever did in my life. I have not yet been able to reconcile myself to Smith's nomination. If the crowd that ran the Houston convention will run the next administration in the event of Smith's election, it makes me shudder to think of it."[6]

The Indiana delegation was chided for wasting no time in climbing on the Smith band wagon, but one of McNutt's friends, Gilchrist Stockton, wondered what effect the nomination had on Democrats in Indiana like McNutt. Stockton wrote McNutt that the Republican party in Indiana was "so rotten that it is almost as difficult for you as any Southerner to feel charitably inclined toward any Republican in an election," and he asked McNutt if there were any chance of Smith's carrying the state.[7]

In his reply, McNutt declared that he felt Smith "has little or no chance to carry Indiana. If he loses the state by over a hundred thousand I am afraid that he will carry the state ticket to defeat with him." McNutt believed that "conditions have been so rotten in Indiana that we have literally prayed for a Democratic state administration. We have a first-rate ticket and, under normal conditions, would have a good chance of winning." But he admitted that no one had a clearly defined idea of what would happen in the fall. "The farmers seem to be embattled. Business is not good. These two factions have carried elections in the past. On the other hand our people have given evidence of strong prejudices and these may outweigh the economic factors."[8]

In the meantime the Hoosier Democrats had nominated Frank C. Dailey for the gubernatorial post against Republican Harry Leslie, and McNutt wanted very much to stump the state for his party. But on account of his high position in the American Legion, he decided not to take an active part in the campaign.[9] Dick Heller of the Democratic speakers' bureau asked McNutt if he could give a few dates during the latter part of the campaign for such speeches. "You could do us a world of good," he wrote.[10] But McNutt replied that although "I should like to see Frank Dailey elected Governor" yet "as long as I hold office in the American Legion and am actively in Legion work I seriously question the advisability of making any partisan political speeches. Politics and The American Legion do not mix, and I am very anxious to keep the Legion out of politics."[11]

Following Dailey's 45,000-vote defeat for the governorship by Leslie, the Indiana Democrats began their search for a potential candidate for 1932. McNutt's election to the national commandership of the Legion made him attractive as a candidate possibility, although the Legion was supposed to be non-political. But it was a recognized fact that Legion affiliation was almost necessary for the attainment of any political ambitions in Indiana at that time, because the veteran vote was so well organized.

Yet McNutt was torn between his intense interest in practical politics and his aspirations in other fields. During the year he was Legion commander he had taken a leave of absence from his teaching duties at the Indiana University law school, although he was still charged with the determination of the administrative policies of the school. All of the other members of the faculty had signed a letter requesting him to remain dean and emphatically stating that no acting dean should be appointed. McNutt found that his new duties demanded all the time available and he wished "that the days were twenty-four hours longer."[12] Early in January, 1929, he left on an extended speaking tour of the United States, and did not return to his dean's office until April. [13]

Just before the San Antonio convention of the Legion, McNutt finished the draft of a new General Corporations

Bill for Indiana, to be presented to the General Assembly in January. The purpose of the revision was to bring the Indiana law in keeping with present-day tendencies and modern thought.[14] At the same time he was forced by pressure of other work to cancel his plans to write a casebook on taxation.[15]

During this period also, McNutt was approached by several education institutions to determine his interest in and availability for certain appointments. One of these inquiries came from Syracuse University, inquiring if there were any possibility of interesting him in the deanship of their newly reorganized college of law, which Dean Pound of Harvard had helped in planning. But Chancellor Flint of Syracuse feared that McNutt was so deeply rooted in Indiana that there would be no possibility of interesting him, although he hoped "that there may be some possible chance that you would enjoy working in this part of the country."[16] There is no indication that McNutt was interested in this situation.

The University of Michigan at this time was searching for a successor to President Clarence Cook Little, and McNutt's name was suggested as a possibility. Governor Fred W. Green, according to one newspaper editorial headed "Keep Politics Out," had suggested to the regents that McNutt "would make a good headmaster for the Ann Arbor school." But the editorial writer hoped "there is some mistake about the story. The task of selecting a new president for the University of Michigan is exclusively a matter for the regents of the institution to handle; and even the appearance of political interference ought to be avoided scrupulously. . . . The regents may very properly ask advice and enlightenment from persons qualified to give them expert help and information in connection with the job they have in hand, but there should be no attempt to 'influence' them."[17]

Apparently Governor Green had endorsed McNutt as Little's successor at the American Legion convention at Lansing. But a story in the Detroit *News* commented on an editorial in the student publication scoring Green, and questioning whether the governor was serious or merely "handing out a bouquet in accordance with the etiquette of the occasion." The editorial claimed that Green "would like to reduce the university to a source of political patronage." The governor was reported to have laughed at the editorial and remarked: "Every time I grow expansive I get into trouble."[18]

The governor's endorsement proved to be more of a detriment than an aid to McNutt's possible candidacy. The reaction against the governor put McNutt completely out of the running, although Frank McHale, a national executive committeeman of the American Legion, and an alumnus of the University of Michigan, who seemed to be his campaign manager, continued to push his candidacy.[19] Another Legion friend of McNutt wrote to McHale that while on a recent visit to Hudson, Michigan, he was able "to stir up the interest of two men who have quite a little influence [with certain members of the Board of Regents] . . . and are now very much interested in having Paul offered the Presidency of the University of Michigan and they are two good Legion men. They promised me faithfully . . . [to use] plenty of pressure in Paul's favor."[20] Evidently such pressure was not sufficient, as no formal offer of the Michigan position was ever made to McNutt.

McHale seemed to be determined to have McNutt receive a firm offer from some educational institution, probably as a springboard to higher services. He had received a letter from his sister, in which she enclosed a copy of a letter of recommendation written by her to Goucher College, suggesting McNutt's name as a possibility for the presidency of that institution. In his reply McHale suggested "that they had better get busy and do something, or else someone would take advantage of their lack of interest." He further suggested that she inform the authorities that McNutt was satisfied at Indiana, but he wasn't being properly compensated, and that the demands on him to uphold the reputation of the school cost more than the office paid.[21]

Dr. Kathryn McHale, who was educational secretary and acting director of the Washington branch of the American Association of University Women, strongly urged McNutt to consider the Goucher offer if it were made to him. The salary, she said, would be "ten thousand, a free house with upkeep, and free service."[22] She enclosed a copy of a letter she had written to acting Goucher president Hans Froelicher on November 16, 1929, recommending McNutt as "the outstanding college presidential material among the various persons around forty years of age considered by the University of Michigan authorities, and was given the offer of that university but refused it for reasons I do not know."[23]

McNutt wrote McHale that he deeply appreciated his sister's interest and efforts in connection with the Goucher vacancy, but he could not bring himself "to believe that I could be perfectly happy as president of a women's college."[24] In a letter to Miss McHale he admitted that "in many respects such a place would be most attractive," but after careful consideration he had come to the conclusion "that I would not be happy in that particular educational field." His interest had always been in co-education and he had been rather outspoken on this subject in spite of the fact "I recognize the outstanding service rendered by such institutions as Goucher College."[25] He claimed that he had had "some very interesting professional and business propositions but have not had an opportunity to give much attention to my personal affairs for over a year." He expected to make a definite decision within the next few weeks as to his future. "My desire is to stay in Indiana. My judgment is that I should leave," he concluded.[26]

By the end of 1929 McNutt had almost reached the decision to enter the active political arena. In the November municipal elections the Democrats won sweeping victories in Indianapolis, Evansville, Lafayette, South Bend, and other Indiana communities. These successes followed quickly in the wake of the stock-market crash of October 29, and the panic which resulted was in turn succeeded by a long period of depression, perhaps the most severe in American history. The Democrats wasted no time in capitalizing on the situation, while the efforts of the Republicans seemed to be a matter of "too little and too late," according to their opponents. This remarkable resurgence displayed by the Democrats in Indiana, as well as elsewhere, indicated that the people were anxious for a change in party control.

The many friends of McNutt, both Republicans and Democrats, now began urging him to become a candidate for governor in 1932. One wrote McNutt that it seemed to him "it might be an opportune time for you to make the race." He was assuming, he said, that McNutt could get the Democratic nomination without a serious fight. He asserted that McNutt was "one of the most finished public speakers I have ever listened to and I am sure that you would be very convincing and effective on the stump. You also have a very amiable way in dealing with your fellowmen. I have known few men in my life with your intellectual attainments who could mix as well as you do. . . . I believe you would have better than an even chance of winning the governorship if you had a united party behind you. If you should make the race and lose, your sacrifice would not be in vain, because

I know your campaign would do much to elevate the politics of Indiana, but also the people of the whole United States would soon have reason to be proud of you."[27]

On January 18, 1930, McNutt wrote Stockton that he had had several visits from delegates from various parts of the state, all begging him to become a candidate for office, "and it looks as if it would be possible to get the nomination for governor or senator without much trouble." But he had not made up his mind that he could afford to get into politics. "I have spent all of my time since graduation from college," he wrote, "in unremunerative public service and for that reason I have not been able to accumulate a [fortune]." He had a strong feeling that the next ten or fifteen years "should be devoted in assuring a future for my family." He claimed that he was seriously considering offers to go to New York or Washington. "If such a move is made," he wrote, "I must forget politics. Even if I stay in this part of the country by reason of making satisfactory connections it may be wise to forget politics."[28]

In referring to the results of the 1929 off-year elections, McNutt thought they indicated future success for the party. "If our forces are properly organized it might be possible to carry the state in 1932. However, the members of the opposition seem to have a happy faculty in forgetting their differences when the stakes are large. 1932 will be such a year with a president, governor, and a senator to elect," he warned. He also predicted that the South would return to the Democratic fold in the national election. "If this happens and the alliance between the western Republican liberals and Democrats continues it is possible to hope for Democratic success."[29]

On February 11 McNutt wrote to his Legion friend Douglas I. McKay, president of the Standard Coupler Company of

New York City and former New York City police commissioner, that a political situation was developing rapidly "but I have given no answer to the delegations which have come to Bloomington. It looks as if the nomination for Governor or United States Senator would be open without much effort and I shall appreciate your advice as the matter develops. I have agreed to make three political speeches within the next few weeks but I have no intention of making any statement concerning personal desires or ambitions at this time."[30]

Several of McNutt's Indiana friends tried to induce him to become a candidate for secretary of state in 1930. Among these was J. H. Heller of the Decatur *Democrat,* who wrote: "While I realize it would be some sacrifice to you I feel it worth it for I am sure it would make you a leader around whom we could build for years to come and that's what our party needs in Indiana."[31] The same sentiment was expressed by Samuel C. Cleland of Fort Wayne, who felt that the secretary of state's office "is the one office in the state wherein an organization can be built which is of value to the Democratic party. In addition to that, if you contemplate becoming a candidate for United States senator from Indiana, it would be invaluable to you. . . . If you decide to become a candidate I feel that the sooner the announcement is made the better position you will occupy in that it may keep some contemplated aspirants out of the field, if there are any."[32]

Joseph M. Cravens, another Hoosier Democratic leader, wrote McNutt that the party was "in great need of an outstanding, magnetic character, a man with elements of leadership around whom it can rally." He felt that McNutt had these qualities. He admitted that the suggestion he was about to make "is not naturally attractive. Yet, it can be tolerated for a short time since it is but a stepping stone to the highest gift the people of our commonwealth can bestow upon one of its citizens, *i. e.*, the United States Senate or the Governorship of our State. . . . I feel that you should allow your name to head the State ticket [secretary of state]. I also feel assured you will be elected in November, two years in this office will afford you splendid opportunity to work up an impregnable organization, preparatory to the '32 campaign. I am not alone in believing you are the best equipped man in Indiana for leadership of the Democratic party. Many others are of the same opinion and have so expressed themselves to me."[33]

William A. Kunkel, Jr., expressed the same ideas in a letter to McNutt on February 18, informing him that he was "the general topic of conversation at the Indiana Editorial Banquet. . . . I discussed the matter with Skitz [Simmons] who says there will be practically no opposition as there will be two or three other candidates who are very weak." Kunkel thought McNutt was "too capable for this position . . . but if elected . . . you will be in the most advantageous position on account of you being able to perfect an organization from the many appointees and commissions that you would control."[34]

Many inquiries about his candidacy for political office were received by McNutt, who finally issued a form letter giving two main reasons why he thought he should not become actively engaged in politics. It was his belief that his candidacy "would give color to the accusations made in every Legion convention in which I have been a candidate and inspired by the Republican State Committee, that I wanted Legion office in order to build up a political background. This is absolutely false as you know." The second reason for not entering politics was the serious illness of his daughter Louise, who had required the services of a nurse for over the past four years. This had been a very heavy expense, and he was reluctant to inflict any additional sacrifice upon his family.[35]

These same sentiments were expressed in a letter to Cravens on March 10, in which McNutt concluded that it would be "unwise to make the race." He would rather have "the friendship of ex-service men than any political office in the gift of the people. It would not be possible to explain to many of these friends if I were to enter a political campaign as a candidate within a year after retirement as National Commander." He realized the office of secretary of state was a powerful one by reason of patronage, "but the fact remains that it is purely a political office and, to accept it, would mean a definite loss of prestige and following." From a financial standpoint he could not afford to accept the office, as the salary was not large enough to maintain his household. He declared if it had not been for employment in two or three important cases and for revenue from public addresses "it would have been impossible for me to meet my expenses for the past four years." He therefore thought he could render a greater service off the ticket than on it.[36]

Others were urging McNutt to become a candidate to fill the vacancy on the Unites States Supreme Court caused by the death of Justice Sanford.[37] Frank White wrote McNutt that he had mentioned it to Frank McHale "telling him your friends here both in and out of the Legion were speaking of you for the vacancy." McHale would be glad to say that friends were mentioning his name "and let the story come out of Logansport." On the other hand White felt sure "that the Indianapolis *Star* would make such a suggestion in an editorial. It could then be picked up and put out on the basis of this editorial. Eddie Lewis or Jack Taylor could in Washington mention it to the Washington correspondent of an Indianapolis newspaper and it might receive better play originating there. Doug McKay might start it. A Legion post might pass a resolution urging this."[38]

White then wrote to John Thomas Taylor at Washington, D. C., asking him to "drop to the correspondents in Washington" that McNutt's name was being considered for the Supreme Court appointment. He believed that the Indiana correspondents there would carry such a suggestion "and coming out of Washington it would get special attention in this state. It would then be picked up by papers in the state and followed with editorials, I am sure. . . . Anything you might do to tip off the Washington newspapermen . . . would be appreciated."[39]

Other friends thought McNutt should turn his political intentions in other directions. Fred A. Wiecking of Bluffton wrote that he had discouraged some talk he had heard about the secretaryship of state "because I have greater ambitions for you and can't help but feel that a term in that office would hinder rather than help you." He felt the time was rapidly approaching "when an ex-service man is going to guide the destinies of the nation from the White House, and I know of no man better fitted by training, background and ability, than yourself. . . . I have been suggesting to Democrats generally that we have a man, in you, whom the democracy of Indiana can sincerely present to our next national convention with the united support of all factions in Indiana and the added assurance of substantial Republican support in the election; and that under his leadership, Indiana will again be back in the Democratic column all the way down the line."[40]

Wiecking also indicated his belief that Al Smith would not be a candidate in the 1932 convention and therefore would lend his support to a midwest or western candidate. He was convinced that McNutt was doing the right thing at the present time in refusing to be a candidate for a state office, but he believed he should give his friends "a chance to start some propaganda toward securing the wholehearted endorsement of our state convention in two years." He had talked to Skitz Simmons "and he feels like I do. This is the time for your friends to start talking."[41]

McKay thought that McNutt's choice should be between the senatorship and the governorship. Of the two he advised the latter, as it was an executive office, and McNutt had "demonstrated a high degree of executive talent, and in a state such as Indiana the record there would be observed beyond its borders." It was his opinion that the United States Senate was becoming increasingly "a hotbed of feuds, from which no great personal opportunity is likely to arise—or if it should, is likely to be other than a target of abuse. . . . A Governor *can* be both efficient and popular. . . . . But I feel that the very atmosphere of the Senate might prove unhealthy or even destructive of the ambitions which your friends entertain for you."[42]

In regard to the Democratic presidential nomination in 1932, McKay thought it was impossible that Smith would run again. "He might rather undertake to influence such loyalty as may be bound to or due him toward the nomination of his successor in the Governorship. And as that brings up the subject of Governor Roosevelt being acceptable to the party, I have conceded him everything, as matters stand, except his health in my estimate of the situation. But that one exception must prove fatal to his chances in my opinion. But unless his recovery is miraculous from now on it simply could not be that the leaders of the party would offer his candidacy as that of one in physical shape to withstand the ordeal of service as Chief Executive. Nor could the deepest sympathy with his affliction offset the lack of confidence with which his prospective usefulness would be viewed by the voters of the party and by those independently inclined."[43]

McKay also mentioned two other possible angles for thought on this subject, although he admitted both were most remote according to his view of the situation. "One would contemplate securing the nomination for President without a preliminary term as Governor or Senator. I do not think this is feasible," he wrote. The other would be a "direct drive on the nomination for Vice President, but that seems to exclude itself as inappropriate to the larger plans contemplated herein," he felt. He believed that if Hoover lived and kept his health, it was almost certain "that he will desire to be reelected. Although off to a bad start, for much of which he is personally responsible, the public memory is generous and the theory of chance is that the closing years of his first term will disclose him in a happier and more esteemed public regard." There was some grave doubt in McKay's mind that McNutt's real chance could come in 1932. If it did, he wrote, so much the better, "but it were wiser to look and plan beyond that time." If McNutt were elected governor in 1932, and had a successful administration, "it would be difficult to deny you the Presidential nomination in 1936," he predicted.[44]

L. G. Balfour, head of a large fraternity jewelry firm in Attleboro, Massachusetts, informed McNutt that at a recent meeting in Boston attended largely by Legion men he had heard "a man who is nationally known make a statement that he was willing to gamble that within the next fifteen years you would be President of the United States. This was quite a coincidence because I have heard this statement several times lately in various sections of the country."[45] McNutt replied that "while the temptation is strong I have determined to be reasonably silent and to keep my feet on the ground for the next few months while the situation develops.

The glamour of public office is overshadowed by the work and grief involved and I think there is far more satisfaction in having a host of loyal friends than in any political preferment."[46]

Another friend wrote McNutt that he believed "if you play your cards cautiously that you will be sitting in a good spot, but . . . there will no doubt be some opposition from the New York Democrats, who will think the candidacy should go to an easterner in order to win New York, if possible. I think it would be a cinch for you to be the candidate for Vice President, but the question is whether you want to do that. In any event, I am sure that you can count on a lot of support from Northern Indiana along any political lines you have in mind. You will get a lot more Republican votes than any other Democrat I know of."[47]

McNutt began his active participation in Indiana politics when he was selected as the keynote speaker at the state Democratic convention in May, 1930. R. Earl Peters, state party chairman since 1926, wrote McNutt that his selection as temporary chairman of the convention had met with "universal approval."[48] McNutt had previously given token support to various candidates who now backed him wholeheartedly for almost any position he wanted. One of these men, Posey T. Kime, who was nominated for judge of the appellate court, expressed the general sentiment toward McNutt:

"Let me say here and now that anything you want, whether it is Governor, Senator, or the 'Big Shot,' I am behind you."[49]

The keynote speech was very well received, and McNutt had many compliments on it. Not in many years had the Republican administration been more soundly flogged by a speaker, and McNutt rose to new heights as a Democratic leader and prophet. He thus established himself as one of the foremost political possibilities of his party, and there followed an enthusiastic discussion of his potentialities as a gubernatorial candidate. The Bloomington *Star* thought it was doubtful "if there is another man in public life in Indiana today who is more genuinely qualified to give his services to his party and his state in the next race for governor."[50]

Pleas E. Greenlee, who was later to play a very prominent role in McNutt's political life, congratulated the keynoter "on the splendid speech you made in the cause of democracy at the convention. It was well received by everyone that I have spoken to and things from now on ought to begin to boom for you." He identified the principles of Jeffersonian democracy as enunciated by McNutt with "the wisdom of Jefferson, the sword of Jackson, the firmness of Cleveland, and the high idealism of Wilson."[51]

Wendell L. Willkie wrote from New York City, congratulating McNutt on "the excellent speech," and declared:

"We are all watching your career with much pride and interest."[52]

McNutt thanked Willkie for his "cordial note" and promised to "call to see you on my next trip to New York to exchange gossip and to discuss the general situation."[53]

Throughout the summer and fall McNutt was actively involved in the political campaign. Peters leaned heavily on him for advice because of his great number of friends in Indiana and his knowledge of the political situation.[54] The party circularized the Legion men in the state with its literature, and certain prominent veterans were consulted. McNutt was made a member of the party's state advisory board.[55] He carried on a vigorous and extensive program of speaking engagements throughout the state.

[85]

Such activities, naturally, were bound to arouse considerable opposition and criticism from the Republican ranks, especially because of McNutt's position as dean of the state university's law school. It was charged that the university was being sacrificed to McNutt's burning ambition to be "the boy Moses who leads the Democratic party of Indiana into the promised land." It was claimed that he was about through with the university anyway, because "it has for him served its purpose, as has the American Legion, as a round in the McNutt ladder to fame."[56] One editorial deplored the fact that he was "dragging the university into the bitter partisan politics which makes enemies and lines up opposition" to satisfy his "vaulting ambitions. . . . For McNutt to use Indiana University as a door mat in one of his grabs for political office and glory . . . is not in accord with the tradition and history on the I. U. campus." It charged that he was "eaten up with political ambition" and was "using the institution . . . for his leaps and scrambles upward."[57]

Serious efforts were made by his opponents to force McNutt off the stump. Various influential Republicans wrote the university trustees, warning them that McNutt's political activities would adversely affect the university. Governor Leslie even threatened to reduce the university's appropriation if McNutt continued. C. M. Niezer, president of the First and Tri-State National Bank and Trust Company of Fort Wayne, wrote McNutt for advice on what could be done to answer the criticism.[58]

McNutt issued a forceful statement in reply to these threats and warnings. As a citizen of the state, he said, he was "entitled to exercise the right of a citizen, including the constitutional rights of freedom of conscience and freedom of speech." He pointed out that no attempt had been made to restrict the political activities of members of the faculties

[86]

of Indiana and Purdue universities, and cited the fact that during his long political career until the day he became governor, Harry Leslie was an employee of Purdue. Likewise, Dean Rothrock and Professor Hanna had held public office without severing their university connections. He declared that his participation in the campaign had been limited to a discussion of official records. He had indulged in no criticism of persons, "although material available for such a purpose is and has been plentiful." He claimed that he had tried to keep the campaign "on a high plane." His conscience was "absolutely clear." He insisted that he had performed his duties to the university and to the state satisfactorily, and had never used his official position "for personal or partisan purposes."[59]

In view of these facts, McNutt did not see how his activities could affect the university adversely "except in the minds of a few blind, unfair partisans and professional politicians." He was convinced that "any possible ill effect is more than compensated by the intense loyalty of those who have been disgusted by the actions of the Republican State Committee." He was sure that "in the event of a Democratic majority in the House of Representatives (and this seems to be a certainty) my activities will bear fruit in the form of lasting benefits to the University." He concluded that the only interpretation he could put on the attack on him was that "any service to the Republican Party is a commendable activity on the part of state employees and members of faculties of state universities but that any service in the Democratic cause is a high crime."[60]

Before the conclusion of the campaign, however, McNutt's opponents resorted to methods which might be considered a form of deliberate and malicious slander and libel, if they were not so downright silly. Elza O. Rogers, chairman of the

Indiana Republican State Central Committee, sent McNutt an open letter which was bitterly sarcastic, in which he revealed that he had been investigating the professor's financial situation. He found that McNutt had received $6,500 a year as dean and instructor, which services "consist of four hours per week for thirty-four weeks in the year, or, in other words, . . . a little over $47.00 per hour. . . . That is a shocking state of affairs," he wrote. He found also that McNutt was "forced to pay in taxes on property you say is worth $800.00, the sum of $33.70 per year, and that there remains unpaid the sum of $16.85. . . . Now I do not want you to be forced to borrow $16.85 to pay your taxes since your salary is only $6,500.00, so I have taken the liberty to relieve you of this burden and have paid your second installment, the receipt for which I enclose herewith, with my compliments." A postscript stated:

"We politicians must help each other."[61]

McNutt considered the letter too small to require a reply, but the Madison, Indiana, *Daily Herald* deplored it as "a last minute effort to divert the voters' attention from the real issues of the campaign as Col. McNutt has been getting under the skin of the hide-bound leaders of the opposition and it has come to the hurting point. The letter is a small, narrow piece of political bunk of the peanut variety and is a libel on the good name of Col. McNutt. . . . Rogers and his followers will learn with regret that their objective will react in the interest of the Democrats on election day as every one loves fair play and no one more than the great army of Legionnaires."[62]

In spite of such threats and attacks, McNutt continued to lead the speaking contingent for the Democrats. He was in great demand throughout the state, and wherever he spoke there was tremendous enthusiasm and interest. He was regarded as the real spokesman for the Democratic machine. Naturally there was increasing talk among the party leaders that he was laying the foundation for a race for the United States Senate in 1932 against Senator James Watson, or the governorship itself.

In the November elections the Democrats won an overwhelming victory in Indiana, as well as in the nation. The state went Democratic by 50,000 votes. Ten Democrats were elected to the thirteen-man Hoosier delegation in Congress. This was a complete reversal of the previous line-up. McNutt claimed the "victory was sweeping and the vindication complete."[63] Typical of the extent of the victory were Morgan County, in which McNutt had grown up, and Monroe County, where he now lived, which both went Democratic, the latter for the first time since the Civil War.

Frank McHale, in his congratulatory letter, gave McNutt the credit for the great Democratic landslide. He thought that "everybody in the state appreciates what you did." He felt that Franklin D. Roosevelt's victory in the New York gubernatorial contest "makes him outstanding and assures the party an undisputed leadership and with you in second place, assures the Democrats of a victory two years from now." It was McHale's personal opinion that McNutt "should start right now, making your connections along that line, as destiny seems to have picked you for this place."[64]

Similar sentiments were expressed by Michael L. Fansler of Logansport, who congratulated McNutt "upon the part you played in the campaign. Everyone feels that you are entitled to anything you want within the gift of the Democrats of Indiana; and while we are talking about that, I wish to say that I stand just where I did in the first instance—the Governorship is the thing." Fansler also believed that "Roosevelt's wonderful victory in New York assures his candidacy for the nomination if his health permits, and I think it would be wise to start a little talk about the nomination for Governor now."[65]

An interesting series of letters now passed between McNutt and Charles L. Wilson, an influential Oklahoma Democrat, in whose opinion "there is only one outstanding figure in the Democratic Party" for the presidential nomination. "That person is no other than yourself," he declared. He had taken the liberty to suggest to his influential friends that the State of Oklahoma get behind McNutt in the 1932 campaign, and this suggestion was taken very seriously and under advisement by the leaders of the state.[66]

In his reply to Wilson, McNutt admitted his interest in the proposition. "No man would or could refuse to be his party's candidate for the highest office in the gift of the people," he wrote. He declared that friends in other parts of the country had made the same suggestion as Wilson, but at a recent meeting in Indianapolis they had concluded that "in view of the fact that Indiana elects a Governor and a Senator in 1932 it was thought best to keep closely in touch with the Indiana situation." His name, he said, "has been connected frequently with both places."[67] Wilson replied that it seemed to him "that it would not be too late to run for either the office of Governor or Senator, if it should happen that you did not obtain the presidential nomination. It would seem to me that the mere fact that you were considered as presidential timber would increase your standing in the State and make a campaign for either of these two offices much easier."[68]

But McNutt's astute political advisor Douglas McKay urged caution, and expressed the opinion that it would be "unwise *at this time* for him [McNutt] to go outside his own state." He thought that "by withholding from the firing line for the while you will to some extent escape being a target whether for machine gun fire or sniper's attack." He felt that by devoting himself intensively to the situation in Indiana McNutt could build there a strength of support that would not accept "no" for an answer. In McKay's letter to Wilson he expressed the belief that "the time for that seems to be now, when there has been a complete reversal of political representation and . . . when a sense of gratitude to Paul is sincere to the point of being ardent. . . . In general," he said, "there is no doubt whatever that Paul has far more than a toe-hold on the ladder leading to the Presidency. But many people must help the ascent—if only to steady the ladder." For the time being McKay thought there should be no attempt, through the medium of publicity, to connect McNutt with the Presidency. "That will come along in due course—indeed be inescapable," he thought.[69]

This letter was apparently a follow-up on one which McKay had recently received from McNutt in which certain developments in the Indiana situation were discussed. Since the death of Tom Taggart, Sr., the state organization had been without a recognized leader, with the result that many local and district leaders now had their ambitions aroused, but the lion's share of the patronage would still be in the hands of the newly elected secretary of state, Frank Mayr, Jr., who would take office on December 1. McNutt considered Mayr a first-rate man "whose intuitions are right but whose real political experience is meagre." According to McNutt, soon after Mayr's election "it became apparent that a group of practical professional politicians in his home city would attempt to control him and, through patronage at his disposal, build up a machine."[70]

McNutt asserted that he and Peters had "asked for nothing but insisted that appointments go to men of unquestioned integrity and ability." But when Mayr announced his major selections without the final word of approval from the state chairman Peters, it was apparent that he had been influenced by his own local group. The newspapers instantly interpreted the announcement as a slap at Peters and McNutt, and a storm of protest from other parts of the state arose immediately. However, Peters and Mayr discussed the matter privately and the situation was cleared somewhat. McNutt claimed he had "no real fear of the outcome but had hoped that no mistakes would be made by the present administration."[71]

By the beginning of 1931 McNutt had definitely decided to become a candidate for the governorship in 1932. During the previous summer he had written to Carl G. Wolflin at Evansville that it was "not at all certain that I want to enter the political arena for any office but, if I do, it will be for Governor in 1932."[72] Events during the next six months, however, especially the results of the November elections, convinced him that he should make the race. He set up a very ambitious speaking schedule throughout the state, and general reaction seemed to be very favorable toward his candidacy for the nomination. One of his admirers sent him a letter with the salutation "My dear Governor *In Futuro*."[73] Michael Fansler wrote him that he was pleased with his decision. The candidate for governor, he wrote, "is always the central figure in the fight to carry Indiana, and a Democratic Governor of Indiana, who is a good campaigner and who has made a good record, is always in a strong position for a Democratic nomination for the Presidency."[74]

One of the major difficulties facing the Democratic Party in 1931 was the lack of a sufficient treasury for campaign purposes, but Dick Shepherd of Logansport approached McNutt with a plan which he believed could be worked out in advance which would take care of the situation locally as well as statewide. He proposed that a McNutt-for-Governor Club be organized in every county in the state, with members contributing $1 to $5 apiece. Twenty-five per cent of the income would go to state headquarters and the rest would be retained in the county for any purpose the local organization would see fit to use it.[75] This suggestion was soon to become a reality.

The main stumbling block in the path of McNutt's ambition, now that he had indicated his interest in the gubernatorial nomination, was the afore-mentioned problem of the patronage. Mayr was now in control, and he used the various automobile license bureaus throughout the state to advance his own personal interests, which included the possibility of his own nomination for the governorship. McHale had arranged for Dick Shepherd, head of one of the license bureaus, to spy on Mayr and his activities.[76]

In the meantime Sherman Minton had heard reports that the so-called "older" Democrats were building a backfire against McNutt, and he urged that something should be done unofficially by McNutt's friends to stem this tide, even though at the time it was still small. He had heard the charge that the "older fellers" were not being treated right, and that McNutt was tied up with Earl Peters. Of course they all were subject to Peters, as he was the state chairman, but many did not like him, and blamed McNutt for his election. Minton thought these arguments were "damned weak, but is the old story of Hans and the dike." He thought it was too early to start an open movement for McNutt, but "it is time to 'dig in' so their barrage gets no casualties." He advised McNutt not to "let them bill you for so many speeches you can talk yourself out."[77]

All of this indicated considerable lack of harmony and dissension within the ranks of Indiana Democrats, although some thought it was a part of a fairly well-organized Republican effort to weaken the opposition before the people. One story circulated the possibility that Peters himself would seek the governor nomination, and McNutt would be given the

Senate nod, instead of Walter Myers, current speaker of the General Assembly.[78] There was also some strong feeling that Frank Dailey would again make the race for the governorship. Dean Barnhart, publisher of the Goshen *Democrat,* wrote McNutt that "steps be taken to avoid this fight, if at all possible, because I fear it means loss of the nomination to both of you, perhaps, and selection of an inferior man."[79]

The political situation in Indianapolis and Marion County was far from satisfactory to the Democrats at this time. The difficulty seemed to center not only around Mayr, but Frederick VanNuys and Frank Dailey as well. Virgil Simmons wrote McNutt that he did not think it had reached a serious stage yet, but "probably some steps should be taken to counteract the influence." To him Bowman Elder was not "a proper party to correct the conditions of Marion County. In fact among some of the younger Democrats he is the cause of the situation."[80]

While all of this intra-party feuding was taking place behind the scenes, Frank White, editor of *The Hoosier Legionnaire,* was importuning McNutt to advise him "preferably a few days in advance when the organization that is being set up will announce your candidacy for governor." He hoped McNutt could get authority to announce it in the Legion paper, "which you know would be a departure." He thought the news value of a former state and national commander coming out for governor would be of sufficient worth to warrant the use."[81]

But McNutt replied that he had come to the definite conclusion that it was unwise to place anything which might be construed as political publicity in the Legion publication. "The policy of keeping the Legion out of partisan politics and partisan politics out of the Legion must be followed," he insisted. "It is fundamentally sound. Any move hinting of a violation of that policy would be misconstrued by the enemies of the Legion and would be used against the organization." He also thought that such publicity would tend to injure the individual mentioned.[82]

In June, Peters wrote to McKay that he had visited practically every community in the state and "the situation is most hospitable to Paul's nomination for Governor." He admitted that there had been some difficulties to overcome, but he could not foresee serious complications. He then discussed the national situation as it was reviewed at a meeting of several Democratic governors at French Lick recently. There was a growing conviction in the middle west and west, he reported, "that some Democrat, not now prominently mentioned, will be in a position to be a strong contender for the presidential nomination. . . . I cannot think of a person who is in a more favorable position, when the time comes, than our mutual friend [McNutt]. . . . The biggest thing we could do is to make possible his selection as key-noter. I am assuming, of course, that his nomination for Governor will be accomplished practically without serious opposition."[83]

Peters thought that if McNutt were given an opportunity to address the delegates at the national convention "there would be a repetition of what happened with respect to William Jennings Bryan [in 1896]." He suggested that literature be prepared portraying McNutt's availability, his background, his wide acquaintance throughout the country, his speaking ability and his executive ability, and have it circulated throughout the country immediately after the state convention and his nomination for governor. He believed this would be most advantageous.[84]

Meanwhile the political situation in Indiana was becoming more confused by the many predictions and rumors which were being made and circulated. Some thought that Peters would seek the gubernatorial nomination and that Frank Mayr was not at all interested in the nomination for governor, and would even refuse to accept it.[85] McHale wrote to McNutt that Earl Peters had asked Frederick Landis, a long-time Republican friend of McNutt's, if he were going to be a candidate for governor. This was at a dinner meeting, and as there were "several Republicans close by" Landis had tried to avoid an answer. Peters then informed him that he would have no business to run against McNutt, but Landis replied that he thought that "it was an open field and that friendships did not enter into it." But Peters had warned Landis that if he got into the race "he would get the worst beating that he ever got in his lifetime."[86]

This made Landis furious, and he told Peters that if he, as chairman of the state committee, was hurling this as a challenge to one who had not declared himself as a candidate, he would announce his candidacy at that meeting, and assured Peters that his folks would know that they had a campaign before it ended. According to McHale, "by that time Peters had come to his senses, and let the matter drop." But McHale reminded McNutt that "while everything looks rosy for the Democrats next year, we must remember . . . that the strongest possible candidate as against you or any other one, in my opinion, would be Landis, and he doesn't even think it would be possible for a Republican to be elected."[87] Later McNutt apologized to Landis, who wrote in reply, "Don't let that banquet incident annoy you, for I have long since forgotten it."[88] It is doubtful if either McNutt or McHale ever forgot the incident.

To McNutt, the political situation in Indiana looked entirely satisfactory. The work of the organization was moving along and the opposition forces had not been able to make much headway. Their strategy seemed to favor McNutt for senator but not for governor, but in a letter to McKay he indicated that his friends "have been able to squelch such talk effectively."[89]

In early August, McNutt received a letter from Earl B. Lambka, secretary of the Michigan City Democratic Central Committee, who asked him point blank if he were going to be a candidate for governor. If he were, he felt that "now is the time for us to get an organization lined up for you."[90] McNutt replied that "unless conditions change I shall be a candidate for Governor." He did not anticipate such a change, however, and agreed that the time had come to quietly start an organization in each county. He expected "to follow the policy of allowing my friends in each county to appoint their own chairman rather than follow the custom of making the appointment myself."[91]

McNutt at this time was still toying with the possibility of some national office, however. The Governors' Conference met at French Lick in June, but Governor Leslie, who was acting as host, did not invite McNutt to attend. After the close of the formal meetings, the members and guests of the conference went to Bloomington to inspect the limestone quarries and mills, where McNutt met the group and took some of his personal friends to lunch and later drove them back to French Lick. In the group was Governor Roosevelt whom he met in the hotel lobby. He introduced himself and had a "most cordial reception."[92]

When McNutt met the party in Bloomington, the newspapermen and photographers swarmed around him. The New York papers were particularly insistent and wanted to know the feeling in Indiana toward Roosevelt. McNutt told them that the New York governor had many friends in Indiana, but that "it was a little too early to say what candidate the

Indiana delegation at the national convention would support."[93]

In August, McNutt wrote to his friend McKay that Governor Roosevelt had sent the New York state chairman, James A. Farley, to Indianapolis to find out if he would be interested in the vice-presidential nomination. Fortunately, he wrote, he did not get the word in time to see Farley "although I made the effort and missed him at the train by five minutes." McNutt thought that the vice-presidential situation would take care of itself, but dropped the hint that his selection as keynoter at the national convention would be desirable.[94]

Early in October, Governor Roosevelt wrote McNutt from Warm Springs, Georgia, inviting him to visit him at Albany or Hyde Park in the near future, as there were "many things I should like to talk to you about."[95] McNutt replied that his program was "full to overflowing," with the first open date being Friday, December 11. He would be glad to visit Roosevelt then, "if it meets your convenience." [96] Roosevelt set up the appointment for December 12, at Hyde Park. [97] In writing to a friend later McNutt said he was to have a three-hour interview with Roosevelt, and the first thing on the program "is to settle the question of leadership in Indiana."[98]

In December, one of McNutt's friends, Arthur Lynch of Columbus, Georgia, wrote him that he had visited Governor Roosevelt at Warm Springs, and while there had a very pleasant talk with Farley about McNutt. He acquainted him "with your splendid charm, marvelous personality, great ability, oratorical powers of persuasion, and told him that you are thoroughly qualified to handle any important posts or assignments the Party may see fit to entrust to you. He was greatly impressed, and said that several others had spoken to him regarding you. . . . I attempted to place you in position for truly large things." He urged McNutt to "hammer at the

Indiana situation thoroughly. I was given to understand that you have it well in hand, both as to gubernatorial nomination and eventual election. You must be successful, because it means so much nationally."[99]

Another friend, Wendell L. Willkie, wrote McNutt from New York City that he had heard from several sources that McNutt was going to be nominated and elected governor of Indiana. He hoped their predictions were correct, "for I shall get better pleasure and pride out of such an happening. Good luck to you," he wrote, "and if I can be of any service, let me know."[100] McNutt replied that "at this time the political situation in Indiana is entirely satisfactory. It must be kept so by vigilance and organization." He felt that it would be much better "to go into the campaign as the unanimous choice of the convention and there are some indications that such a result can be brought about."[101]

Meanwhile McNutt's governorship band wagon was gaining momentum. His Legion friend John Wheeler wrote from Crown Point on August 6, attaching a clipping from the Hammond *Lake County Times*, verifying McNutt's possible candidacy. He said there was no longer any conjecture about it.[102] And in September, McNutt received a letter from his friend Bernhard Knollenberg of New York City, offering to campaign for him in and around Richmond and Wayne County, Indiana.[103] Although he had not yet officially announced his candidacy, McNutt became embroiled in various controversial issues. On October 12 he spoke at Franklin on the public utility question, and declared that strong regulation or ownership was necessary to protect the public. In one of the many letters he received in regard to his ideas, William T. Young complimented him on his speech. "It is no time for a man who is lacking in courage to enter public service," he wrote. "There never was a better time to say something.

Where you will lose one vote on the utility question, you will gain an even hundred. There is not the least doubt about what is right on that question, and where the people stand. I am for you and intend to do everything I can for you. You said something at Franklin. You are right. I have heard a number of favorable comments this morning and it is doing you a world of good."[104]

Another letter came from C. C. Shipp, Indianapolis, who also congratulated McNutt for making the utilities issue one of the planks in his platform. "It's high time that some candidate possessed of the courage of his convictions should take a bold stand against the utility interests of this state," he wrote. "The various commissions, created for the purpose of controlling such interests are misnomers or else the very purposes for which they were created have been aborted. You are to be congratulated on the stand you have taken. It's a serious step but one taken in the proper direction. It proves conclusively that you not only 'preach' but believe in the Jeffersonian principle of 'Government of, by and for the people.' "[105]

In the same vein Joseph W. Kimmell, mayor of Vincennes, wrote McNutt commending him for the speech, "since it is one of the fundamental principles of our party to oppose special privilege. . . . Our legislatures for a number of years have been absolutely controlled by the utility interests. Our utility legislation has been written by utility lobbyists. Under our present laws, the public is practically helpless to protect itself from extortionist utility rates. We need a legislature that will write our utility laws in the interest of the public, and then we need a Governor that will name a Public Service Commission without dictation from the Insull interests. This is a live issue in Indiana. . . . The Democratic party and its leaders cannot afford to 'pussy-foot' on this issue. . . . There are just two big questions before the people of Indiana today. One is . . . the utility queston; the other is taxation. The Governor who can lead us to a right solution of these two problems will immediately become a national figure in American politics. I have every confidence in your patriotism, honesty and integrity, and wish you the utmost success."[106]

This appraisal of McNutt was not shared by all, naturally. A very scathing denunciation was sent to him on November 7 by H. K. Cuthbertson of Indianapolis, who was a member of the Public Service Commission. He bitterly criticized McNutt's stand on the utilities issue, and accused him of making assertions which were not supported by facts. He referred to McNutt as a "demogogue," which he defined as "an insincere politician, orator or leader, who stirs up popular prejudice to gain office or influence." He challenged him to debate the utilities issue with him, and assured him that "if you are elected Governor of Indiana, which I feel that Divine Providence will never permit, that at any time you call my attention to my inability to serve the public I shall gladly resign my office."[107]

Many letters were received by McNutt, condemning Cuthbertson's attack on him. One warned, however, that McNutt should not get into any debate or newspaper discussion with his opponent. He had a strong issue in the public utility question, and the people would be with him, but the utilities would fight him all the way, with Cuthbertson as their mouthpiece.[108] Another declared that McNutt would be derelict in his duty if he did not change the personnel of the Public Service Commission after his election as governor. He felt that Cuthbertson's move "has more back of it than just vindictiveness. I believe it is a move sponsored by the public utilities to get you in the hole."[109]

Another friend wrote McNutt that Cuthbertson's attack

on him would be to McNutt's advantage. "There is nothing in this wide world that will keep you from being the next governor of Indiana if you can keep such skunks as this jumping onto you through the papers," he wrote. It was his belief that the Public Service Commission of Indiana had been bought and paid for. In the 1931 session of the General Assembly, he recalled, Cuthbertson, then a state senator, "was the advocate of the public utilities in the senate and helped to put their measures across which we took pleasure in killing in the House of Representatives. As soon as the Legislature was over Cuthbertson was appointed as a member of the Public Service Commission—a man practically unknown in Indiana—to complete a set-up to control the Commission. This has been done. . . . Let him roar. The more he says the better it will suit and let your friends prod him just enough to get him to roar some more and then at the proper time take him into town. He sure is some damphool [sic]."[110]

One writer expressed the feeling that Cuthbertson's remarks "will be taken with a grain of salt" by those who knew him,[111] and another wrote McNutt he hadn't talked to a single person Republican or Democrat "who isn't enthusiastic in his support of your stand on these public service corporations. The common people do not know all, but they do know enough about them, that they are ready to follow you in a fight against the unfair tactics employed by these corporations and the support given them by the public utilities commission."[112] Still another warned McNutt that if he got into a controversy with Cuthbertson "there will be no end of it."[113] Many others wrote McNutt along the same lines. One even suggested reducing the expenses of the state by the general dismissal of commissioners "which are a burden upon the taxpayers of Indiana, without value received."[114]

McNutt did not reply to Cuthbertson, who wrote him an

11-page single-spaced typed letter the following March, in which he declared that it was his honest conviction that "with you presenting yourself as a candidate for Governor on the Democratic ticket the very principles of government are not only threatened, the very structure of our form of government is not only threatened, but in addition to that the very principles of democracy are being cast aside, and in their stead is plainly seen the cold hand of ambition, that for the purpose of gaining its own ends has no respect for government, no respect for persons, no respect for principles and no respect for the truth. . . . Your entire record is the record of a dishonest and ambitious politician, and there is not one place in your career where you can point out that you have ever done one act or performed one deed that was actuated by a desire upon your part to render any public service. . . . Your campaign now is the campaign of a coward and only consistent with your past actions. . . . Your whole public career has been marked solely by ambition and every thought that you have expressed and every act done by you has been actuated by the cold hand of ambition."

In concluding his vituperative letter, Cuthbertson said that "the time has arrived in this country when men of your type should withdraw themselves from public life until such a time as you are able to gain sufficient strength to cease to be guided by the cold hand of ambition, and until the time comes when you can speak the truth and set aside cowardice and hold yourself out as an American citizen in every sense of the word as qualified to represent the citizenship of this State or any community as a public official. I also have an abiding conviction that the time has arrived when the rank and file of democracy in Indiana should realize that in keeping faith with the principles of democracy and with those whose memory still remains as a guiding light to the conduct of men in public office and aspiring to public office, yourself and Mr. Earl Peters should be removed from any further consideration by the Democratic Party as men who are worthy to be called leaders."[115]

In the meantime friends were suggesting that McNutt set up an organization for his forthcoming campaign. Pleas Greenlee, business manager of the Michigan City *Evening Dispatch,* offered to give his full time to the organization of the campaign. Although Skitz Simmons had suggested that two men be put in the field, Greenlee was sure he could do the job himself. "I know the fellows," he wrote, "and it is not like going out into strange territory. Then, too, these fellows, I think, have confidence in me, and it will not be so hard for us to have a real organization in a few months." If McNutt had someone else in mind, or some other plan, he was willing to step aside, Greenlee said. "Your success means everything to the Democratic party, not only in the state, but will have a bearing on the nation, as well, and I am for anything that will be for the best results," he declared.[116]

It was absolutely essential that such an organization be set up quickly, if McNutt expected to gather strength for his candidacy. He advised Hugh A. Barnhart of Rochester that it was necessary to have harmony in the ranks. "We face desperate foes this time," he said, "and must gain strength by desertions from their ranks." He was of the opinion that the appearances of trouble in the Democratic group "have been created, for the most part, by forces around the Secretary of State's office. Apparently the policy has been 'rule or ruin.'" But McNutt insisted that despite the fact that many of the activities had been directed against him personally, that no efforts be made to replace Mayr as secretary of state.[117]

Frank Dailey was again expected to announce his candidacy shortly, and it was predicted that this would hurt Mc-

Nutt's chances,[118] although some thought that it would make no difference, except to make the McNutt forces work a little harder. Dailey's alliance with the Mayr crowd would probably hurt him, and it was difficult to understand "why he would ally himself with a gang that fought him so bitterly and only want him to pull their chestnuts out of the fire." But McNutt was warned to keep an eternal vigilance.[119]

Early in January, 1932, McNutt was advised by McHale that Mayr had indicated to him that he would again be a candidate for secretary of state, and suggested that to eliminate any embarrassment to all candidates on the ticket, Peters not be retained as chairman, as the Republican party would make their attack on Peters, instead of the candidates, thus strengthening McNutt's own position.[120]

Two days later McNutt wrote his friend Val Nolan that he was opening an office in the Chamber of Commerce Building in Indianapolis. No name would yet appear on the door and the address would be a post office box. Pleas Greenlee was appointed executive secretary and would give his entire time to the program. It seemed advisable to take such a step at this time "in order to effectively organize our forces and to assure no change in the present satisfactory conditions." McNutt also confided to Nolan that several men who had approached Dailey "were beginning to feel their efforts were futile."[121] A third major contender for the governor nomination was John Frederick, president of the state Chamber of Commerce, but there was very little evidence of any strength to his candidacy.[122]

There were some in the party, of course, who refused to recognize factions. Samuel C. Cleland of Fort Wayne declared in a letter to McNutt that he was "getting tired of having everyone who desires to be a candidate for office from the Justice of the Peace on up through, tie their wagon onto your star. I do not know why every Democrat in the state who seeks to obtain an office should expect you to carry along with your own candidacy theirs as well. . . [They] are constantly peddling the tale that they are a McNutt candidate. The only logical effect this can have is to weaken your position with people against whom they are obliged to run in the Primaries, and I do not think it fair to you. You don't need the help of anyone. You can stand on your own feet without the help of anyone else."[123]

"A cold-blooded analysis of the chairmanship fight" led McNutt to believe that Peters would win by at least two to one and maybe five to one. He wrote Val Nolan that "recent developments have all been favorable" to him. As far as he was concerned, he could not and would not forget "that he [Peters] is and has been absolutely loyal to me." He cited the old political adage that "you cannot beat a man unless you have someone to beat him with." As for the members of the Mayr group, he had been told that they had softened their attacks on him, but he was inclined to look upon them as "Greeks bearing gifts."[124]

McNutt formally announced his candidacy for governor in February. The official announcement declared:

"In response to the repeated requests of friends, party leaders and workers in every county of the State I have determined to offer myself as a candidate for the Democratic nomination for Governor. In doing so, I am prompted by the duty, which rests on every citizen, to heed the call of public service and to serve the State to the best of my ability. This duty is especially strong during periods of great stress, such as the present. It is necessary to restore confidence in government and to make it an useful instrument for all the people rather than a burden. I believe that the Democratic party is the proper agency for attaining these ends and that it is ready for the great tasks and heavy responsibilities which await it.

It is my desire to be useful in the accomplishment of these high purposes."[125]

Members of the American Legion of the State of Indiana formed the nucleus of the McNutt-for-Governor organization. Frank M. McHale was the head of the group, and Pleas Greenlee, who had been Adjutant of the Legion, was secretary. Pat Manion, Dean of the Notre Dame University Law School, Clarence Jackson, past state commander of the Legion, and Sherman Minton, were also among the leaders in the organization.

For the next three months, McNutt carried on a very extensive speaking program in every part of the state. He addressed the meetings of numerous bar associations, and gained the support of many lawyers who used their influence in helping to build the McNutt organization. Another group to whom McNutt appealed were the teachers and others interested in education. They looked upon the McNutt candidacy with considerable favor.

McNutt became known as the champion of the people and particularly of their civil rights. Although born and reared a Methodist, and married to a Christian Scientist, he was one of the very few individuals who was a Protestant who had the courage to condemn the Ku Klux Klan as being un-American. These were the days when the Klan in Indiana boasted a membership of a half million, or roughly one-fourth the total population. The result of McNutt's stand was that the Jews, the Negroes, and the Catholics looked upon him as their champion, although others thought he was jeopardizing his political future by attacking the Klan as un-American. According to Frank M. McHale, in all the public offices McNutt was to hold, he was an American first and a Methodist and Democrat second. He felt deeply that unless the rights and privileges of the people were protected that it would not be worth while for anyone to be in public office. The quality of being just, granting every indiviual the right to think politically, and to join the church of his choice, and being fair to all people regardless of race, color or creed, was predominant in his thinking. This was not just a quality or a political gesture on the part of McNutt. He felt it and he lived it.[126]

One of the many letters of best wishes following McNutt's candidacy announcement came from Wendell L. Willkie, who said he would be happy to contribute to his campaign funds, "both for the nomination and for the election." He was very anxious to see him elected, he wrote, "both because of old friendship and also because I have predicted for years that you would succeed grandly. I guess we all like to see our predictions come true— particularly so when they involve a friend of years standing."[127] In March, Willkie sent Bowman Elder a check for $250 as a contribution to McNutt's campaign fund,[128] and the following month he wrote to Pleas Greenlee, offering to send additional money if needed.[129]

McNutt's efforts against Mayr were overwhelmingly successful. On May 14 Peters was re-elected state chairman, and immediately called for party harmony. McNutt's chances for the nomination at the state convention were thus greatly enhanced. When the state committee met, McNutt and Peters were able to have the order of nomination at the convention reversed to allow the gubernatorial nomination to come up first, rather than the United States Senate nomination. Clarence "Pat" Manion of the Notre Dame University law school was chosen as keynote speaker and John McFadden of Rockville was designated as permanent chairman of the convention. Wray Fleming was appointed publicity director for the campaign.

Meanwhile "McNutt-for-Governor" Clubs were being established all over the state. The preamble for the club was:

"We, the voters of Indiana, who believe that our great Hoosier State will be best served by having as its chief executive—a MAN who can restore that state to its rightful place in our republic; a MAN who can re-establish confidence in state affairs and promote the general welfare; a MAN who has demonstrated the qualities of leadership that are needed in these momentous times—and, who believe that Paul V. McNutt embodies all the characteristics and qualities necessary to accomplish these purposes, do associate ourselves together in a 'Paul McNutt for Governor' Club, and pledge our every effort to promote his candidacy to the end that he may be nominated and elected Governor of the State of Indiana."[130]

These clubs were most effective in arousing interest in McNutt's campaign, not only for the nomination, but for his election in the fall.

But McNutt did not take his nomination as a foregone conclusion. There were still too many political opponents within his own party, and he could not feel safe until he had received the nomination at the June convention. His strength among the delegates appeared to be increasing, although there were still some powerful forces which had not yet been won over to his camp. But on May 11, McNutt wrote his friend Henry E. White at Franklin that it looked as if he would go into the convention "with at least 1181 out of the 1559 delegates."[131]

On the eve of the convention John Frederick denied the rumor that he would withdraw from the nomination.[132] But Wood Posey, mayor of Terre Haute, dropped out, and just before the balloting the next day he threw his support to McNutt, declaring that his action was prompted by the conviction that the number of delegates pledged to McNutt "offers an insurmountable obstacle." Soon thereafter Frederick also withdrew "for harmony's sake."[133] Following Pat Manion's stirring keynote address, John C. McNutt nominated his son Paul for governor, and pandemonium broke out. The nomination was seconded by Wood Posey, and Henry White, chairman of the Johnson County delegation, moved the nomination by acclamation. McNutt and Peters were now in absolute control of the convention, and their choices for nomination for other offices prevailed. M. Clifford Townsend was selected as the nominee for lieutenant governor on the first ballot.

McNutt accepted the nomination "with a spirit of humility, deeply conscious of the responsibility the honor entails. I pray Divine Providence for the courage and wisdom the task demands. My friends also asked for this nomination. They fought a good fight, one not marred by discord. I appreciate their attitude. I am profoundly grateful to my friends and I shall not forget."[134]

Only one case of disharmony appeared in the convention. Walter Myers, speaker of the General Assembly, was defeated by Frederick Van Nuys 938 to 670 for the United States Senate nomination, to oppose James E. Watson. The McNutt-Peters forces had supported Van Nuys because of a personal feud between McNutt and Myers. The story had been circulated that Myers had at one time embarrassed McNutt before a farm audience by giving McNutt's farm speech verbatim, leaving McNutt without anything appropriate to say.

Among the many letters and telegrams which McNutt received on his nomination, one or two significant ones should be mentioned. James A. Stuart, managing editor of the Indianapolis *Star*, declared McNutt's campaign had been an "inspiration to our party, and thus to the whole state."[135] In his reply, McNutt thanked Stuart for the friendly attitude of the *Star* which had been more than helpful, and he was profoundly grateful. He hoped he would have the benefit of Stuart's advice as the campaign progressed.[136]

Another congratulation came from Ralph F. Gates, commander of the Department of Indiana, American Legion, who was later to become Republican governor.[137] And Mc-Nutt's Republican opponent, Fayette County circuit judge Raymond S. Springer, wrote him that it was "a fine thing for two friends to seek the same office and maintain the spirit of friendship and comradeship which has characterized their relations through the years. I know that we can demonstrate to the people that it is possible to keep a campaign on a high plane."[138] Springer had also been very active in the American Legion, especially as its first commander in Indiana. During the campaign he refused to attend any Legion meeting, saying that he "would rather suffer defeat than to have any one man say that I had ever brought politics, even in a remote degree, into our great organization."[139]

Commenting on McNutt's nomination, the South Bend News-Times prophesied that "nothing short of a political upheaval or a social cataclysm can prevent his securing this high office for which he is so well prepared." According to this newspaper, the entire state needed a complete overhauling, and McNutt had an opportunity to be "the best governor Indiana has had for half a century."[140]

The convention itself was noted for its youthful leadership and the preponderance of Legion men. Although the ghost of Thomas Taggart still hovered over the assemblage, the former leaders were not in power. The convention, to all outward appearances, lacked the old-time leadership. The platform, which was about the only thing determined by the older heads, unhesitantly ventured into new governmental paths. It made an open bid for Farm Bureau support by taking up the income tax idea, and then complied with all organized labor's demands, advocating abolishment of prison contract labor, definition of injunction in individual disputes, liberalization of the compensation laws, and condemnation of "yellow-dog" contracts. It favored old-age pensions, and solicited the support of the Indiana League of Women Voters by recommending a new registration law. It also called for strengthening of the state banking laws, denounced the highway commission, and urged an end of the fee system for county officials.

The platform also advocated removal of municipally-owned utilities from the jurisdiction of the public service commission. But the platform-makers refused to go along with the farmers who would have all appointments made by the governor subject to approval of the state senate. A proposal to have the party favor a referendum vote on the eighteenth amendment in 1932 was defeated. Thus the Democrats went along with the Republicans in taking the wet-and-dry issue out of the campaign. Following the state convention, McNutt delayed his campaign for the fall election long enough to attend the Democratic national convention in Chicago. The previous December he had been requested by John H. Stelle, assistant treasurer of Illinois, to use his influence with the National Committee to bring the convention to Chicago. Illinois was considered a doubtful state by the Democrats, and holding the convention in Chicago, after a lapse of twelve years, was expected to help toward a Democratic victory in 1932. Whether or not McNutt acted on this request is not certain, but Chicago was selected as the site of the convention.

In the six weeks prior to the convention, a series of letters passed between McNutt and prominent Democrats regarding the possible nomination of Governor Roosevelt for the presidency. Farley wrote McNutt indicating that Howe S. Landers, formerly of Indianapolis, was very much interested in the candidacy of Roosevelt, and was anxious to see him nominated. For that reason he was writing to urge McNutt to use every effort he possibly could to try to get Indiana's delegation instructed for Roosevelt. He felt that the New York governor "has many admirers in your state and we are satisfied here that there should be no difficulty in getting a resolution through [the state convention] instructing your delegates to support him."[141] Two weeks later Farley again wrote McNutt, asking for confidential information as to the situation in Indiana regarding an instructed delegation for Roosevelt.[142]

In his reply to Farley, McNutt recognized that Roosevelt had many staunch supporters in Indiana, but he had found an overwhelming majority of the Democratic leaders feeling that they should not be hampered by instructions.[143]

Abram Simmons of Bluffton, recalling the political conditions of the parties in 1884, wrote to McNutt that he felt it would be proper for the state convention to endorse Roosevelt, as he was quite sure he would be the nominee. In his opinion such a move would be a great political advantage for Indiana in the event of Roosevelt's election. Not only would Roosevelt win the election, he felt, but the chances of the Democrats' carrying the state would be much increased.[144]

Another letter came to McNutt from Mary W. Dewson, representing a group called "Friends of Franklin Roosevelt." She had heard from all quarters that the sentiment in Indiana was very strong for Roosevelt, and she asked McNutt to do all that he could at the state convention to have the delegates to the national convention instructed for the New York candidate. "It is the feeling of Governor Roosevelt and his friends that an instructed delegation is a matter of great importance in order to further prove the hopelessness of any attempt to bring about a deadlocked convention such as destroyed all chance of Democratic success in 1924," she wrote.[145]

Other convention matters were discussed by McNutt in a letter to his friend McKay. A place as one of the delegates to the national convention had been left open for him, he wrote, "but I have made up my mind that it would be wiser to give the place to someone else. I will be present and will be consulted on all moves made and can go onto the floor at any time if necessary with a proxy." He reported that the Indiana group had been deluged with callers and visitors from New York. Cornelius Vanderbilt, Jr., had been in the state twice. Farley had called on Peters with two definite propositions. One was that McNutt be made chairman of one of the convention committees, but he was not interested. The other was that McNutt be made the nominee for vice president. McNutt's reply was that he was not interested in this either.

The result of all this was that Indiana would have an uninstructed delegation, "containing a liberal sprinkling of Smith sympathizers." It was McNutt's opinion that the delegation's vote "might be Roosevelt 20, Smith 10, if no effort were made to influence its decision." He concluded that these activities and offers "indicate rather clearly that the Roosevelt forces are not as sure of themselves as their publicity might indicate. The action of Indiana is very important to them. All of this makes our action stronger."[146]

McKay answered that Roosevelt was not wanted as the candidate, and it was his belief that if he were nominated, he could not be elected, although many Republicans in New York were unhappy about Hoover. McKay urged McNutt to persuade the Indiana delegation "with all the power you can command" to remain open-minded on the choice of the standard-bearer.[147]

Thus Indiana sent an uninstructed delegation to Chicago, although it was generally felt that they would support Roosevelt as a last resort. Yet McNutt received many telegrams from leaders throughout the state, opposing support for Roosevelt. One wired that "Roosevelt's nomination would be a calamity to the party and nation at this time," and Republicans who wanted to vote with the Democrats in this election "simply will not support him," and he would not even receive the united support of his own party.[148] Evans Woolen wired McNutt that it was his earnest conviction that "our best chance both in the nation and the state lies in the nomination of Newton D. Baker, and my hope that he has substantial votes from Indiana on the first ballot."[149]

At least the Indiana delegation was in a position to bargain with Roosevelt and Farley, until the large state delegations began to jump on the Roosevelt bandwagon, which made his nomination a certainty. Indiana was therefore considered a late-comer, and as a result both Farley and Roosevelt never forgave McNutt for the part he played in the use of such delaying tactics. This was one mistake made by McNutt which was to have fatal consequences later on.

McHale gives an interesting account of Indiana's role in the Chicago convention which he claims was misunderstood by both Roosevelt and Farley. McHale was chairman of the Hoosier delegation, and R. Earl Peters was state chairman. According to McHale, Farley has been given more credit than he deserves for the nomination of Roosevelt, for he had a "natural" candidate. Although a personal friend of McHale's and a great leader, Farley contacted neither McNutt nor McHale at the convention, but relied on the statements of Peters.

The following story is here told for the first time, as reported to the author by McHale. Anton J. "Tony" Cermak, then mayor of Chicago, was the chairman of the Illinois delegation, and Edward Kelley, at that time the Park Commissioner, sub-chairman. Kelley and Cermak, McNutt, Tom Taggart, Jr., and McHale meeting prior to the voting, realized that Roosevelt was the outstanding candidate. It was agreed that Illinois would have a candidate of their own, and they would hold their votes together and scatter a few, and Indiana would do the same.

The Scripps-Howard papers had as their general counsel Newton D. Baker. Roy Howard had asked McNutt and McHale to give some votes to Baker, and it was agreed to give him eight votes on the first ballot. This was more than he received in all the rest of the midwestern states. It was very obvious to the Indiana leaders after the third ballot that Roosevelt would go over on the next vote. Illinois and Indiana had agreed to "steal the show" and Cermak was authorized whenever the vote became close, to take to the platform and cast the solid vote of both Illinois and Indiana for Roosevelt. Illinois, of course, came first in the roll-call.

McNutt and McHale went to see Cermak and Kelley toward the end of the third ballot when it became obvious that they could change the vote and put it over on the next ballot. Cermak looked into the empty galleries and realized that it would be a terrible thing for the Democratic Party to nominate the next President of the United States with an empty gallery, and it would be devastating as far as the city of Chicago was concerned, with their problems of unpaid school teachers, firemen, and policemen. It was agreed to wait and move for adjournment.

Adjournment was voted for, and it was decided to reconvene at four o'clock the next day. In the meantime, John Garner of Texas and William McAdoo of California got together and they cast the vote of California and Texas for

Roosevelt. Mayor Cermak attempted to cast the vote of Illinois and Indiana for Roosevelt, but McHale says, "We missed the boat and never got credit for what we thought was a major piece of strategy. Had we been able to accomplish it, both Indiana and Illinois would have been favored by the Roosevelt administration, whereas they were not."[150]

During the gubernatorial campaign in Indiana, McNutt was vilified as "a lawyer who never tried a case and a soldier who never fired a gun." He conducted a vigorous campaign, although it was somewhat unorthodox. One political writer described his tactics as follows:

"He arrives at the country courthouse or operahouse just before the meeting begins. Legion trumpeters await him. As he enters they sound a fanfare. He makes his speech, and retires immediately to the accompaniment of another fanfare. No wait for handshaking and backslapping. . . . His manner is that of a field officer, dignified, superior and aloof. This is new to Hoosierdom politics but because it is new the pose goes over. It is so convincing that everyone is convinced that McNutt is a very big man. That he will be elected is more than likely. And then look out for him in the 1936 Democratic National Convention when the ex-service men will demand the vice presidential nomination, as they will in the Republican Convention."[151]

A scurrilous but interesting attack was made on McNutt in a broadside headed "Does Indiana Want a Left-Handed Governor?" It was circulated by the Republican party, which compared Professor McNutt's record of promises and performance. According to this sheet, he had promised to "keep faith with you," but he had personally profited on some private deals with Legionnaires; he favored care for the unfortunates, but he had charged $50 for a speech he made at the Veterans' Children's Home at Knightstown; he had pledged economy, but he had been the most expensive dean the Indiana University law school had ever had and the most expensive national commander of the American Legion; he favored protection for the consumer in public utilities matters, but he had written the 1929 corporation law which gave utilities even greater power; he said he favored better banking laws, but the 1929 corporation act allowed bank owners to escape double liability for forming holding companies; he favored protection for the worker, but he had charged $100 a day to settle a labor dispute; he branded the tax burden as unfair and intolerable, but he had paid no taxes in 1929 and 1930, and only $50 for 1931; he favored a $1.50 tax law, but used his influence to kill a bill in the special session of the state legislature. Such was McNutt's record as analyzed by this broadside.[152]

Nevertheless McNutt and his fellow Democrats won an overwhelming victory in the November elections, both nationwide and in the state. McNutt's plurality was 192,330, although Roosevelt's plurality in the state was only 189,447. McNutt's majority was 157,345.[153] The Democrats also gained all twelve Congressional seats; Van Nuys won the Senate contest. The Democrats also were now in control of both houses of the General Assembly by huge margins—the Senate 43 to 7, and the House 91 to 9.[154] McNutt was expected to have smooth sailing for his program as Indiana's thirty-third governor.

Among the congratulations received by McNutt on his victory was one from his friend Wendell L. Willkie, sent from Greensboro, North Carolina. The telegram predicted that McNutt would "make good with a bang."[155] Another came from Judge Springer, and in reply McNutt wrote that he was more than glad that the two of them were able to demonstrate to the people of Indiana "that two friends could go through a spirited political contest without marring in any way the relationship between them. You kept your personal campaign on a high plane." McNutt concluded:

"In meeting the great tasks and the grave responsibilities which are ahead I hope that I may have the benefit of your advice and counsel. We can continue to work together for the common good."[156]

James M. Curley, mayor of Boston, wrote McNutt shortly after the election that he recalled with much pleasure his recent visit to Indiana in behalf of Roosevelt and the entire Democratic ticket, and he was grateful to the electorate for the cordial reception accorded him. "The splendid victory achieved by the Democratic Party in this contest presents an opportunity for service which, I am certain, under the leadership of Franklin D. Roosevelt, with your assistance and other leaders of the party, will be forthcoming. The opportunity is great; the party responsibility is even greater. God grant that we may measure up to the fondest wishes and highest aspirations of the entire people of the United States," Mayor Curley concluded.[157]

Notes for Chapter 3

[1] Letter to McNutt from Gilchrist B. Stockton of Florida, April 13, 1928. McNutt Collection.

[2] George Ade to George Freeman, New York City, July 10, 1928. McNutt Collection.

[3] McNutt Collection.

[4] *Ibid.*

[5] *Ibid.*

[6] Stockton to McNutt, August 6, 1928. McNutt Collection.

[7] McNutt Collection.

[8] McNutt to Stockton, August 18, 1928.

[9] McNutt Collection.

[10] Dick Heller to McNutt, August 24, 1928.

[11] McNutt to Dick Heller, August 27, 1928.

[12] McNutt to Herbert F. Goodrich, University of Michigan Law School, Ann Arbor, Michigan, December 3, 1928.

[13] Memo from Miss Margaret K. Green, secretary Indiana University School of Law, January 15, 1929.

14 McNutt Collection.

15 Letter to McNutt from West Publishing Company, January 4, 1929.

16 Chancellor Charles W. Flint, Syracuse University, to McNutt, January 25, 1929.

17 Clipping, no date, no place.

18 Detroit *News*, February 14, 1929.

19 Letter to Frank McHale from T. Hawley Topping, Field Secretary, the Alumni Association of University of Michigan, March 14, 1929.

20 Letter to Frank McHale from R. E. Snoberger, Goshen, no date.

21 Letter to McNutt from Frank McHale, November 19, 1929. McNutt's salary 1928-29 was $6,500. He requested $9,000 for the next year but only $7,000 was granted, same as Hugh Willis.

22 Kathryn McHale to McNutt, November 26, 1929.

23 McNutt Collection.

24 McNutt to Frank McHale, November 26, 1929.

25 *Ibid.*

26 *Ibid.*

27 Gilchrist B. Stockton to McNutt, December 6, 1929.

28 McNutt to Stockton, January 18, 1930.

29 McNutt Collection.

30 McNutt to Douglas I. McKay, February 11, 1930.

31 J. H. Heller to McNutt, February 15, 1930.

32 Samuel C. Cleland to McNutt, February 20, 1930.

33 Joseph M. Cravens to McNutt, February 17, 1930.

34 William A. Kunkel Jr., Montpelier, Indiana, to McNutt, February 18, 1930.

35 McNutt to Kunkel, February 21, 1930.

36 McNutt to Cravens, March 10, 1930.

37 Frank A. White, editor of *The Hoosier Legionnaire*, Indianapolis, to McNutt, March 11, 1930.

38 McNutt Collection.

39 White to John Thomas Taylor, March 14, 1930.

40 Fred A. Wiecking, Bluffton, to McNutt, March 22, 1930.

41 *Ibid.*

42 Douglas I. McKay, New York, to McNutt, March 24, 1930.

43 *Ibid.*

44 *Ibid.*

45 L. G. Balfour, Attleboro, Massachusetts, to McNutt, April 7, 1930.

46 McNutt to Balfour, April 11, 1930.

47 C. A. Beal, LaPorte, Indiana, *Herald Argus*, April 7, 1930.

48 R. Earl Peters to McNutt, May 9, 1930.

49 Posey T. Kime, Evansville, Indiana, to McNutt, June 14, 1930.

50 Bloomington *Star* (no date).

51 Pleas E. Greenlee, Shelbyville, Indiana, to McNutt, June 12, 1930.

52 Wendell L. Willkie, New York City, to McNutt, July 9, 1930.

53 McNutt to Willkie, July 9, 1930.

54 Peters to McNutt, July 30, 1930.

55 Peters to McNutt, September 26, 1930.

56 Bedford, Indiana, *Mail*, October 23, 1930.

57 Editorial in Noblesville *Ledger*, October 24, 1930, taken from the Bloomington *Telephone*.

58 C. M. Miezer, Fort Wayne, to McNutt, October 17, 1930.

59 McNutt to Miezer, October 22, 1930.

60 *Ibid.*

61 Elza O. Rogers, Indianapolis, to McNutt, October 24, 1930.

62 The Madison, Indiana, *Daily Herald*, October 27, 1930.

63 McNutt to Douglas I. McKay, November 7, 1930.

64 Frank M. McHale to McNutt, November 4, 1930.

65 Michael L. Fansler, Logansport, to McNutt, November 6, 1930.

66 Charles L. Wilson, Oklahoma City to McNutt, November 6, 1930.

67 McNutt to Wilson, November 15, 1930.

68 Wilson to McNutt, November 24, 1930.

69 McKay to Wilson, December 15, 1930.

70 McNutt to McKay, November 25, 1930.

71 *Ibid.*

72 McNutt to Carl G. Wolflin, July 9, 1930.

73 Walter R. Arnold, South Bend, to McNutt, January 12, 1931.

74 Michael Fansler, Logansport, to McNutt, January 20, 1931.

75 Dick Shephard, Logansport, to McNutt, November 25, 1930.

76 Frank McHale to McNutt, April 18, 1931.

77 Sherman Minton, New Albany, Indiana, to McNutt, March 11, 1931.

78 McNutt to T. S. McConnell, Fowler, Indiana, *Benton Review*, March 20, 1931.

79 Dean L. Barnhart, Goshen, to McNutt, May 21, 1931.

80 Virgil M. Simmons, Bluffton, to McNutt, May 14, 1931.

81 Frank A. White, Indianapolis, to McNutt, May 7, 1931.

82 McNutt to Frank A. White, May 18, 1931.

83 R. Earl Peters to McKay, June 12, 1931.

84 *Ibid.*

85 Val Nolan, city attorney of Evansville, to McNutt, June 18, 1931.

86 Frank McHale to McNutt, July 21, 1931.

87 McNutt Collection.

88 Landis to McNutt, August 4, 1931.

89 McNutt to McKay, August 6, 1931.

90 Earl G. Lambka, Michigan City, to McNutt, August 3, 1931.

91 McNutt to Lambka, August 6, 1931.

92 McNutt to McKay, June 6, 1931.

93 *Ibid.*

94 McNutt to McKay, August 6, 1931.

95 Franklin D. Roosevelt, Warm Springs, Georgia, to McNutt, October 7, 1931.

96 McNutt to Roosevelt, October 27, 1931.

97 Roosevelt to McNutt, November 4, 1931.

98 McNutt to Arthur Lynch, December 9, 1931.

99 Arthur Lynch, Columbus, Georgia, to McNutt, December 9, 1931.

100 Wendell L. Willkie, New York City, to McNutt, December 9, 1931.

101 McNutt to Willkie, December 16, 1931.

102 John Wheeler, Crown Point, Indiana, to McNutt, August 6, 1931.

103 Barnhard Knollenberg, New York City, to McNutt, September 8, 1931.

104 William T. Young, Indianapolis, to McNutt, October 13, 1931.

105 C. C. Shipp, Indianapolis, to McNutt, October 13, 1931.

106 Joseph W. Kimmell, Vincennes, to McNutt, October 13, 1931.

107 H. K. Cuthbertson, Indianapolis, to McNutt, November 7, 1931.

108 James E. Perry, Indianapolis, to McNutt, November 8, 1931.

109 B. B. Shively, Marion, Indiana, to McNutt, November 8, 1931.

110 H. H. Evens, New Castle, to McNutt, November 8, 1931.

111 Robert D. Smith, Wabash, Indiana, to McNutt, November 8, 1931.

112 Omer Wooldridge, M. D., Columbus, Indiana, to McNutt, November 11, 1931.

113 Walter S. Chambers, Business Manager, New Castle *Courier-Times*, to McNutt, November 9, 1931.

114 Harry Burris, New Castle, to McNutt, December 9, 1931.

115 Cuthbertson to McNutt, March 11, 1932.

116 Pleas Greenlee, Michigan City, to McNutt, December 14, 1931.

117 McNutt to Hugh A. Barnhart, Rochester, Indiana, December 24, 1931.

118 W. N. Berryman, Frankfort, Indiana, to McNutt, December 26, 1931.

119 Ralph N. Smith, LaPorte, Indiana, to McNutt, December 28, 1931.

120 McHale to McNutt, January 16, 1932.

121 McNutt to Val Nolan, Evansville, January 18, 1932.

122 McNutt to W. H. O'Brien, Lawrenceburg, Indiana, January 21, 1932.

123 Samuel C. Cleland, Ft. Wayne, Indiana, to McNutt, January 23, 1932.

124 McNutt to Val Nolan, January 27, 1932.

125 Typed sheet, no date, Indianapolis *News*, February 6, 1932. McNutt Collection.

126 McHale to author.

127 Willkie to McNutt, February 19, 1932. McNutt Collection.

128 Willkie to Bowman Elder, March 31, 1932.

129 Willkie to Pleas Greenlee, April 7, 1932.

130 Circular. McNutt Collection.

131 McNutt to Henry E. White, May 11, 1932.

132 Indianapolis *News*, June 26, 1932.

133 *Ibid.* June 21, 1932.

134 *Ibid.* June 21, 1932. Cincinnati *Inquirer*, June 21, 1932.

135 James A. Stuart to McNutt, June 21, 1932. McNutt Collection.

136 McNutt to Stuart, June 22, 1932.

137 Ralph F. Gates to McNutt, June 22, 1932.

[138] Raymond S. Springer to McNutt, June 22, 1932.

[139] Springer, Connersville, to Frank A. White, September 27, 1932.

[140] South Bend *News-Times* editorial, June 22, 1932.

[141] James A. Farley, New York City, to McNutt, May 3, 1932.

[142] Farley to McNutt, May 18, 1932.

[143] McNutt to Farley, June 13, 1932.

[144] Abram Simmons, Bluffton, to McNutt, May 19, 1932.

[145] Mary W. Dewson, New York City, June 2, 1932.

[146] McNutt to Douglas I. McKay, June 15, 1932.

[147] McKay to McNutt, June 22, 1932.

[148] R. A. Shively, Indianapolis, to McNutt, June 29, 1932.

[149] Evans Woolen to McNutt, June 30, 1932.

[150] McHale to author.

[151] Clipping from the Providence, R. I., *Journal,* sent to McNutt from E. B. Rowbottom, Veterans Administration, Providence, October 14, 1932.

[152] Broadside in McNutt Collection.

[153] Indianapolis *News,* November 10, 1932.

[154] *Ibid.*

[155] Wendell L. Willkie, Greensboro, North Carolina, to McNutt, March 10, 1932. McNutt Collection.

[156] McNutt to Raymond Springer, November 10, 1932.

[157] Mayor James M. Curley, Boston, to McNutt, November 14, 1932.

CHAPTER IV

Depression Governor

Paul Vories McNutt was inaugurated Indiana's thirty-third governor in an outdoor ceremony on January 9, 1933, the fourth Indiana University man to be elected head of the state. He presented a most striking personal appearance as he took the oath of office. His six-foot frame was crowned with a mass of silver-white hair, and his facial features were those of a Greek god. Some even thought he looked like a movie matinee idol. Judge Walter E. Treanor, chief justice of the Indiana Supreme Court, administered the oath.

When McNutt assumed the reins of office it was generally thought that even he, with all his dash and verve, never would be able to achieve the changes in state government he had promised in the campaign. His party had been almost demoralized during the long period of Republican rule, and the spirit of defeatism seemed to have permeated its ranks.

Many students of Indiana politics believed that McNutt would be forced to spend most of his term getting rid of hold-over officials named by his predecessor for four-year terms. Because of the tremendous patronage difficulties which faced him, there was no guarantee that he would be able to effect a workable administration. There was also the uncertainty as to what course the new legislature would pursue. It was almost solidly Democratic, but its lack of experience made it most unpredictable.

Indiana, perhaps as much as any state, felt the full force of the depression which had followed the stockmarket crash of October 29, 1929. There was widespread suffering as the result of business failures, and extensive unemployment. Farmers lost their land due to their inability to repay loans or to pay taxes, and general economic chaos ran rampant throughout the state. Savings accounts dwindled to nothing in many cases, and with the loss of jobs and income, real economic hardship ensued. Indiana had her share of bread-lines and soup-lines. Mobs often congregated on the steps of the Statehouse. Schools were closed and the teachers were unpaid. Every problem which faced the nation faced the new government in Indiana.

The prestige of the state of Indiana was at a low ebb. Political scandals had rocked the state. Governors and other public officials in high places had been accused of corrupt practices in government. Departments of government were so disorganized and costly that the taxpayers were spending hundreds of thousands of dollars for services that did not benefit them. No one was responsible for the conduct of state government, and the "buck" was passed in every crisis. All of this was reflected in curtailed tax income for the state and municipal governments.

Such was the situation in Indiana when McNutt became governor. His inaugural address stressed the theme of economy for his administration. His speech was considered a masterpiece in statecraft. "The change in government," he said, "for which we have prepared, is here. It carries with it tremendous responsibilities and the possibility of far-reaching consequences. It offers an opportunity to prove that government may be a great instrument of human progress. It is a ray of hope which heartens us as we follow a path dark with ominous shadows." Under such circumstances, he said, "I assume the great office of Governor of my native state with unaffected humility, conscious of limitations but sincere in my desire to serve all of the people according to the best of my skill and ability. I pray God that I may be given the wisdom, the courage and the strength to perform the duties of the office and to lead the way toward the satisfactory completion of the important tasks to which all of us must now set our hands."

McNutt continued:

"The situation must bring forth a new, a greater, a continuous patriotism on the part of all citizens. Some look upon patriotism as a thing reserved for periods of armed conflict.

They wait for the blare of martial music, the sound of marching feet, and the rumble of the caisson to quicken the pulse and inspire supreme devotion to the common cause.

They are sustained by the excitement of the moment, and lose all interest in public matters when hostilities cease. Such intermittent attention to the general welfare does not satisfy present needs."

To McNutt, the struggle to restore economic equilibrium "is as grim and as real as any war. It calls for the same unselfish service, energy, intelligence, and solidarity. It requires the same willingness to give all that we are and all that we hope to be without thought of reward save the accomplishment of high purpose. It demands something more—a critical and searching examination of all governmental agencies to see which, if any, have outlived their usefulness." McNutt thought that this was "the time for perfect candor—no bragging, no pretense that things are better than they are, no tolerance of what should not be tolerated." With all his heart he desired such patriotism for Indiana.

The new governor pioneered practically all the laws which afterwards President Roosevelt was given credit for instituting. In other words, the first legislature of the McNutt administration started on January 9, 1933, and ended on March 6, 1933, two days after Roosevelt had taken his oath of office.

Anticipating the Roosevelt New Deal utterances by two months, McNutt declared it was possible "to know the truth without fear, to meet a crisis with indomitable courage. . . . Yet there are those among us who are afraid, who listen to prophets of evil. They profess to see the end of representative government, now rudely challenged by communism, fascism, and some think by technocracy. They say that democracy in theory is not democracy in practice, that popular sovereignty is an illusive concept, that the right to have a voice in government is not a prized possession. I wish to be counted among those who deny such doctrine. I believe in the destiny of democracy as a system of government, believe in it more profoundly than in anything else human. . . . This is a testing time for representative government. Our high enterprize is to prove it sufficient in every circumstance and for every task which can come to free people. We face a magnificent opportunity in which we, as lovers of freedom, dare not fail."[1]

The new governor outlined the immediate tasks that faced the state government if the depression were to be overcome. As he saw it, the task was "To provide food, clothing and shelter for the destitute, the aged and the infirm; to lower the cost of government and simplify its operations; to reduce and redistribute the burden of taxes; to maintain an adequate system of public education; to promote the efficient administration of justice; to strengthen necessary social agencies; to remove special privilege from the seats of power; to offer every assistance in restoring economic equilibrium; and to regain confidence in ourselves and in our institutions."[2] McNutt said:

"It is true that a government of the people may become corrupt and be used for selfish and private purposes. But whenever this has happened the voters have finally risen in their might to demand a change, a recognition of 'equal rights for all, special privileges for none,' and a return to high standards of official morality and administration."[3]

This was quite obviously an attack on the preceding Republican administrations.

McNutt emphasized the fact that man does not live by bread alone. "Things of the spirit are likewise necessary," he said. "But it is significant that, through the ages, hungry people have been in the vanguard of every revolt against the established order. A hungry man is never rational in his attitude toward the life of the community or toward his own life." Therefore, he believed that the most important business of government was "to make those adjustments which guarantee to every man the right to live as a normal human being." For this end it was imperative "that all unite in adopting a constructive program, unhampered by factions within or differences between parties, unmindful of selfish interests or propagandist associations. The purpose must be restoration rather than destruction, healing rather than harm. The lives and fortunes of the people are at stake."[4]

McNutt declared he had complete faith "that the people of Indiana are equal to the occasion, that they have a spiritual energy in them which will carry through any crisis however great. They have been sorely tried before and their experiences have left them steadfast, serene, unconquerable."[5]

When McNutt addressed the joint session of the General Assembly the next day, he again called for "a critical and searching examination of all governmental agencies." He insisted that "Every item on the budget must be subjected to the most critical examination in the performance of your duty to reduce the cost of government and simplify its operations." He urged "an immediate survey of the administrative department of government with a view to reducing the number and size of commissions, boards, and bureaus, and the number of offices, officials, and employees."[6]

These recommendations were based on a first-hand study McNutt had made shortly after his election. He had visited all the state institutions and had made an inventory of the situation as he found it. He thus had become fairly familiar with the needs of the state in this regard.[7] A month before he took office, he met with the newly elected Democratic legislators and discussed with them his proposed recommendations. These changes included certain consolidations and departmental transfers in the executive branch.[8]

From the very beginning McNutt insisted that economy in the cost of government and the simplification of operation would be the goal of his administration. He demanded that the chief executive be given strong powers to cope with the emergency facing the state. To accomplish his purposes he formulated a wholesale executive reorganization bill for the consolidation of overlapping departments, bureaus and commissions, reducing the number from several scores to about eight. Its purpose was not only to reduce the cost of government, but also to promote greater efficiency of operation. Its real purpose, however, was obviously to give McNutt a much greater control over the patronage, by creating a truly formidable political machine entirely dominated by him.

McNutt's executive reorganization bill and other centralizing measures were recognized by the legislators as "must" bills, to be passed by both houses under suspension of the rules, so well drilled was the Democratic majority. His critics and even his friends were amazed at the rapidity with which some of the bills were enacted into law. Often an important bill would appear seemingly from nowhere, be introduced into the House, sent to the Senate, passed again and signed, all on the same day. (It must be remembered that the Democrats outnumbered the Republicans 43 to 7 in the state senate, and 91 to 9 in the House.) It was said that often the legislators had to await publication of the bills to know what they had actually passed.[9] Such unorthodox methods were bound to cause voices to rise in protest. Some of the anti-McNutt Democrats strongly objected to this slow centralization of power as being foreign to the principles of the Democratic party.[10]

The executive reorganization bill was probably the most important and far-reaching of all McNutt's "must" proposals. Its title is interesting:

"A bill for an act concerning the executive including the administrative department of the government of the State of Indiana; repealing all acts and laws in conflict herewith and declaring an emergency."[11]

This so-called "Mussolini" bill provided for the consolidation of all 168 of the state governmental agencies into the following departments: executive, state, audit and control, treasury, law, education, public works, and commerce and industry. The governor would be given absolute authority over the departments. The "ripper" provision of the bill allowed him to discharge any employee or officer at his discretion. He was given the power to appoint or commission all officials except the deputies of the six elected officials. This meant that the governor could remove at his pleasure and discretion all but twelve officials in the entire state administrative organization. Only officials holding constitutional offices, and their deputies, were immune from the governor's power.

Such sweeping dictatorial powers were justified by Mc-Nutt as being necessary "to simplify the laws providing for the operation of the executive, including the administrative department, to eliminate duplications of activities, to effect radical reductions in personnel of officers, employees, and servants of the state of Indiana, to concentrate responsibilities in the elective offices, and to reduce the costs of executive and administrative government."[12]

There seemed to be at first general approval of the measure. The Indiana State Chamber of Commerce, the Indiana Farm Bureau, the Indiana Manufacturers' Association, and the State Federation of Labor were among the many organizations indicating their support.[13] They believed that such a measure would create more efficiency and economy in government by eliminating overlapping functions and duplications.[14] The support of such organizations assured the immediate and favorable attention of the legislature.

Not everyone, however, was so enthusiastically in favor of the proposal. Some of McNutt's political opponents, even in his own party, considered the proposed legislation a device to cripple them politically. Frank Mayr, Jr., who had long been jealous of McNutt's meteoric rise to power, was again the secretary of state, and he realized that if enacted into law, the bill would deprive him of his great patronage power over the automobile license division. A three-man board, composed of the governor, the lieutenant governor, and the secretary of state, would make all decisions affecting the Department of State, in which case Mayr would be in the minority. Nevertheless there was such universal approval of the measure that Mayr could not cause its defeat, and it passed both houses with little opposition.

About the only real opposition to the bill came from a group of one Democratic and seven Republican senators who

[131]

challenged McNutt to show how greater economies would be effected under his plan. They charged that the bill would "build up the greatest machine ever known on the face of the earth unless it was Nero's."[15] Several attempts were made to amend the bill, but all failed. McNutt persuaded his many friends, including McHale, who was not even a senator, Anderson Ketcham, the Democratic floor leader, Virgil Simmons, another non-member, and Pleas Greenlee, his executive secretary in charge of patronage, to use their influence among the legislators.

As a consequence of their activities the bill passed the House 80 to 15 on February 2, 1933, after the third reading, and it cleared the Senate 39 to 7, in spite of Republican charges that it would cause an increase in expenditures and "the development of the greatest political machine in politics." Others warned that it was invalid and contrary to the Constitution of the United States. The final passage with some slight amendments was completed on February 3. McNutt immediately signed the bill into law the same day, although he said there would be no immediate sweeping changes in the present governmental set-up, as he had until June 30 to regroup the 168 divisions of the state government.[16] It had taken only a week to accomplish the bill's introduction, passage, and signing.

As a part of his own "executive" department, Governor McNutt retained control of the division of safety, including the state police department, the automobile theft fund, the bureau of criminal investigation and identification, the fire marshal's department, the dry cleaning department, the state athletic commission; the adjutant general's division, including the armory board, battle flag commission, Grand Army of the Republic, the naval militia, Soldiers and Sailors Monument, Spanish War Veterans and Veterans of Foreign Wars; the state board of accounts, the budget department, the board of clemency, the board of state charities, poor relief commission, industrial aid for the blind, the free employment commission, Governor's yearbook publication, the state probation department and all state institutions. Thus, directly the governor controlled some of the most important features of the state government.

Details of operation of each of the institutions was placed in the hands of a separate commission. But McNutt still had a firm grip on each institution, because the members of each commission served at the will of the governor. Thus McNutt could immediately remove any commissioner who did not go along with his wishes.

In spite of McNutt's statement that he would not effect any sweeping changes immediately, he wasted no time in clipping the wings of Frank Mayr, Jr. Ten days after he had signed the bill, he ordered the creation of a division of public safety under his supervision, to be composed of the state fire marshal's department, the state motor police, and the bureau of criminal identification, all formerly within Mayr's jurisdiction.[17]

The next day McNutt took further steps against Mayr by certain personnel shifts among license plate distributors, parole agents, etc.[18] This was followed by the dismissal of twenty workers in the state motor police division,[19] and the transfer of the automobile license division from the secretary of state's office to the Treasury Department. Mayr was thus deprived of virtually all his patronage, and McNutt was in supreme control.

By April 14 the entire state government had been reorganized into eight central departments. Governor McNutt was branded by some as a Fascist dictator, but he insisted that the state government must be run as a business, and the people of Indiana had made him the business manager of the State.[20] Some of his supporters claimed that the office of governor had formerly been so limited in its powers that gross inefficiency had resulted. In the election of 1932 the people had demanded a change, and this change had been accomplished through the election of a general manager, and therefore McNutt's activities were justified by the decision of the voters.

As stated previously, Governor-elect McNutt, shortly after his election, had visited all the state institutions and made a detailed study of their problems. Just before he was inaugurated, he met with the newly elected Democratic members of the legislature and outlined the recommendations he intended to propose for consolidations and transfers of departments in the statehouse. The executive reorganization act was the result. But the increased powers which it gave the governor created serious problems. There were 35,000 applicants for the 3,000 jobs to be filled. Under the circumstances, it was virtually impossible to satisfy every jobseeker, even the most loyal among the Democratic party workers. Many members of the 1933 General Assembly were rewarded for their services by being appointed to lucrative state and federal positions,[21] while Republicans were dismissed, although in some few instances the boards were made bipartisan. An attempt had been made to have the reorganization act declared unconstitutional, but this failed,[22] and organized Democratic opposition to McNutt dwindled to nothing, although Republican opposition was still quite strong. By the end of his first six months in office, McNutt had practically completed his reorganization of the state government.

One of the avowed purposes of the reorganization act, according to McNutt, was to reduce the cost of government. But its opponents seriously questioned that any appreciable economy would be effected. McNutt himself predicted that the new plan would show a saving of $3,000,000 a year for the general fund, principally through the dismissal of state employees, yet it was admitted that scores of new jobs would be created under the new administration. There was wide speculation as to the new savings which the new program would realize,[23] although it was estimated that McNutt had saved the state about $400,000 a month in the first six months of office,[24] and McNutt asserted in August of his first year that the general fund was greater by $762,780 than the previous year, largely because of better budget control.

Actually, there seems to be considerable proof that there had been a real reduction of governmental costs during the first half year of McNutt's administration. The Indianapolis *News* declared on August 22, 1933:

"Reduction of expenditures totaling $3,362,750.48 was set forth by the McNutt administration for the first seven months of 1933 in a financial compilation prepared by Floyd C. Williamson, auditor of state. The comparison was made against the first seven months of 1932, although officials admitted they could not separate the savings made by the special 1932 legislative session, and those that could be attributed to the state governmental reorganization act."[25]

Of course it is extremely difficult, if not impossible, to say exactly how much money was saved by McNutt's program. Nevertheless it is obvious that the elimination of overlapping and useless boards and the consolidations of others must have resulted in some economy. Whether the savings in expenditures was the result of the reorganization act or greater efficiency otherwise in administration, or some other factor, it is true that Indiana was in a far better financial condition when McNutt left office in 1937 than when he became governor in 1933. In January, 1933, there was a deficit in the general fund of a little over $3,400,000.[26] Four years later, the general fund had a surplus of $17,000,000.[27] Regardless of the reasons, Indiana had been put on a sound financial basis.

In order to properly and objectively evaluate the entire governmental reorganization machinery of the state, the 1933 General Assembly passed a resolution providing for the appointment of a committee to make a study of the situation. McNutt appointed such a committee in January, 1934, composed mostly of academic personnel from the state's educational institutions. In their report, released in 1935, the committee declared that the Indiana administrative system as it existed before 1933 "was excessively decentralized and disintegrated." They declared that the Reorganization Act of 1933 and the executive order which was issued under it "accomplished both greater centralization and greater integration."

According to the report, centralization was increased "by giving him [the governor] power to appoint and remove," therefore making him the effective head of government. But the committee criticized several phases of the program. Some dissimilar services were consolidated which should remain separated. Other agencies were allowed to act as district units with almost complete autonomy. The committee thought there was little to be gained "by having an intermediate supervisory authority set above the lower operating units such as those of health, conservation, public utilities, and workmen's compensation." The committee also felt that "a second kind of control over operating units might have been placed in the hands of the newly created departments through the power of appointment and removal. Under the Reorganization Act, however, this form of control was vested exclusively in the chief executive."

In its recommendations, the committee declared:

"It is in view of the considerations above set forth that the conclusion is reached that the Reorganization Act may have carried the principle of integration somewhat too far. This conclusion is substantiated by the experience in other states which have had effective reorganization."

Illinois was cited as an example of a state which first set up nine departments and almost immediately added two more. The number was further increased later. The number ran from twelve to twenty in other reorganized states. In view of all these considerations, the committee recommended "that the administrative services of Indiana be grouped into thirteen departments."[28]

Governor McNutt's reorganization program was not the only piece of legislation he had introduced early in his administration, although it did act as a portent of future important recommendations which were later enacted into law. Even before President Franklin D. Roosevelt inaugurated his so-called "New Deal" program of relief, recovery, and reform, Governor McNutt had begun such a program in Indiana. Indeed, many of the federal measures which were later enacted into law had their origin in Indiana, and nearly all of them required state action before they could be implemented for the benefit of the people. The McNutt administration supported the Roosevelt policies enthusiastically.

One of the most controversial laws passed in the 1933 session of the General Assembly was the Gross Income Tax. It was bitterly attacked by the Republican Party and the Retail Merchants Association of Indiana. There is no question that McNutt did use dictatorial powers in having this act passed. The bill embraced over one hundred typewritten pages, and not more than ten members of the legislature out of 150 had read or studied the measure. But the day it was laid on their tables at 9 a.m., the retailers association sent out wires to all the merchants in the state and promised to march upon the Statehouse the next day—5,000 strong.

Meantime McNutt had suggested that this bill be presented to a caucus of the Democratic members of the House and Senate. Senator Chambers, who owned the two newspapers in New Castle, was to present it and explain it to the members of the legislature. But unfortunately the merchants in his home town advised him that if he did not withdraw his support, or if he took an active part in support of the legislation, they would start a new newspaper. So on the morning that the caucus was to be held, Chambers notified McNutt that he would not appear at the caucus.

McNutt then contacted McHale and asked that he explain the bill to the legislature. McHale, of course, was not an employee of the state or of McNutt, but he had volunteered his services to McNutt. He had almost complete charge of the legislative program, and worked on the eighth floor of the Indianapolis Athletic Club, which was commonly referred to as the "Bill Factory." He appeared before the legislature and spent two hours presenting the bill and answering questions from all those present. He read the wire from the merchants' association and stated that the bill would have to be enacted into law before midnight of the day it was introduced.

Ordinarily a bill that size and so controversial and so much an innovation would take six or seven weeks, but because the Democrats had such a large majority, they were asked to pass it and enact it into law under suspension of the rules, without changing a word or punctuation. The result was that the bill became law and was signed by McNutt the same day. The next day over 3,000 marched on the Statehouse in protest, but the following day 7,000 farmers appeared at the Capital and cheered McNutt for giving them the first relief they had from the heavy tax burden.

The Republican Party in the next campaigns attacked the gross income tax law, but in the meantime it became so popular that no party or individual has attempted to advocate its repeal.[29]

Even before the national government acted, Indiana under McNutt's leadership passed a measure calling for the legalization of the sale of beer and wine. The bill, which repealed the "Wright Bone-Dry" prohibition law of 1917, passed on March 2, 1933, and was to become effective on the repeal of the federal prohibition laws, such as the Volstead Act and the Eighteenth Amendment.[30]

Shortly after Roosevelt became President, the national Congress modified the Volstead Act permitting the sale of 3.2 beer and wine in states that had repealed their own prohibition laws and had provided for such sales. Thus on April 7, 1933, beer and wine became available in twenty states, including Indiana.

In the meantime, the General Assembly had provided for a statewide referendum to vote on substituting the Twenty-first for the Eighteenth Amendment. As a result, a convention of delegates elected by the people met in Indianapolis on June 6, 1933, and ratified the Twenty-first Amendment, which did not become effective, however, until December 5, 1933.

In legalizing beer and wine, the Legislature legalized also the sale of medicinal liquor which Congress had also sanctioned. Indiana remained on a medicinal liquor diet until the 1935 General Assembly authorized, in what is now regarded as the basic regulatory act, the sale of spirits by the drink. Previously the legislators were fearful that the public would go on a "binge" after fifteen years of prohibition, and they insisted that beer sales be confined to bottles. It took a tortured opinion from the attorney general to correct this error.

Under the 1933 law, all out-of-state beer was channeled through ten importers who were licensed by the excise commissioner. The latter was appointed by the governor. These importers were chosen from the ranks of sturdy Democrats and loyal McNutt Republicans. McNutt therefore had complete control over the patronage. The 1935 legislature changed the name of the importers to Ports of Entry, and provided for the licensing of from fourteen to one hundred.

Naturally there was considerable opposition to the 1933 law and those that followed. Many people were violently against the return to the manufacture and sale of intoxicating liquors, while others opposed it because it denied the rights of local option, even though the "open saloon" and the tavern in rural areas were eliminated.[31] Still others resented the very close alliance between the Democratic party and the liquor traffic, and Governor McNutt himself was severely criticized for his part in the enactment of the legislation, especially because it increased his power over the patronage.

Of course this Alcoholic Beverages Act was controversial. McNutt early in his governorship had promised that draught beer would never be sold in Indiana while he was governor, and that he would not allow an "open saloon" to exist. Under his Port-of-Entry system, McNutt made a private monopoly of all beer that entered Indiana from other states. In each of the districts into which the state was divided, McNutt designated one man or corporation to be "importer" for that district. Each "importer" bought "foreign" beer for whatever price he wanted to pay, and sold it to Indiana dealers for whatever he could get. The profit was his. It was unlawful for anyone to compete with the "importer." This Port-of-Entry system was not repealed until 1939, long after McNutt had left the governorship.

Another measure which became law in Indiana before the

federal government acted was the one providing for an old-age pension system. McNutt had promised such relief in his pre-election campaign, and the general assembly of 1933 enacted it into law. It provided payments up to $180 per year for indigent citizens over 70 years of age. The following year a special session of the legislature brought the payments in line with the national program, with compensation for the unemployed, the blind, the dependent, and the aged provided by the federal, state, and county governments.

McNutt's political power was augmented by the city skip-election bill, introduced into the General Assembly on February 27, 1933. This called for the postponement of the 102 city elections from 1933 to the following year. Its purpose was to extend the terms of the city administrations, sixty percent of which were Democratic, for an extra year, thus insuring the continued predominance of the party in municipal affairs. It would also give McNutt additional power over the patronage so that he could further dominate the party and control subsequent elections. Naturally the Republicans bitterly attacked the proposed legislation, but McNutt cited several precedents to justify his demands. He estimated that the one-year postponement of municipal primaries and elections would save the taxpayers nearly a quarter of a million dollars. The bill passed the house on March 1, 1933, by a vote of 73 to 13, and the Senate approved it the same day. McNutt affixed his signature immediately.[32] The Republicans challenged the constitutionality of the law in the courts, but it was upheld and remained on the statute books until 1941, when it was finally repealed by the Republican majority in both houses of the General Assembly, during the administration of Henry F. Schricker, the Democratic governor. [33]

The Reorganization Act of 1933 and the Skip-Election Law of the same year proved to be politically shrewd moves on the part of Governor McNutt. He was now firmly entrenched in power, and was in a position not only to control the Democratic party in Indiana, but also to implement his ideas of government. Yet such an ambition would cost money, and he began to effect schemes to increase the funds of the party for such purposes. As a consequence the Hoosier Democratic Club was organized. This was an organization made up of all the Democratic state and local appointive and elected officials for the purpose of securing their active political cooperation in McNutt's program. This immediately was dubbed the "Two Percent Club" because each member was required to contribute that percentage of his salary each month to the organization or "machine."

There seemed to be a difference of opinion as to whether membership in the club was voluntary, or required of all those holding state or local political jobs. It was said that if an employee failed to "contribute" he would be dismissed summarily. Thus McNutt could at once rid himself and his administration of any "disloyal" appointees, and cause the defeat of "reluctant" elected workers at the next election. Yet Pleas Greenlee, who was in charge of the patronage, claimed that many employees did not belong to the Hoosier Democratic Club, and that no one had ever been disciplined for failure to "kick in."[34] There is no doubt, however, that McNutt knew who were members and who were "disloyal."

Although the Democratic State Committee refused to assume any responsibility for the Two Percent Club, it willingly accepted the benefits of its treasury. The money was used to reduce party deficits and to aid the party in financing its political campaigns, as well as to assist in carrying out the party's program. It was the feeling of the leading Democrats that it was much better to have the rank and file of loyal

Democrats pay their share toward the activities of the party, than to depend on the support of big business interests.

Naturally there was considerable criticism of the Two Per-cent Club both from within and outside of Democratic ranks. The state Corrupt Practices Act forbade employees and offi-cials to make political contributions, but this did not deter the collections of assessments. The Indianapolis *News* in August, 1933, openly charged the Club with violating the Corrupt Practices Act.[35] McNutt attempted at first to cir-cumvent this charge by having the organization changed from an incorporated to an unincorporated group, and then had the Corrupt Practices Act amended so as to exempt such clubs, corporate or otherwise, whose function it was to aid or assist in political activities generally, provided, however, that the exemptions should not excuse those clubs whose purpose was to sponsor or promote individual candidates.[36]

Thus the Two Percent Club was legalized, but it was soon to come under attack by the Republicans. It was one of the few laws sponsored by McNutt and enacted by the General Assembly, which were later repealed. McNutt defended the law when it was attacked in the 1934 campaign. He stated that everyone recognized that money had to be spent in large amounts in building a political organization. He declared that political parties had two choices—either to get the money from those who were interested in the party and particularly those who were working in the administration and had jobs, or they could get contributions from privileged groups. Mc-Nutt preferred to get the money from the workers and dedi-cated Democrats, and those interested in good government.[37]

Although the Two Percent Law was repealed, making such contributions illegal, both the Democratic and Republican parties continue to use it in some form when in power to col-lect funds from their workers, but neither party ever accuses or attacks the other in regard to the practice. As a matter of fact, McNutt's open-and-above action seems to have been the right thing to do, and the people in politics generally accept this method of raising funds.

It was about this time that Governor McNutt began to give indications that he and R. Earl Peters, the state Democratic chairman, were coming to the parting of the ways. It seems that McNutt felt that Peters was now a stumbling-block to the governor's further political aspirations. They differed over various political issues, and neither could tolerate opposition to his views. Peters insisted that the fund of the Hoosier Democratic Club, amounting to approximately $10,000 per month, be assigned to the state committee to help pay off its deficit from the 1932 campaign, which amounted to more than $35,000. He saw no justification for raising $120,000 a year from state employees when the obligations were only a fraction of that amount, and he asked that the assessments be reduced by half.

McNutt decided to put the issue squarely in the lap of the state committee for final decision. In the meantime he assured the members of Indiana's congressional delegation that the money would be used to satisfy the debts and obligations of the state committee. He further claimed that the Republicans had been doing the same thing for some time, and "if the Republican party spends $100,000 on propaganda, certainly the enthusiastic supporters of the Democratic party and the state administration have the right to raise money to be used for their own purposes and to maintain their own party platform."[38] This charge against the Republicans was branded as "unquestionable inaccuracy" by Burrell Wright, treasurer of the Republican state committee. He said it was characteristic of McNutt "to be careless whenever talking about other people's money."[39]

The Democratic state committee met on October 9 to dis-
cusss the situation. They adopted a resolution setting up a
subcommittee of three members to supervise the funds of the
Two Percent Club. When the committee was appointed it
was found that McNutt, Peters, and Senator Van Nuys were
all represented. This was a blow to Peters. The resolution
gave this special committee the power to determine the
amount of funds to be raised and the disbursements thereof,
and "such powers so conferred shall not be delegated to any
person or persons and said committee is hereby authorized to
employ such agencies as are necessary in carrying out the purpose of the committee."[40] The conference postponed for the
time being a definite ruling on the Hoosier Democratic Club,
but the following month the Van Nuys-McNutt forces cooperated in endorsing the Two Percent Club.[41] Peters thus lost
control of the state committee, and resigned as chairman. He
announced his candidacy for the Democratic nomination for
the United States Senate on November 14, 1933. Dr. Carleton
B. McCulloch, an Indianapolis physician who had been the
Democratic candidate for governor in 1920 and 1924 was immediately elected unanimously to succeed Peters as chairman.[42]

Peters fully expected that the state committee would support his candidacy for the nomination, but Governor McNutt
and his forces refused to endorse him. It was a part of Mc-
Nutt's strategy to dispose of Peters as the power in Indiana
Democratic politics, so that he himself would have a clear
track toward undisputed supremacy. Publicly he stated that
the election of the party's nominee was his main concern, after
the party had made its choice. Even McNutt's friend Senator
Van Nuys refused to take sides in the nomination fight, thus
almost alienating himself from McNutt. Perhaps both were

playing politics with the party. Van Nuys was willing to leave the matter entirely up to the state convention itself.[43]

In the meantime McNutt himself was being urged by some to make the race for the Senate nomination, although he issued a statement that he had not been, was not, and would not be a candidate. "I have a job and I was brought up to finish any job I started," he said.[44] Shortly thereafter Sherman Minton, who had been appointed by McNutt as the public counselor for the Indiana Public Service Commission became the fifth contender for the nomination.[45] But McNutt continued to appear as a strong contender. Pleas Greenlee, his patronage secretary, sent a form letter to many McNutt backers, urging them to be especially diligent in working for the state administration program. "It is imperative," he wrote, "that state legislators are elected who will not be too individualistic in their thoughts, but rather who will be 'ball players' and go along for our program," and that convention delegates be elected "who will listen to you and follow the Administration wishes," and that precinct committeemen are elected "who will give us a loyal county organization." Greenlee concluded his letter by stating that the governor was very anxious to know "the true political situation in your county."[46]

The Democratic state committee chose June 12 as the date for the state convention at Indianapolis.[47] McNutt was chosen temporary chairman to give the keynote address and introduce Van Nuys, who was designated permanent chairman. This was considered a setback for Peters' chances for the nomination, although a month before the convention, Peters claimed that he already had more than enough votes to guarantee his nomination. This claim was vigorously denied by Frank McHale. Naturally both factions predicted victory at the convention. McNutt himself did not openly suppport any candidate, but it was well known that he was opposed to Peters.

It was generally conceded that the McNutt faction was the dominant one in the two or three weeks before the convention. When Dr. McCullough resigned as state chairman, Omar Jackson was elected to the post on May 19. This move was not opposed by Peters, who still insisted he would win the support of the majority of the convention delegates.

Although Representative Louis Ludlow entered the race as the ninth candidate, the contest began to appear as a fight between the McNutt, Peters, and Van Nuys forces for control of the convention, with Greenlee supporting Minton and Albert H. Cole favored by McHale. The McNutt-Van Nuys forces were unable to reach agreement on a candidate. Indianapolis mayor Reginald H. Sullivan was supported by Van Nuys, while McNutt believed that Minton was the only man who could stop Peters.[48] As far as he was concerned, this was absolutely essential.

The Democratic state convention of 1934 got off to a good start, although Lieutenant Governor Townsend presided due to the absence of Senator Van Nuys, who was ill. Governor McNutt set the tone in his keynote speech, in which he strongly defended his administration. He called for the adoption of a constructive program to "speed recovery during this critical period and furnish a lasting foundation for the future prosperity and welfare of our people. . . . Today the militant and victorious Democracy of Indiana meets to review its unparalleled record of achievement and to chart the course for the next biennium," he said, and "to adopt a constructive program which will speed recovery during this critical period and furnish a lasting foundation for the future prosperity and welfare of our people." The Democratic program for the future, he claimed, included three great objectives: "The security of the home, the security of livelihood, and the security of social insurance."

According to McNutt, the pledges of the Democratic platform of 1932 constituted a program for the effecting of these
objectives. "These pledges were carried out by a Democratic
General Assembly with fidelity and intelligence," he claimed.
"Relief was and is the first problem. All welfare agencies
were consolidated and a definite program adopted providing
for the creating of public employment clearance facilities
and the coordination of unemployment and poor relief activities with a view to the more effective use of state, county,
city and local resources for relief purposes." He claimed that
the administration of poor relief in Indiana had been conducted "impartially and with the interest of the unemployed
at heart. At the same time it has been managed in a careful
and thoughtful manner with due regard to the conservation
of public resources."

In reviewing the accomplishments of the past seventeen
months, McNutt declared that his administration had solved
most of the pressing problems which existed early in 1933:
"In keeping with the promises of the Democratic platform, it
had deferred most of the mandatory tax levies, fixed standard
salaries for public officials at lower levels, returned fees to
general tax funds, established a moratorium on additional
bonded indebtedness, adopted a deferred payment plan for
delinquent taxes, enacted a voters' registration law to preserve
the sanctity of the ballot and to carry out the mandate of
the constitution, passed an anti-lynching law, reformed the
poor relief laws, established old-age pensions, liberalized the
workmen's compensation law, removed the competition of
prison labor, prohibited 'yellow-dog' contracts, repealed the
obnoxious Wright bone dry law, passed an excise tax, controlling the sale of beer and providing machinery for revenue
and regulation in respect to the sale of spiritous beverages

after repeal, and prepared for additional reforms by the appointment of a commission on governmental economy."[49]

In conclusion, McNutt maintained that the issue in the 1934 campaign was "between chaos and order." The Republican party, he claimed, "proposes to destroy the credit of political subdivisions, repudiate honest obligations, abandon the needy and helpless and cripple the performance of the necessary functions of government. The Democratic party proposes to continue the orderly processes of government, maintain the credit of the state and its political subdivisions, keep the schools open, care for those who hunger and are in want, promote economy, insure the proper integration of functions among the different governmental units and continue the march toward complete economic rehabilitation of our people."[50]

Peters, who was ahead on the first ballot, was unable to secure the nomination for the Senate and he was soon passed by Minton, who was finally nominated on the fourth attempt.[51] Peters' strongest opponent after the first ballot appeared to be Clarence Manion, who claimed that he had the backing of the administration. When Peters released his supporters there was a general swing to Minton with the blessing of McNutt, who was now in full control of the party organization in the state. From then on, Peters was no longer an effective influence in Indiana politics, although he was given an important federal post in the state.

The convention adopted a platform which gave a general approval to the McNutt administration and urged the continuance of the gross income tax law, creation of a nonpartisan liquor commission, and repeal of the direct primary law.[52]

Governor McNutt's complete control of the convention was now viewed as the "culmination of his far-sightedness in obtaining from the legislature a grant of power giving him complete control over state patronage," through the passage of the 1933 state executive administration act. In commenting on the situation, the Indianapolis *News* observed that formerly the political power of the governor had usually diminished as his term progressed, but this trend was now reversed, as a result of the 1933 act, and the governor was now limited only by "statutory inhibitions preventing summary dismissal of state personnel."[53] Thus Governor McNutt was hereafter in a position to dominate the selection of the nominee for United States senator and even the decisions of the national conventions.

The Democratic campaign opened officially on September 11, 1934. McNutt gave a great deal of his time and energy in speaking for his party's slate, but at the same time he used the campaign as a device for justifying the acts of his own administration, in answer to what he claimed were "the deliberate misrepresentations of a hostile press in dealing with the accomplishments of the state administration."[54] The governor himself came in for considerable criticism, rather than Minton, the candidate. McNutt's political machine, his Two Percent Club, the reorganization act, and other McNutt accomplishments were denounced severely.

McNutt conducted a very interesting campaign in the 1934 election, which caused the Republicans to resort to rather unusual methods. According to Frank McHale, Republican marching clubs were formed, and they attended every rally where McNutt spoke. The governor insisted that wherever he spoke the party organization issue an invitation in the newspapers for all the citizens to attend his meeting, and after his speech he would answer any question that anyone in the audience had concerning his administration. He insisted that he would first be given the right to speak. Afterwards he would usually say to the audience that all the people were invited by their governor, and he was responsible for his stewardship, and they were his especially invited guests. He then asked that they be accorded every respect and courtesy that would be extended to any guests visiting their homes. He was generally able to answer all questions satisfactorily.

One of the first such meetings was held at Broad Ripple in Indianapolis, and the Republican Irvington Marching Club of 1,000 advertised that they would be present. When they appeared, McNutt finally quieted them down until he had finished his speech. He then stated that he would remain there until morning, if necessary, answering questions and asked his friends to accord the marchers every courtesy. He answered questions for about two hours.

This sort of campaigning took place all over Indiana. At first, the Republican state organization encouraged people to go to the Democratic meetings prepared to ask embarrassing questions, and even printed some questions in the newspapers in advance and furnished individuals with questions to ask. Finally the crowds became so large and McNutt was so completely the master of the situation that the Republican organization ordered all their various committees throughout the state to discourage this type of attack, because it was only popularizing McNutt and he was becoming the people's champion.

In the meantime, McNutt was being attacked by the Republican editorial organization. One of the members who attacked him most was the publisher of the Fort Wayne *News-Sentinel*, Oscar Follinger, who attacked McNutt personally. Unfortunately for the gentleman, in the midst of the campaign while he was on a hunting trip in Canada, he was killed.

The publisher of the Washington, Indiana, newspaper who was on the platform committee of the Republican state committee, had worked all one night before the Republican convention, writing a platform and planks that attacked McNutt. This involved a lot of detail and conferences. On the way back to Washington the next day, he fell asleep at the wheel of his car and went off the road and was killed.

The most dramatic and unfortunate of the incidents of the campaign occurred when McNutt was speaking at Richmond, Indiana. The doctor who was assistant to the superintendent of the mental hospital at Richmond issued a statement attacking McNutt and the Two Percent organization. He stated that he did not contribute although requested to do so, and that he did not intend to contribute, and that McNutt did not dare to fire him because he knew so much scandal about the administration which he would expose if he were fired.

When McNutt received this information from the Associated Press, he wired the doctor that he was discharged. In the wire which McNutt turned over to the press, he stated that he would be in Richmond about ten days before the election, and that the doctor would be invited with his friends to attend the meeting at the armory and expose McNutt or ask him any questions.

The night of the meeting in Richmond, the armory was filled with about 6,500 people, and it was estimated that there were at least that many on the outside who could not get in. When McNutt had finished his talk, he asked for questions, and after quieting the crowd, he called on the doctor who, he said, was his especially invited guest. He asked him to state what his charges were or ask any questions. The doctor was given a microphone and he started mumbling, and McNutt asked him to speak up louder, that he couldn't understand what he was attempting to say. As the doctor started to talk again, there was a gasp in the crowd—the doctor in his excitement fell dead.

Thus the three men who had most violently attacked Mc-
Nutt in the campaign had all died suddenly, with the result
that the Democrats were fearful of resentment against them.
But as the vote turned out, there was no evidence of such resentment against the type of campaign McNutt had conducted.

In the election on November 6, 1934, the Democrats again
won a sweeping victory throughout the state, although not
by such a landslide as in 1932, when the plurality of the
state officials was approximately two hundred thousand, instead of fifty thousand. Arthur Robinson, the Republican candidate for the senate, was defeated by Sherman Minton by
44,823 votes. It was generally conceded that Minton had
won largely through the personal popularity of Governor Mc-
Nutt. The Republicans elected only one representative to
Congress, Fred Landis.[55] In the General Assembly, the
Democratic majority was reduced to 65 to 35 in the House,
and 38 to 12 in the Senate.[56] This statewide Democratic
victory of 1934 was a good omen of things to come in 1936.

Governor McNutt now had two more years in his term.
Those years were spent in implementing the legislation already
enacted, and preparing for the elections of 1936. The Indiana
Constitution prohibits the governor from succeeding himself,
so McNutt could not use the possibility of re-election as a
political device. But he still exercised considerable political
influence in the state, and was expected to play a dominant
role in the forthcoming Democratic convention and election.
Yet his work as chief executive was not quite finished. He
made the most of his last two years in the gubernatorial chair.

When the general assembly met in January, 1935, they
were faced with the repeal of the direct primary law, which
had been one of the planks in the Democratic platform. The
platform stated:

"It should be repealed and legislation enacted safeguarding the selection of party candidates by representatives of the party, and thereby save more than $1,000,000 to the taxpayers of the state biennially."

Repeal was also favored by the Republicans.[57]

Yet Louis Ludlow, who represented the Eleventh District in Congress, claimed on December 18, 1934, that if Indiana repealed the law, it would be the first state "to take this reactionary backward step from popular government to boss rule." He thought that repeal would virtually exclude women from participating in the nominating process.[58] Many other Democrats, including Senator Van Nuys, opposed the repeal of the measure, as did organized labor, the Indiana Farm Bureau, and the Indiana League of Women Voters. [59]

Governor McNutt made no reference to the primary law in his message to the joint session, however, and it was therefore concluded that he was not in favor of its repeal. He did feel, however, that it was the legislature's problem, and not his.[60]

In spite of overwhelming Democratic opposition, however, a Republican-sponsored bill to repeal the primary law was introduced into the Legislature on January 31, 1935. The Republicans were determined to stand behind their platform, in spite of the fact they were in the minority. Senator Henry F. Schricker, the Democratic caucus chairman, declared:

"In response to what we believe to be the popular demand of the people, the Democratic senators in caucus decided unanimously that the Indiana primary law shall not be repealed and that this action meets with the approval of the Governor."[61]

A resolution to this effect was then adopted by the legislature by a vote of 35 to 11. Only one Republican favored the measure. On March 11 the House voted to postpone repeal indefinitely.[62]

[154]

Another important issue which had been given much publicity in the previous months was whether or not the offices of governor and United States Senator should be included in the primary. A bill to include these offices in the primary was introduced into the senate and referred to the committee on elections February 11. Both Democrats and Republicans feared the power of McNutt in the state convention, and thus hoped that this power might be curtailed or eliminated if such nominations should be made in the primary. Senator Van Nuys, who favored the change, broke with Governor McNutt, who vigorously opposed the move.

McNutt firmly believed in the convention system for choosing United States senators, governor, and some other state offices. State-wide primaries, as is evidenced in other states, allow small cliques to dominate the selection of candidates for public office. In theory, the primary may seem the more democratic way, but McNutt thought otherwise, since with each small group endorsing its candidate—sometimes candidates with the same name—the voters can be confused. McNutt believed that the only fair and equitable way is for a political party to choose its candidates at a convention of representative delegates from throughout the state.

An attempt to prevent a vote on the measure was made when the president *pro tempore* called for the adjournment of the Senate, thus preventing the elections committee reporting the bill, but this method was unnecessary. The elections committee reported the bill without recommendation, and consequently the bill was killed.[63] This was a great victory for the McNutt administration. It thus appears that McNutt had supported the wishes of the people in not urging the repeal of the direct primary law, but when opposing forces threatened to increase the law's power and thereby reduce the governor's control over nominations, he brought about the amendment's defeat.

During the last two years of his term, Governor McNutt had considerable difficulty with the patronage, especially in regard to various federal programs in the state. Over 700 positions were involved in the federal farm census alone in Indiana. Nominations for these positions were submitted to Commerce Secretary Daniel C. Roper in December, 1934, by the Indiana Democratic congressmen. Governor McNutt believed that such nominations should be made by him, but Senator Van Nuys opposed any attempt to usurp congressional power over the federal patronage. The senator thus lined himself squarely against the governor in favor of the members of the House. Roper then accepted the list as drawn up by the congressmen, and thus McNutt suffered one of his worst defeats.[64]

However, McNutt's defeat in this matter apparently proved to be a victory. The month following, James A. Farley, chairman of the Democratic National Committee, proposed that in the future all federal appointments in Indiana be approved by the state committee. This suggestion was immediately opposed by Senator Van Nuys and most of the Indiana congressional delegates, who felt that they were better qualified than the state committee to screen applicants for federal jobs. For the time being, at least, Farley's proposal was sidetracked.

The question of McNutt's successor in 1936 soon became a red-hot political issue. Both Greenlee and Townsend, the lieutenant governor, were strong potential contenders, but it was expected that Van Nuys would try to liberalize the organization against the McNutt forces, although McNutt was still recognized as the leader of the party. Early in 1935 McNutt was asked whether Greenlee had the approval of the state administration for the nomination, but he replied that no one had the "go" sign.[65] Even Senator Van Nuys was expected to join the anti-McNutt forces in reorganizing the state committee. He declared that he would "carry the fight for the liberalization of the organization and for the election of delegates to the state convention of 1936 into every county in Indiana.[66]

During the sessions of the Indiana Democratic Editorial Association annual meeting in August at French Lick, efforts were made by the leading political figures of the state to reconcile the differences between McNutt, Van Nuys, and Greenlee. McNutt's friends apparently were opposed to Greenlee's gubernatorial ambitions, and seemed to favor Lieutenant Governor Townsend instead. As a result of shrewd political maneuvering, McNutt emerged from the meeting as the undisputed leader of the party.[67]

Yet Greenlee insisted even as late as December, 1935, that the majority of the delegates to the state convention favored his candidacy, and he charged that the rank and file of the Democratic machine would follow him and not McNutt. When Greenlee officially opened his campaign on January 1, he was retired as executive secretary within forty-eight hours, although he did not resign. His dismissal was approved by McHale, Elder, Wayne Coy, Virgil Simmons, head of the conservation department, Senator Van Nuys, and William Kunkel, Fort Wayne publisher. Thus one of the most bitter campaigns in the history of Democratic politics was launched.

McNutt was chosen temporary chairman of the June 1936 Democratic convention, and gave the keynote address on June 16. Just before the convention opened, he predicted that Townsend, who was favored by the state administration,[68] would be nominated on the first ballot, although Greenlee asked, "what does Paul know about politics?"[69]

During the balloting, the convention became a regular Donny-brook with a full-fledged fist fight marring the proceedings, but at the end of the first ballot, Townsend had 904½ votes, which was less than twenty shy of the required 923. These were added when Greenlee and the other contenders dropped out, and Townsend was elected. Henry F. Schricker, the administration's candidate, was chosen for the lieutenant governorship on the first ballot. He was a long-time member of the party and a loyal McNutt supporter. The Republicans nominated Raymond S. Springer as their gubernatorial choice.

During the campaign the party was generally united in supporting Townsend, in spite of opposition from some quarters of the state. McNutt was very active as usual, and joined Van Nuys, McKinney, Peters, Minton, and even Greenlee in making speeches in behalf of the slate. The Republicans attacked the Two Percent Club and the McNutt administration in general. But the Democrats again carried the state in November, partly because of the Democratic sweep in the national elections. Townsend's majority was 180,968, which was less than Roosevelt's plurality in Indiana.

However, the national issues and national candidates dominated the political scene. Franklin D. Roosevelt and John Nance Garner were again the Democratic candidates, and advocated a continuance of the New Deal program. Alfred M. Landon and Frank Knox were their Republican opponents. Roosevelt carried the state by an almost 250,000-vote margin. All but one of the 12-man Hoosier delegation in the national House were Democrats, and the party elected twenty-three state senators to three Republicans. It was truly a New Deal victory on the state and national levels.

Just before the election the noted Washington columnist David Lawrence suggested a federal inquiry into "The Two Percent Club." He charged that the Roosevelt-Garner ticket had benefited from this fund "because very little money was to be sent into the state by the Democratic national committee inasmuch as the state Democratic organization is interested in keeping the state organization for a straight ticket combination. Governor Paul V. McNutt, who is the boss of the state organization, having played very close to the New Deal and believing that he might outstep Governor George H. Earle of Pennsylvania for the 1940 Presidential nomination, has been trying to carry Indiana for Roosevelt by keeping the state organization on its toes for the national ticket." McNutt denied that the rates in the club were as high as 2 per cent. "I pay the highest on my salary of $8,000 a year," he said, "and I contribute $12 a month. . . . The books are open. They show precisely what has gone to the state committee."[70]

Governor McNutt had won the general approval of labor during his four-year term.[71] When he first took office, he was the idol of labor. He consulted continuously with labor leaders and generally accepted their recommendations without question. The city of Indianapolis at that time was the headquarters of many labor organizations, including the Teamsters' Union, which was the largest of all, the Carpenters' Union, the Barbers' Union, and the Typographical Union. It had been the headquarters of the Miners' Union, headed by John L. Lewis. The Teamsters were headed by Dan Tobin, and the Carpenters by William Hutchinson, a Republican.

At the time that McNutt took office, there had been no favorable legislation to speak of on behalf of labor, but McNutt brought employee and employer together and enacted legislation which gave each equal rights at the conference table and before the bars of justice. He saw to it that business was fairly protected.

Prominent labor leaders claimed that McNutt had given labor in the state its Bill of Rights. During a total of 125 legislative days, he had approved forty-four bills of benefit to labor. Many of these laws were of a pioneering nature, enacted prior to federal laws on the same subject, and some of them set the example for similar laws by other states.

The keystone law in this Bill of Rights was the so-called "Anti-Injunction Law," enacted after having been strongly advocated by McNutt in his gubernatorial campaign. Previously the laws of Indiana had permitted the granting of injunctions against employees in labor disputes almost at the whim of the presiding judge. The discretion granted him was extremely broad. The new law permitted the issuance of an injunction only after five days' notice and a definite showing in open court that there was imminent danger to life and property. It also forbade the use of the state police in labor disputes.

The law had the effect of legalizing picketing within the state, and at the same time, outlawed numerous city ordinances which had provided against picketing. It also prohibited the notorious "yellow dog" labor contracts which had been used for years to oppress labor by unscrupulous employers.

In order that Indiana's workmen, its aged, blind and other beneficiaries might promptly receive the benefits of the Federal Social Security program, Governor McNutt called a special session of the General Assembly in March, 1936, which enacted what are known as the Unemployment Compensation Act, the Public Welfare Act, and the Child and Maternal Health Act. Indiana was the ninth state to take such action. Most of the other states waited for the regular sessions of their legislatures.

Governor McNutt did not always win the approval of labor, however. There was considerable labor unrest in the coal-mining and industrial areas during the early years of the

Thirties, due to the general economic conditions prevailing. The miners' union was attempting to organize the non-union workers in the eleven coal-mining counties of the state. In the resulting violence, the mines were being dynamited and the laborers were shot at from ambush with an average of twelve killings a year.

Soon after McNutt became governor, he declared martial law in these eleven counties, and ordered General Elmer "Pete" Straub, head of the state national guard—and afterwards on General Dwight Eisenhower's staff in World War II—to police the area. A skeleton group of twenty-four men was brought together and housed at Shakamak State Park. These men of course had officers in addition to the soldiers, and each night they rode through these counties and maintained law and order.

Shortly after Governor McNutt had declared martial law, the newly elected president of the Miners' Union and all the representatives of labor in the state came into McNutt's office. They demanded that the governor withdraw the troops from Shakamak Park. When the head of the union finished speaking, McNutt asked, "Aren't you the individual who, when campaigning for the office of president of the miners' union of the State of Indiana, told your members that once you were elected you would make that white-haired SOB in the State House remove the troops from Shakamak Park?" The president of the union pounded the table and said:

"You're damned right I am, and I mean every word of it."

McNutt then told him to go back and tell the members of the various locals that he had called upon that individual in the State House and that he—the Governor of Indiana—had said to the president of the union, "You get the hell out of this office and don't come back in unless I send for you, and the troops will remain in Shakamak Park and will police these eleven counties as long as you are president of the Miners' Union."

Later, at a conference held in Sullivan, Indiana, the president asked Fred Bays, the Democratic county chairman, if he couldn't meet McNutt on the platform, as there would be about 5,000 people present, and shake hands with him. This was arranged, and when he met McNutt, the latter stated to him that he was willing to take the troops out of the park. Two days later, this same individual called on McNutt, and when asked if he had made the statement, McNutt replied, "Yes," and the president then asked him when that would take place. McNutt replied, "Just as soon as you resign as president of the Miners' Union." The individual replied that he did not intend to resign. McNutt stated:

"If you do not, the troops will remain and the rest of you can go out and tell the members of the Miners' Union that as long as this man is president, the troops will stay, but if they elect someone else, I will take the troops out of Shakamak Park."

As a result another president was elected and the troops came out of the park.[72] For this action against labor, Norman Thomas branded McNutt the "Hoosier Hitler."

In spite of strong censure from the American Federation of Labor on October 14, 1935, in a resolution criticizing McNutt "for his un-American and unconstitutional usurpation of power in declaring martial law which, in effect, has put the National Guard in a position of strike-breaking agencies," he again declared martial law early in 1936 because of strikes in Floyd and Clark counties. He explained that under his oath of office, troops must be called to keep order in a general strike.

Terre Haute, Indiana, was the scene of considerable labor unrest during McNutt's governorship. A general strike was called in that city. The police were run off the streets, stores closed, and milk wagons upset; Governor McNutt declared martial law, but only after he had obtained written request from all the city officials asking for the troops. Within twenty-four hours, he placed 128 men in jail in Vigo County and would not release them on a writ of habeas corpus. He was upheld in this action by the Federal District Court in Indianapolis.

Though McNutt had called out the National Guard three times, he refused to intervene in twelve other cases when local officials insisted that the situation had got out of hand. He refused to use the Guard to break a strike in Bloomington.

One other incident in connection with labor should be mentioned. In 1935, a May Day riot was threatened at South Bend. A delegation of public officials from that city, including the mayor, chief of police, Chamber of Commerce president, and businessmen met Governor McNutt in his office on the Sunday prior to the threatened riot, and asked him to send the National Guard to South Bend. The governor promised to send the troops providing that he first could send one man to the city to ascertain if they were necessary. He then called Indianapolis Mayor Reginald Sullivan and asked if he could borrow Michael Morrissey, chief of police of Indianapolis. Morrissey went to South Bend and insisted that the police bring in the twenty-one labor leaders to a room at the Oliver Hotel. After being introduced to them by the chief of police, he asked the chief to leave. Then for an hour Morrissey talked with the men representing labor.

When he had finished talking with the men, Morrissey recommended to the governor and to the mayor and to the South Bend group that labor be permitted to parade on May Day, and that the parade be headed by a group of policemen in uniform. He got the labor group to agree that the American flag and the flag representing the labor union be carried in the parade by men in uniform who had served in World War I. This was agreed upon. The line of march Morrissey suggested should be about three miles long and the pace should be pretty fast, so as to exhaust the individuals but not to restrain them. This was done over the objection of the mayor and the chief of police of South Bend. However, Morrissey's recommendation that this would be a peaceable solution of the problem was a correct one. The parade took place and outside of a little heckling, that was the end of the threatened May Day riots in South Bend. This is just another proof of the way McNutt understood and handled labor.

Several years later when President Franklin D. Roosevelt was seeking a chairman for the War Manpower Commission to deal with labor and business, he sought the advice of several labor leaders, including Samuel Gompers, of the A. F. of L., Phil Murray of the CIO, John L. Lewis of the Mine Workers, Dan Tobin of the Teamsters' Union, and William Hutchinson of the Carpenters' Union. Roosevelt was almost shocked to learn that almost all suggested McNutt. Industry was for McNutt, as well as the labor leaders. Finally, over the objections of Lewis, McNutt was chosen Manpower Commissioner.[73]

McNutt's labor policy was generally supported by public opinion to such an extent that Republican and anti-McNutt Democrats, who attacked McNutt on every other ground, did not attempt to make a serious issue of his labor policy.

There was no police force in Indiana before 1933, and McNutt immediately recommended to the legislature that a state police force be formed. Al Feeney, formerly captain of the Notre Dame football team, was its first head.

McNutt was always very much interested in public education, and insisted on a drastic revision of the state's tax system to meet the emergency facing the schools in the depression period. He argued that "Children are born and grow up in periods of depression as well as in periods of prosperity. They have but one chance that cannot be postponed. Roads and buildings may wait, but certainly not the children."[74]

When McNutt became governor, both state and local government had so collapsed that one of the main responsibilities of government, education, faced a grave crisis. Teachers were serving without pay, and some schools had closed early. But McNutt insisted that the schools remain at maximum excellence regardless of the economic situation. One of the first acts of the McNutt administration was to provide each teacher with state funds, in addition to the amount collected locally from property taxes. Thus the schools, especially rural, were kept open the entire term.

The McNutt administration also enacted into law a measure making the office of lieutenant governor a 12-month job. Prior to that time, the lieutenant governor served only 61 days plus the 40-day special session. In 1935 this was made a full-time position, and the lieutenant governor since then has devoted his full time to the office with specific duties assigned to him. He is in charge of the State Fair, the fairgrounds, and is responsible for agricultural and industrial development in the state. The result is that the lieutenant governor ever since has found the office a very helpful stepping-stone to becoming governor.

Just before he left office in 1937, McNutt issued an order transferring the administration of the state benevolent, penal and correctional institutions to the state department of public welfare, thus placing them on the merit system, with Wayne Coy as acting director.[75] This was a shrewd political move which relieved the pressure on McNutt and at the same time assured him of further control of the party, even when he was no longer governor.

In reviewing McNutt's four-year term as governor of the Hoosier state, the general consensus of opinion seemed to be that he did a job that everyone agreed couldn't be done, in spite of all his dash and decision. It had been felt that he would be obliged to use up much of his term before he could rid himself of holdover officials—but of course the general reorganization legislation took care of the possibility. He worked tirelessly in carrying out his administrative duties. He was a hard campaigner, and a popular orator. His organizing ability was exceptional. Because of his almost complete domination of the legislature, his critics branded him as an uncompromising tyrant. They charged that no such thing as compromise was in his soul, although the facts did not bear this out.

Although McNutt had many severe critics, he was generally considered a good governor. [76]

Unfortunately in the past, more than at present, people generally looked upon politicians as unscrupulous, dishonest, and those who amassed fortunes because of special privileges and illegal acts. Naturally when McNutt became governor, his personal enemies checked every facet of his life, both social and political. They screened him as no other man in Indiana had ever been screened before because they knew that he was politically ambitious.

After four years, and to the present day, neither McNutt nor anyone connected with him was ever involved in any scandal. Most of the men associated with him went on to become successful in business and in their professions. Many a time McNutt was compelled to tell a man who had been very loyal to him and who was seeking an appointment that he was not the type of man who could handle public office or trust, and that in refusing him appointment, it was in order to protect the individual as well as the State of Indiana. Mc-Nutt had the courage to make decisions with a total disregard for the political effect resulting therefrom.

While he was governor, McNutt kept in close touch with the problems of the day. He had a weekly meeting with his department heads, the lieutenant governor, and with the eight men who formed his political organization. He was the first governor to meet daily with the press. During the sessions of the legislature, he held a press conference twice daily, and the reporters were permitted to ask any question concerning the subject matter of the day. He counseled with the heads of labor, industry, the merchants' association and other groups, and was in constant touch with the reaction of the people. He was more concerned with what the people across the tracks thought than he was with what the people on North Meridian Street in Indianapolis thought.[77]

McNutt was very popular with the independent voters while governor of Indiana, and he numbered many Republicans among his friends. In his fairness he was able to attract to his administration some outstanding individuals who were available at the time because of general business conditions.

For example, McNutt had men in his official family like Perry McCart, general counsel of the Monon Railroad, as chairman of the Public Service Commission, and James Adams, a banker from Whitley County, on the State Highway Board. He appointed as head of the Gross Income Tax Division Clarence Jackson, who afterwards became head of the state Chamber of Commerce, and recently retired as chairman of the United Life Insurance Company. Frank E. McKinney was a young man in the McNutt administration and became national chairman of the party. He is now chairman of Indiana's largest national bank, American Fletcher. McKinney is perhaps one of the closest men to former President Harry S Truman, who often refers to him as the greatest chairman the Democratic Party has ever had.

McNutt was able to start many other men on their road to prominence because of his many contacts. Judge John Kern, former mayor of Indianapolis, became chief justice of the United States Tax Court. He was the only man ever to have been re-elected to that office three times by the other members of the court. John Scott, a Republican, was placed on the Federal Power Commission. Wayne Coy, who was associated with McNutt as under-secretary in his office, became associated with the Public Works Administration and assistant to Harry Hopkins. He was afterwards assistant to President Roosevelt and chairman of the Federal Communications Commission. Sherman Minton was the public counsel for McNutt and later became United States Senator, assistant to the President, and then Associate Justice of the United States Supreme Court. Several appointments to the federal bench were McNutt men. Two of them went to the Circuit Court of Appeals in Chicago.

McNutt's entire four years in the governor's office were marked by tireless, dynamic energy. Frequently he was at his desk until noon and then spoke in some distant state that night. He was a fearless air traveller, although he did not pilot a plane himself.

On many occasions he showed he considered himself "just one of the people." In the summer of 1936 when he was to address a meeting of the Indiana State Bar Association at Lake Wawasee, he was delayed by numerous duties at his office and found that in order to arrive in time for his scheduled address it would be necessary to fly. Landing at the isolated Wawasee airport he found no one to meet him to drive him to his destination. The only method of transportation was a large oil truck and the driver offered to "give him a lift."

"That's good enough for me," the governor said, and they were off. The truck sailed up the driveway to the fashionable hotel. The attendants were horrified that a truck driver should have the audacity to approach the hotel doors, then blinked their eyes when the governor appeared.

Governor McNutt had the peculiar faculty of being able to refresh himself by "cat-naps." It was not unusual for him to sleep in the back seat of an automobile going eighty or ninety miles an hour. He could throw himself on a bed for a few minutes before a banquet or speech and go to sleep immediately. This ability enabled him to be what was generally recognized as one of the most active governors the state has ever had.

McNutt had a keen sense of humor. In his press conferences he was at ease and often his boisterous laugh rang out at some reporter's quip, but he never demeaned himself. He looked on the governorship as a post of dignity and consequently he sometimes appeared to the public as being haughty. He was far from that. He was companionable, but he wanted performance and he expected it from his appointees.[78]

One of the kindest things that McNutt did during the depression was the manner in which he took care of some widows of prominent members of both political parties. Up to 1933 there was no provision for a widow of a former governor. Harry Leslie, who had preceded McNutt in the office, had died, and his estate was penniless. Mrs. Leslie now found herself without funds and with no business training. McNutt got a job for her in the auto license department. He then initiated legislation with the support of the Republicans, headed by Ralph Gates, who later became governor, for a law which is now on the statute books which pays a widow of an Indiana governor $3,000 a year as long as she lives.[79]

In summing up McNutt's term as governor, it might well be said that he had won the adjective "terrific" in the familiar description of him as "tall, tan, and terrific." It has truly been said that no governor has ever driven a program more energetically through a legislature than did McNutt. He had come into office on the anti-Hoover wave of 1932, when the people were demanding action to fight the depression, and he gave it to them through his overwhelmingly Democratic legislature. Most of his proposed legislation was ratified, and most of it has stood the test of time, in spite of fierce criticism. Even his political enemies have admitted that he raised revenue, paid the school teachers and other state employees, bolstered county governments, and administered relief work effectively. When McNutt left office, a $17,000,000 surplus was in the state treasury.[80]

Notes for Chapter 4

For much of the material included in this chapter, credit is given to Rand Burnette, "Paul V. McNutt: A Study of Machine Politics, 1928-1937," an unpublished Master of Science thesis, University of Wisconsin. Lent to author.

[1] Paul V. McNutt. "Inaugural Address of Governor Paul V. McNutt of Indiana," delivered in Indianapolis, January 9, 1933. (Indianapolis 1933).

[2] *Ibid.*

[3] *Ibid.*

[4] *Ibid.*

[5] *Ibid.*

[6] Paul V. McNutt. "Message of Governor Paul V. McNutt to the Seventy-eighth Indiana General Assembly," delivered in Indianapolis January 10, 1933. (Indianapolis 1933).

[7] Indianapolis *News*, November 15, 1932.

[8] *Ibid.* December 26, 1932.

[9] Indianapolis *News*, July 12, 1934.

[10] *Ibid*, January 26, 1933.

[11] *Ibid.* January 27, 1933.

[12] *Ibid.*

[13] *Ibid.* January 29, 1933.

14 McNutt Papers, Indiana State Library.

15 Journal of the Indiana State Senate during the Seventy-eighth Session of the General Assembly (Indianapolis 1933) pp. 276-277.

16 Indianapolis *News,* February 3, 1933.

17 *Ibid.* February 13, 1933.

18 *Ibid.* February 17, 1933.

19 *Ibid.* March 1, 1933.

20 *Ibid.* May 25, 1933.

21 *Ibid.* March 15, 1934.

22 *Ibid.* March 25, 1933.

23 *Ibid.* April 13, 1933.

24 *Literary Digest,* July 15, 1933.

25 Indianapolis *News,* August 22, 1933.

26 *Ibid.* January 10, 1933.

27 *Ibid.* January 8, 1937.

28 *Report of the Indiana State Committee on Governmental Econo*my (Indianapolis 1935) pp. 44-45.

29 McHale to author.

30 Indianapolis *News,* March 2, 1933.

31 John D. Barnhart and Donald F. Carmony, *Indianapolis from Frontier to Industrial Commonwealth,* 2 vols. (New York 1954) Vol II, pp. 479-480.

32 Indianapolis *News,* March 2, 1933.

33 Barnhart and Carmony, p. 493.

34 McNutt Papers, Indiana State Library.

35 Indianapolis *News,* August 30, 1933.

36 Burnett Manuscript.

37 McHale to author.

38 Indianapolis *News,* September 27, 1933.

39 *Ibid.* September 28, 1933.

40 *Ibid.* October 10, 1933.

41 *Ibid.* November 14, 1933.

42 *Ibid.* November 15, 1933.

43 *Ibid.* February 13, 1934.

44 *Ibid.* February 16, 1934.

45 *Ibid.* February 22, 1934.

46 McNutt Collection. Pleas Greenlee to William Storen, Indianapolis, March 6, 1937.

47 Indianapolis *News,* March 13, 1937.

48 *Ibid.* June 13, 1934.

49 McNutt Collection. Indianapolis *Star,* June 13, 1934. Pamphlet, *Facts for Every Democrat.*

50 *Ibid.*

51 Indianapolis *News,* June 12, 1934.

52 *Ibid.* June 12, 1934.

53 *Ibid.* June 13, 1934.

54 *Ibid.* August 11, 1934.

55 *Ibid.* November 7, 1934.
56 *Ibid.* November 29, 1934.
57 *Ibid.* January 17, 1935.
58 *Ibid.* December 18, 1934.
59 *Ibid.* January 14, 1935.
60 *Ibid.* January 11, 1935.
61 *Ibid.* January 31, 1935.
62 *Ibid.* March 12, 1935.
63 *Ibid.* February 25, 1935.
64 *Ibid.* December 13, 1934.
65 *Ibid.* April 11, 1935.
66 *Ibid.* June 4, 1935.
67 *Ibid.* August 12 and 17, 1935.
68 *Ibid.* May 23 and 25, 1936.
69 *Ibid.* June 6, 1936.
70 *Ibid.* October 15, 1936.
71 "Labor Record of Paul V. McNutt", pamphlet, Indiana State Library.
72 McHale to author.
73 McHale to author.
74 Quoted in Alva Johnston, "I Intend to be President," *Saturday Evening Post*, March 16, 1940.
75 Indianapolis *News,* January 14, 1935.
76 Indianapolis *News,* January 17, 1937.
77 McHale to author.
78 From Harold Feightner's files. Lent to author.
79 McHale to author.
80 Indianapolis *News,* December 15, 1936.

CHAPTER V

High Commissioner

When McNutt left the governorship in 1937, various offers were made to him, including the presidency of Indiana University. He had also been offered a $50,000-a-year job as consultant with a large business house in the East. But he had higher ambitions in the national arena. He was mentioned for the Secretaryship of War; so certain was Harry Woodring, Acting Secretary of War (and former governor of Kansas), that McNutt would become Secretary, that he did not move into the offices of the late Secretary Dern until McNutt had accepted another appointment.[1]

President Roosevelt invited McNutt to a conference in Washington regarding an appointment as High Commissioner of the Philippines, which carried a salary of only $18,000 plus $10,000 for maintenance of the household. But the foreign post appealed to McNutt—although the Islands were over 8,000 miles away, he was thinking of the Presidency in 1940. He was encouraged to accept the appointment by his friend McHale, who was also thinking of 1940. McNutt could return to the United States at the appropriate time, and he needed

[173]

a federal job if he wished to remain in the political limelight and gain national prominence.

Just before the appointment, Frank McHale and Bowman Elder had gone to Washington from New York City to discuss future plans for the governor. They were prepared to offer him a $50,000 job with a five-year guaranty as head of the New York Stock Exchange. In the lobby of the Mayflower Hotel, McHale and Elder met Frank Murphy, Governor-General of the Philippines, who informed them that he had just come from the White House where he had learned that McNutt had been offered the new position of High Commissioner to the Philippines, and that he was to let President Roosevelt know his decision the next day.

McHale and Elder then went up to McNutt's room and informed him of the $50,000-job offer. McNutt turned to McHale and said, "Frank, money never made anyone happy or satisfied. As you know, I do not have very much money. [His estimated wealth at that time was between $30,000 and $35,000.] I want to ask you a question and I want you to be very fair and try to be conservative in your reply. What are my chances of being elected President four years from now, in 1940?" McHale then stated to him that his chances were about 100 to 1 against him. "In other words," McNutt said, "you mean to state that I am one man in 100 that has a chance to be elected President in 1940, of 145 million people?" McHale said that was about right. Then McNutt repeated that money never made anyone happy or satisfied, and he would never be happy or satisfied until he had his chance at running for the Presidency.

McNutt then asked McHale to go home to Indianapolis that night and talk to Mrs. McNutt, as he had to make a decision and tell the President the next day. The next morning when Elder and McHale were eating breakfast with Mrs. Mc-

Nutt, she broke down and cried. She had formerly lived with her father in the tropical part of Mexico, and she hated the climate, and the illness of her father made her uneasy to go so far away. (Her father passed away while she was in the Philippines.) But when McNutt telephoned her, "she was a champion because she greeted him and said she thought it would be a wonderful appointment and hug the President for her, and that the two of them could spend the next couple of years on their second honeymoon." When she hung up, "she broke down and cried," and said, "I never want it to be said that I ever stood in Paul's way. I have always tried to go along and I'm very proud of him and I know how dedicated a man he is, and I only hope the people of Indiana and the nation realize this." And so McNutt accepted the appointment as High Commissioner of the Philippines, at the youthful age of forty-five.[2]

The White House looked upon the acceptance as a victory, because it was felt that the post definitely sidetracked the handsome former governor for 1940. In their glee, White House officials indicated the truth of often-repeated rumors that Roosevelt intended to break precedent and run for a third term, and he wanted no interference from McNutt.[3]

In the meantime, Dr. William Lowe Bryan, who had long been president of Indiana University, was expected to retire soon, and McNutt's friends were urging that he spend only a year or so in the Philippines, during which time a temporary president would be appointed to succeed Bryan, and then McNutt could return to the States and become head of his alma mater. This was expected to be an excellent springboard to the presidency of the United States.[4]

Ever since the United States had acquired the Philippines from Spain at the conclusion of the Spanish-American War in 1898, promises had been made to withdraw American sovereignty over the Islands and to recognize their independence as soon as a stable government could be established. Many Filipino insurgents, however, under the leadership of Emilio Aguinaldo, refused to accept American sovereignty over the Islands, and continued their armed fight for freedom until their leader was captured by the American army in 1901. A civil administration then followed the military government. In 1916 the Jones Act was passed, establishing an elective senate in place of the Philippine Commission, and vesting the supreme executive power in a governor-general appointed by the President of the United States. This act reaffirmed "the purpose of the people of the United States to withdraw their sovereignty over the Philippine Islands and to recognize their independence as soon as a stable government can be established therein."[5]

Yet the years following World War I brought major differences of opinion regarding Philippine independence. The official view in Washington was that the Filipinos were not yet ready for complete independence, but American economic and labor interests were strong for immediate independence to free themselves from competition from Philippine free trade and the influx of Filipino labor into the United States. Many leaders in the Islands feared that independence would cut them off economically from the United States, and they would therefore be forced to pay higher tariffs.[6]

The Jones Law of 1916 is generally considered the first covenant between the people of the Philippines and the people of the United States. Its preamble, which contains the promise of freedom, reads:

Whereas it was never the intention of the people of the United States in the incipiency of the war with Spain to make it a war of conquest or for territorial aggrandizement; and

Whereas it is, as it has always been, the purpose of the

people of the United States to withdraw their sovereignty over the Philippine Islands and to recognize their independence as soon as a stable government can be established therein; and

Whereas for the speedy accomplishment of such purpose it is desirable to place in the hands of the people of the Philippines as large control of their domestic affairs as can be given them without, in the meantime, impairing the exercise of the rights of sovereignty by the people of the United States, in order that, by the use and exercise of popular franchise and governmental powers, they may be the better prepared to fully assume the responsibilities and enjoy all the privileges of complete independence . . . .[7]

Following the 1932 election, the Philippine independence movement gained momentum. The Hawes-Cutting Act was passed by a Democratic Congress on January 13, 1933, over President Hoover's veto. The act provided for independence after twelve years. The Philippine legislature, however, rejected the measure in October on the ground that its real aim was to exclude Philippine products and labor from the United States. On March 24, 1934, Congress passed the Philippine Commonwealth and Independence Law, commonly known as the Tydings-McDuffy Act, which substantially re-enacted the Hawes-Cutting bill, but provided for the removal of United States military posts and the settlement by negotiation of the future status of United States naval bases. This act was unanimously accepted by the Philippine legislature on May 1. Under its authority, a convention met on July 30 to frame a constitution, which President Roosevelt approved on February 8, 1935, and which was ratified on May 14. Manuel Quezon was elected the first president on September 17, 1935. July 4, 1946, was the date set for the complete political independence of the Philippines.

The Tydings-McDuffy Act did not give precise and final answers to all questions of future Philippine-American relations, but it did go far in establishing the guide lines for an orderly and mutually satisfactory transfer from Commonwealth to independent status. After a ten-year period of gradual withdrawal, all United States control over the Islands was to be severed, although the United States was to be allowed the continued use of naval reservations and fueling stations. These were to be negotiated after July 4, 1946. Future commercial relations were to be determined before that date.[8]

Under the terms of the Tydings-McDuffy Act, the President of the United States was authorized to appoint a High Commissioner to the Commonwealth of the Philippines, who "shall be the representative of the President of the United States in the Philippine Islands and shall be recognized as such by the government of the Commonwealth of the Philippine Islands, by the commanding officers of the military forces of the United States, and by all civil officials of the United States in the Philippine Islands. He shall have access to all records of the government or any subdivision thereof, and shall be furnished by the Chief Executive of the Commonwealth of the Philippine Islands with such information as he shall request."[9]

The act also provided that in the event the Commonwealth failed to pay any of its bonded or other indebtedness or the interest thereon when due or to fulfill any of its contracts, the United States High Commissioner "shall immediately report the facts to the President, who may thereupon direct the High Commissioner to take over the customs offices and administration of the same, administer the same, and apply such part of the revenue received therefrom as may be necessary for the payment of such overdue indebtedness or for the fulfillment of such contracts."[10]

The United States High Commissioner was required to render to the President and Congress of the United States an official report annually, "and at such other times as the President may require." He was authorized "to perform such additional duties and functions as may be delegated to him from time to time by the President under the provisions of this Act." He was to receive the same compensation "as is now received by the Governor General of the Philippine Islands, and shall have such staff and assistants as the President may deem advisable and as may be appropriated for by Congress. . . . The salaries and expenses of the High Commissioner and his staff and assistants shall be paid by the United States."[11]

The High Commissioner who represented the President of the United States in the Philippines was faced with a most delicate task. He was to give as much help as possible to the Filipino people largely by personal influence and suggestion rather than by constitutional authority. According to one expert on Philippine-American relations, "The exercise, no matter how tactful, of even such residuary power as remained in American hands was frequently an irritation to the Filipinos. Quite understandably they wanted to see the Philippine flag at the top of the masthead and not underneath the American flag."[12] It was only natural that delicate situations constantly arose.

In commenting on the office, one of the leading experts on Philippine history has declared:

"In glamour, opportunity, and difficulty the High Commissionership is one of the great American offices. The welfare, the very destiny of a young nation . . . and the vital interests and the honor of the United States in the Eastern Hemisphere may hang upon the statesmanship of this distant representative of the President. In practice, the success of the High Commissioner in serving both his country and the Philippines will depend to a considerable degree upon the relations which exist between him and the Philippine chief executive. Ideally, both the High Commissioner and the Commonwealth President will feel that under normal conditions the former has the three rights and only the three rights attributed by Walter Bagehot to the British constitutional sovereign: the right to be consulted, the right to encourage, the right to warn. Acknowledged as possessing these rights by a statesmanlike Philippine President and exercising them wisely, a properly qualified High Commissioner will need no others in the ordinary conduct of his office. Indeed, he should have no others, for the High Commissioner is not intended to be a super-president of the Commonwealth."[13]

Just before President Roosevelt appointed McNutt as High Commissioner, the Philippine press speculated considerably about the possible successor to retiring High Commissioner Frank Murphy. The Manila *Herald* editorialized that one qualification for anyone who would successfully perform the duties of the office was "complete familiarity with the Filipino people, their psychology, institutions, and the general historical background of their current political life."

According to this editorial, the powers of the High Commissioner under the Tydings-McDuffy Act were vague, and "where they seem explicit are full of dynamite."[14] His powers of intervention "must be cautiously exercised. The powers of general supervision (without control), specifically to be informed and to seek information on the affairs of the Commonwealth can well be extended, in the hands of an officious High Commissioner, beyond limits that are neither legal nor desirable."[15]

The editorial insisted that the most important consideration in the appointment of the High Commissioner should be "the continuity of the policy already established of sympathetic cooperation rather than of inquisitorial obstruction. No stranger will satisfy this specification, but a man already familiar with our institutions and attentive to our aspirations. It is to be hoped that the Philippine post will be spared the usual considerations that dictate the distribution of political plums to the victor's friends. As it happens, the High Commissioner job is one of the most highly prized positions within the gift of the President of the United States, and it is just possible that our wish and welfare may not count as heavily in the choice of the man as they should."[16]

In spite of this feeling on the part of the influential Philippine press, President Roosevelt appointed McNutt as High Commissioner to the Islands. There is little profit in speculating on the reasons and motives which prompted this selection, although it may be taken for granted that political consideration was not absent in rewarding a deserving Democrat for services rendered. It is no more than fair to assume that the choice was prompted at least in large part by McNutt's record. He was considered an able administrator. He had a broad cultural background combined with practical experience in public affairs. He was thus able to approach his task in the Islands with sympathy and understanding.

One of the reasons why the Philippine legislature had declined to accept the original Hare-Hawes-Cutting Act was the vagueness regarding the powers of the High Commissioner. Yet the Tydings-McDuffy Act reiterated these provisions, which named the High Commissioner the "representative of the President of the United States in the Philippine Islands," but which did not precisely specify what authority may be "delegated to him" by the President. But it was certain that the High Commissioner could not exercise any power over the Philippine Government which was not assigned to him directly or vested in the President by the Tydings-McDuffy Law or some other United States statute. Thus the powers of both the President and his representative were limited.[17] As early as August 3, 1936, President Quezon declared:

"Let it be clearly understood that no American official

from the President of the United States down to the High Commissioner has any authority, powers, prerogatives or privileges in the Government of the Commonwealth except those granted by the Independence Law."[18]

The Manila *Tribune* editorialized:

"The powers of the United States High Commissioner are defined in law with sufficient vagueness to permit almost any interpretation of their extent. Both Murphy and Jones [J. Weldon Jones, acting High Commissioner following Murphy] chose to impose strict interpretation, and to function in a way that gave the widest possible leeway to officials of the Commonwealth government. McNutt will be at least as careful in the interpretation of his powers as Murphy and Jones have been. It is natural that his appointment should be, as it universally is, in official circles, welcomed."[19]

The Manila *Bulletin*, in an editorial, declared that it was natural that there should be some disappointment that the appointment was given to one not Philippine trained and not familiar with the important problems with which his official duties would bring him into immediate and intimate contact. "However, no one has been so blind to realities of political appointments as to assume that politics would be ruled out and the more important questions of training and special qualifications made the deciding factors. If politics were not considered, if special fitness and proven qualifications had been the deciding factors, . . . J. Weldon Jones would have been named High Commissioner several weeks or months ago."[20]

The *Bulletin* continued:

"If a political appointment had to be made . . . it is fortunate that the man selected should be one with as favorable a record as that of Mr. McNutt. [He has] keenness of mind to give him distinction, ability to grasp political problems with a mastery to make him a leader among executives, a personality to carry him forward in his political career with spectacular speed. . . . His appointment thrusts him into the center of the stage in a historic drama in which the problems are internationally involved and the whole plot most intricate, and with the staging of the drama already far advanced."[21]

Rumors continued to circulate that McNutt would use his appointment as a stepping-stone to the Presidency in 1940, and thus his sojourn in the Philippines would be of short duration. But when asked about his plans for 1940, he parried all questions, even though some observers expected him to remain only a year or two before returning to the States to reenter politics. McNutt himself declared:

"I am going to do my job in the Philippines. How long I stay there depends on the President. I did not ask for the job, and I am not going there with any selfish purpose. I have no axes to grind. I am facing the task with the utmost humility. I propose to study all phases of the Philippine-American problem. I consider it a great honor to represent the United States, a nation of 140,000,000 people, and I look forward with pleasure to meeting President Quezon."[22]

While the *Bulletin* was encouraged that the Philippine post should be filled by one considered presidential timber, yet "we frankly cannot see this position in the light of a White House stepping stone. To put it in that light is to threaten this office with an injustice. The place here needs a man of ability and all the related favorable qualities, but the task is not such as to render it a White House build-up, unless it is to be considered on the wrong plane. This post needs a man with the qualities that could take him to the very top, but a man who has the sense of service to cause him to place his duties here above all considerations of where he is going."[23]

However, the *Bulletin* assured McNutt a cordial welcome as he faced the big task which his new office presented. He had "a mind of his own," and was obviously "a fighter of high caliber." "He should get along well with both Americans and Filipinos." He was "far from the blustering, domineering type of political boss who might be expected to hold the Democratic leadership of a state." He was rather the "diplomatic type—suave, polished—well educated—scholarly—possessing a mind of his own."[24]

In a speech delivered at a popular banquet in his honor at the Jose Rizal Tennis Memorial Stadium on August 20, 1937, on his return from the United States, President Manuel L. Quezon gave his opinion of the new High Commissioner. "I had the high honor," he declared, "of being present when High Commissioner McNutt took the oath of his office. I congratulated him then and offered him my best wishes and cooperation. He reciprocated my sentiments. Now, I offer my felicitations to the Filipino people for the appointment, to the important post of High Commissioner of the United States in the Philippines, of a man who has proved his unusual talent and capacity, his noble character and high ideals in many a field—amongst scholars, soldiers and governors. I confidently predict his success in his new undertaking."[25]

President Quezon continued in a jocular vein:

"Let me add in strict confidence that High Commissioner McNutt is also an expert in another line, although in this one, I dare say, I am his superior as you will readily see. One night, soon after I had the pleasure of meeting him, a mutual friend of ours invited us to a poker party in Washington, and we have become friends ever since, for a good game of poker tests good fellows and makes friends of them. It was on that occasion that our cooperation started, for we licked everybody and divided between us the winnings of the evening—I getting the major part."[26]

Speaking in earnest, President Quezon said:

"As the representative of the President of the United States, the High Commissioner naturally takes precedence over the President of the Philippines, even though they are of equal rank. The High Commissioner is entitled to the recognition of all the officials of the Government of the Commonwealth in his capacity as representative of the President of the United

States. . . . If and when a time should come that the President of the United States should, under the law, intervene in the affairs of the Government of the Commonwealth, and the President should designate the High Commissioner to act for him, there would be no question as to the compliance on our part with the orders of the President."[27]

President Quezon continued:

It is my pleasure and purpose to take counsel with High Commissioner McNutt whenever I feel that it will be convenient or necessary. I also look forward to his suggestions and advice whenever in his opinion he can be of help by giving me such advice. It is my hope that he will always feel free to speak to me frankly. . . . I am sure that the High Commissioner and I will bend every effort . . . to make sure that the friendship, mutual respect, and affection which have characterized that relationship in the past will grow as the day of our final political separation approaches, and that every rising sun thereafter will set on a happier and greater America and Philippines, bound closely together by everlasting ties of cultural and spiritual as well as commercial association."[28]

McNutt's appointment to the Philippines post was not universally accepted at home, however. The pacifists especially were opposed to his selection. In a note to President Roosevelt they protested his military background and his attitude toward labor. F. J. Libby, executive secretary of the National Council for the Prevention of War, wrote to President Roosevelt that McNutt would add to General MacArthur's "militarization" of the Philippines, and urged that the nomination be withdrawn from the Senate.[29]

But the protests of the pacifist groups were ignored, and the Senate confirmed the appointment on February 23. During the debate, Senator Lynn J. Frazier, Republican of North Dakota, asked whether McNutt had ever called out the Indiana National Guard in labor troubles, and Senator Frederick Van Nuys, Democrat of Indiana, replied that McNutt had once summoned the National Guard in a labor strike to avoid violence. Frazier then withdrew his objection, and the appointment was accepted.[30] On February 27 McNutt took the oath of office in the office of Secretary of War Woodring. Among those present at the ceremonies were Philippines President Manuel Quezon, Secretary of War Harry Woodring, Philippines Resident Commissioner Quinton Paredes, and Major-General Douglas MacArthur, military adviser to the Philippine Commonwealth.

Just before McNutt's arrival in the Philippines, the Manila *Bulletin* reprinted editorials from several American newspapers. One from the Boston *Evening Globe* declared:

"In this choice of McNutt, the President is giving added distinction to one of the most striking political figures of the Middle West. He has received frequent mention as Presidential timber for 1940 or later. Of McNutt it may be said that his comparative youth and known abilities make it likely that he will have a political future..

And the Lafayette (Indiana) *Courier Journal* gave much credit for the appointment to Mrs. Roosevelt, who threw her support to McNutt. It was understood that Postmaster General James A. Farley, national chairman of the Democratic party, who had favored the anti-McNutt faction in Indiana, opposed the appointment. Farley was also a foe of Frances Perkins, Secretary of Labor. Mrs. Roosevelt supported Miss Perkins against Farley's attacks, and favored the McNutt appointment in order to strike against Farley. Mrs. Roosevelt's influence apparently convinced the President that he should appoint McNutt.[31]

High Commissioner McNutt and his family sailed from San Francisco for Manila on April 3 on the *President Hoover*. With a staff of eighteen, including Wayne Coy, who was afterwards assistant to the President and chairman of the Federal

Communications Commission, they arrived in the Philippines capital on April 25, after a stopover in Hawaii. Little fanfare greeted the party. In conformity with McNutt's desires, the ceremonies were simple, with no formal speeches. While a squadron of army planes flew overhead, the group left the ship by launch after meeting Acting Commissioner Jones. Others in the welcoming party included Jorge D. Vargas, secretary to President Quezon, Captain Melville F. Grant, United States Army, and Lt. Hunter Wood, Jr., United States Navy. Then followed the inspection of the guard of honor, 31st Infantry, and the customary nineteen-gun salute. Fewer than four hundred spectators were on hand for the ceremonies, but McNutt's simplicity and straightforwardness and his ever-ready smile made a favorable impression upon those gathered to welcome him. "El Nido," the E. A. Perkins residence on Dewey Boulevard became the temporary home of the High Commissioner.

An interesting story concerning the arrival was written by McNutt to McHale, who related it to the author. Father John O'Hara, who was then the president of Notre Dame University, where McNutt had delivered the commencement address the year before, was a classmate of the Bishop of Manila, who greeted McNutt in full regalia. Following the blessing, the Bishop then said to the new High Commissioner: "We would like to honor you with a Pontifical Mass in the next week or two, preferably on Sunday." The Mass was held the second week and afterwards the red-carpet full pontifical Mass was celebrated. Following the Mass, while awaiting the arrival of the Bishop, the party went to the home of President Quezon for cocktails and brunch, during which time Quezon turned to McNutt and asked, "What did you think of our services?" McNutt smiled and said, "Well, I thought they were excellent, but where do you get that 'we' stuff, because you

wear a 'cheese-knife' as a Mason and Shriner, the same as I do."
And Quezon said, "Don't you know, Mr. High Commissioner,
that we Catholics in Spain and the Spanish countries were
always permitted to continue our membership in the Masonic
Lodge?"

After receiving the official call of the Philippines' vice
president, High Commissioner McNutt then officially returned the call at the Malacanan Palace. He immediately
thereafter plunged into the toughest job of his career to date.
He was faced with almost insurmountable problems. One
difficulty concerned the educational program. Teachers and
other government workers on the islands were protesting
against an amendment of the pension laws and the liquidation of various funds. Some 27,000 teachers were involved.
Many of them had either retired or were eligible for retirement at the date of the liquidation on November 14, 1936.
They protested against the reduction of their pensions, the
shortening of the pension period from life to twenty years
after retirement, the power of the government insurance board
to cancel pensions unless the retired teachers were indigent,
and the insufficient balance in the fund. Many of the retired
teachers had already returned to live in the United States.[32]

Another problem which was brought immediately to the
attention of the High Commissioner was the attitude of certain Spanish groups in the Islands regarding the civil war in
Spain. One group had recognized the rebel government, while
another remained loyal to the official government. Still another problem was the question of the modification of export
taxes which would hasten or retard the economic and financial
adjustments facing the Islands. There was also the question
of the practicability of the neutralization of the Philippines.
Another major issue was whether reciprocal trade relations
with the United States would help Philippine economy.[33]

In his first press interview after arriving on the field of duty, McNutt said in effect that his policy and his course of official action would be "expressive of the assumption that the laws now in effect are to be carried out." In other words, he would comply with the letter and the spirit of the Tydings-McDuffy Act as it stood and would not attempt to amend it by precedent, nor act on the assumption that it would be modified. As to interpretations, he indicated that he had received written instructions from the president and that these specific instructions would be his guide in the application of the law. He displayed a friendly and sympathetic attitude which presumably harmonized with his instructions.[34]

In general, McNutt gave the impression of a definite disinclination to meddle unduly in Philippine domestic affairs or to proceed beyond the bounds fixed by the letter and the spirit of the laws defining and outlining his prerogatives. He also gave the impression of a clear comprehension of the duties and prerogatives of the office to which he had been appointed.

This general attitude immediately endeared McNutt to the Philippine people. The tone which had characterized his conduct and comments ever since his appointment inspired confidence and built respect for him and for the office which he held. The Philippine lawmakers especially were favorably impressed by his personality and attainments. His views on Philippine-American relations were praised in all circles. Political and business leaders almost unanimously agreed with him on the subjects which he discussed, even though he did not agree with President Quezon that the period of Commonwealth should be shortened. It was fully expected that McNutt's administration would be satisfactory from both American and Philippine standpoints. The Filipinos felt fortunate that President Roosevelt had appointed such an outstanding American to the High Commissionership.[35]

In his new role, however, McNutt faced a sharper test than he ever did as governor of Indiana. It was his duty to carry out the Roosevelt policies in the Philippines and to maintain a state of good will. This was no easy task. It demanded all the diplomacy at his command. It was infinitely harder for him to placate all the disturbed factions in the Islands than it was for him to smooth the troubled waters of the political sea in his own state. His admirers and those generally interested in the outcome of the American experiment in the Orient watched his every move.

The Manila *Tribune* expressed the general attitude toward the new High Commissioner:

"Here, in the midst of the new uncertainty, is one responsible authority who refuses to be stampeded, and who holds firmly to the proposition that the existing law still exists. Mr. NcNutt deserves the country's gratitude. . . . There is no doubt where he stands. . . . On the basis of his expressed views he can count on the support and cooperation of all elements, since he approaches his task with a confidence and a sureness which all should be willing to share."[36]

Before leaving Washington, McNutt had studied thoroughly the whole problem of the Orient in general and the Philippines in particular, and had become exceptionally knowledgeable in regard to the problems of the area. He had become convinced that Philippine economic independence had to be achieved before political independence could be realized. He was in favor of a much greater diversification of crops as the first step in remedying the economic faults which existed. He also believed that the Islands must be neutralized, and that there must be a readjustment of trade relations with the United States. Many Filipinos, however, insisted on the early political independence of the Islands.

While McNutt was attempting to cope with the more serious tasks facing him, he created a furor over some relatively minor issues. One of these was a note which he sent to all the foreign diplomatic officials in the Islands, asking that they route all their correspondence with the Commonwealth government through his office. He was entirely within his authority, of course, and his action was upheld by the State Department, which declared it a routine matter. The Iloilo *Times*, however, declared that McNutt was not given such orders by the United States government, and charged that the letter was issued on McNutt's own initiative and without instructions from the State Department.[37] The order stirred considerable reaction in some quarters, especially when McNutt followed this by another order in which he insisted that in the future all official toasts should be drunk first to the United States, then to President Roosevelt, then to High Commissioner McNutt, and last to the Philippine president.

An editorial declared that "McNutt seems to be developing quite a knack for drawing fire from local political circles over what may be termed tremendous trifles. It seems that at a recent ball, the host offered a toast to President Roosevelt, then to President Quezon, and then to the High Commissioner McNutt. And that strikes the Commissioner as all wrong. The order, he states, should be Roosevelt, then McNutt, then Quezon.

"As could be expected . . . indignant cries of protest have followed. President Roosevelt is toasted to the accompaniment of the American National Anthem, and if a toast for High Commissioner McNutt is to follow that, it would mean two toasts for the United States and two renditions of the American hymn, before a toast is offered to President Quezon and the Philippine hymn is played.

"We are sure High Commissioner McNutt does not have good reasons for his circular. The American anthem starts out, 'Oh say, can you see?' A hearty affirmative answer might be invoked after the first and second drink. But if the same question was proposed after the third (whiskey sodas being what they are), we are not quite sure about ready response.

"Furthermore, we have a feeling President Quezon himself would prefer to be toasted last. If his name was proposed at the very first drink, some people might toast him just to be polite. If his name was sung out for the second drink, government officials might toast him because it would be the better part of valor to do so. But if after taking in three or four whiskey sodas in their system, people still drank to his health, it would be because they felt like doing so."

Another editorial declared:

"We must also grant that Mr. NcNutt came over with just the shade of a complex in his psyche of which a certain overconfidence natural in a man of his various gifts and abilities has likewise unwittingly betrayed him into prompt exploitation and this even before he has had a chance to get familiar with the lay of the land. It cannot be denied that his first month in the Philippines has given flower to rather unhappy miscalculations. If only he had acted as he had professed long before he arrived; that he approached his Philippine responsibility with humility and a high sense of adventure. Now it is obvious that his thoughts lie elsewhere.

"We can only remind Mr. Paul McNutt . . . that Filipinos are decidedly easy to get around if one knows a little secret which any oldtimer is only too willing to divulge to the 'humble' newcomer. We are only some 14,000,000 here, but we can be mighty particular about the gestures designed to put anything over on us. We like them a trifle more subtle than circulars to friendly foreigners in our midst."[38]

Naturally, diplomats wondered why McNutt insisted on such procedure. Even though he apparently acted on orders from the State Department, which feared loss of face for the United States if the Commonwealth president were ranked higher than the American President and his representative, the

Above.

Governor and Mrs. Paul V. McNutt and daughter Louise. Courtesy of Miss
Thelma Sines, Logansport, Indiana.

Below.

Governor Paul V. McNutt at his desk in the Statehouse, Indianapolis. Lent
by Miss Thelma Sines.

Above.

McNutt attempts to quiet the crowd at the Democratic National Convention in 1940. Shortly after his name was placed in nomination for the Vice Presidency he declined the nomination in favor of Henry A. Wallace, who had been chosen by President Roosevelt.

★ ★ ★

Left.

Secretary of Agriculture Henry A. Wallace and McNutt chat at the Democratic National Convention July 19, 1940. Federal Security Administrator McNutt withdrew from the Vice Presidential race in favor of Wallace.

Upper left.

Chairman Alben Barkley raps for order at the 1940 Convention, when the delegates interrupted McNutt while he tried to decline the nomination. McNutt waits patiently for order to be restored.

Lower left.

A moment before order is restored, McNutt stands reverently in deep meditation and prayer, apparently realizing the significance of his next move.

Above.

McNutt declines the nomination, after the wildly-cheering crowd allows him to speak. The delegates interrupted him several times during his speech, in which he yielded to the wishes of President Roosevelt.

Above.

Scene at the Democratic National Convention in Chicago, showing McNutt attempting to address the delegates.

Lower.

President Roosevelt's war-time Cabinet. Reading clock-wise around the table: Harry Hopkins (light suit), Lend-Lease Administrator; Frances Perkins, Secretary of Labor; Philip Fleming, Federal Works Administrator; Vice President Henry A. Wallace; Fiorello L Guardia, Civil Defense Administrator; Paul V. McNutt, Federal Security Administrato Jesse Jones, Secretary of Commerce and Federal Loan Administrator; Harold L. Icke Secretary of the Interior; Postmaster General Frank C. Walker; Henry L. Stimson, Secreta of War; Cordell Hull, Secretary of State; President Franklin D. Roosevelt; Henry Morge thau, Secretary of the Treasury; Attorney General Francis Biddle; Frank Knox, Secreta of the Navy; and Claude R. Wickard, Secretary of Agriculture.

Left.

General John J. Pershing and Paul V. McNutt, National Commander of The American Legion, in Paris, 1928.

Above.

American Legion National Commander Paul V. McNutt tossing a flower on the grave of the Unknown Soldier in Paris, 1928.

Left.
Paul V. McNutt has an intimate chat with Presidential Advisor Bernard Baruch.

Right.
Governor Paul V. McNutt with his parents, Judge and Mrs. John C. McNutt, at the governor's mansion in Indianapolis.

Left.

Paul V. McNutt and his daughter Louise.

Center.

First Lady of Indiana, 1933-1937, Mrs. Paul V. McNutt. Lent by Miss Margaret Paddock, Greenwood, Indiana.

Lower right.

Miss Louise McNutt in Manila.

Below.

A little comedy between High Commissioner McNutt, Philippine President Quezon, and Mrs. Mc-Nutt.

High Commissioner McNutt dancing with Mrs. McNutt, who is wearing the traditional Philippine costume.

Left.

High Commissioner and Mrs. Paul V. McNutt at a social gathering with Philippine Vice President Osmena in Manila.

Above.

The High Commissioner's residence and garden in Manila.

★ ★ ★ ★ ★ ★ ★ ★ ★ ★

←*Across the page.*

This picture appeared shortly after the toasting incident, which occurred soon after McNutt arrived in the Philippines as High Commissioner.

★ ★ ★ ★ ★ ★ ★ ★ ★ ★

Across page, upper left.
Paul V. McNutt as a grade school pupil in Martinsville, Indiana.

Across page, upper right.
Paul V. McNutt as a high school student in Martinsville, Indiana.

Across page, lower left.
Paul V. McNutt as a college student.

Across page, lower right.
Paul V. McNutt as an officer in World War I.

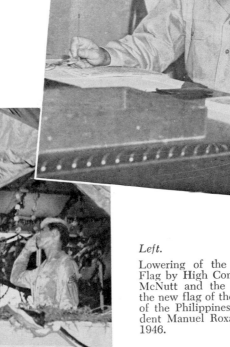

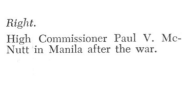

Right.

General Douglas MacArthur welcoming Ambassador Paul V. McNutt on the latter's visit to Tokyo in 1947.

Left.

Indiana Senator Frederick Van Nuys, President Franklin D. Roosevelt, and Governor Paul V. McNutt exchanging pleasantries at dinner.

★ ★ ★

Above.

President Franklin D. Roosevelt and Paul V. McNutt.

War Manpower Commissioner Paul V. McNutt.

incident was no laughing matter, even though President Quezon was amused, and saw no diplomatic crisis. Several foreign consuls asked their home governments for a ruling on the issue.

As a result of these two directives, an amusing bit of verse entitled "Voice from the Philippines" appeared on the editorial pages of the New York *Sun* May 24:

> I am the High Commissioner—
> My name is Paul McNutt;
> For form I am a stickler, and
> I will not stand a cut;
> All letters to officials of
> The Isles I must see first,
> And glasses must be raised to me
> By all men with a thirst.
> Oh form is form and dignity
> Must not get in a rut,
> For right is right and fair is fair
> And Paul McNutt's McNutt!
> So three loud cheers for Uncle Sam
> From palace, home and hut.
> And four loud cheers for Franklin D. —
> And five for Paul McNutt.[39]

At least one member of the Philippine National Assembly branded McNutt as an "enigma." He was puzzled by the High Commissioner's actions and utterances, which he called "intriguing, enigmatic, ununderstandable and puzzling.. . . His decisions and utterances are so strange that they do not seem to fit into the conditions obtaining here."[40]

Some years later, in reviewing the activities of the several High Commissioners, Joseph Ralston Hayden declared that McNutt "by vigorously vindicating certain American rights which had been called into question demonstrated that if firmly and tactfully used the authority of his office would be respected without question or rancour by the Commonwealth Government and all other elements in the Philippine community. By the exercise of vigorous leadership as the ranking American (and the ranking official) in the Islands, Mr. Mc-Nutt further strengthened the High Commissionership."[41]

Yet an editorial appeared in the Manila *Herald* shortly after the diplomatic crisis, which was headed "Descent into Oblivion," in which McNutt was accused of being "impatient with the unostentatious position which he occupies on the local political stage. He seems to be cramped by the comparative quiet and obscurity of his little nook. Used to riding high in the wide political prairies of Indiana, with state troops at his beck and call, and a machinery for declaring martial law such as only a former commander of the American Legion can properly appreciate, he must feel suffocated in the close quarters which have been allowed him under the Tydings-McDuffy Law. For a man, furthermore, whose dearest ambition was to become Secretary of War, and thus be at the head of the nation's armed forces, the Philippine job, with its too civilian, too passive, too diplomatic, character, must prove somewhat irksome.

"The attempts, therefore, to increase by definition and by statute, the prerogatives of his office must be examined against the background of the man's personality. The reports and insinuations of his anti-liberal tendencies are many, and it may be profitable to discover how such tendencies will likely vent themselves in the field of public action. If . . . Mr. McNutt should conceive it to be his duty to enlarge American authority in the Philippines in the face of growing Filipino autonomy, merely for its own sake, and out of a desire to meticulously stick to the letter of the law, he is certain to run into difficulties and possible trouble."[42]

By contrast, another editorial, headed "Common Sense— A Filipino's View," declared that the stand taken by McNutt "is absolutely correct, if it is to be judged by the wording of the Tydings-McDuffy Act. . . . It is time to clear the atmosphere. There is too much muddled thinking in our midst. . . . To High Commissioner McNutt I extend my most sincere congratulations for having upheld the authority of the United States in this country, and I have no doubt in my mind that he will always uphold American authority without impairing Filipino autonomy."[43]

Another editorial stated that "Under normal conditions . . . the United States High Commissioner is a mere ceremonial official performing ceremonial functions. And it is certain that every attempt on his part to resort to specific and reserved powers, by either presidential delegation or petition, will be scrutinized and resisted, unless conditions fully warrant his action. He cannot be blamed, to be sure, for making the most of his normal powers, but the fuss already raised over nothing is a sample of what would happen if an unwarranted attempt were made to transcend the ceremonial limits. The Filipino people, one can feel sure, will be generous with forms but they will jealously guard over the substance of their autonomy."[44]

One correspondent wrote in the Manila *Herald-Tribune Mid-Week Magazine* that McNutt was better known for his frankness than for what he had accomplished after one month in the Philippines. He charged that the High Commissioner "answers in a curt and clear manner every query newsmen put to him and uses no diplomatic language that may give double meaning, thus saving himself from future embarassment. . . . This dignified, grey-haired leader . . . means business. He will be a hard nut to crack, so that Commonwealth officials will have to watch their steps in their official dealings with him. . . . He is . . . a man who sticks to his guns, firm in his convictions, and sincere in his purpose."[45]

The Manila *Bulletin* reprinted an editorial from the Brooklyn, New York, *Eagle*, which pointed out that McNutt was acting on specific instructions from Washington, "which feels it is vital that the United States maintain its prestige at Manila throughout the present transition period until the Philippine independence becomes an actuality in 1946. . . . It would be a serious matter for the United States to lose face in the Far East while it continues to be responsible for the Philippines, but it will be hoped that the incident will not develop anything in the nature of a diplomatic crisis. In the meantime Mr. McNutt will doubtless come in for considerable ribbing for seeming to insist on social precedents that most Americans will regard as rather upstage and silly."[46]

The *Bulletin* also reprinted an editorial from the New York *Herald-Tribune,* which considered McNutt's action "as it should be and as immemorial custom in the East prescribes. Out there prestige and 'face' count for much. Each unwarranted concession which the American administration makes to the Filipinos in their efforts to acquire face results in a loss of prestige for the American government and for American individuals. Had Commissioner McNutt permitted himself to be ranked after the President of the Commonwealth it would have been regarded as a confession of weakness on his part. He and the American government would both have lost face. . . . If the President fails to uphold the Commissioner he might as well wire that gentleman to pack up his trunks and return to Indiana. As High Commissioner, Governor McNutt would have ended his usefulness."[47]

Former High Commissioner Frank Murphy summed up the situation well when he predicted that the longer McNutt stayed in the islands "the higher he will be regarded." He praised McNutt as a man of "ability and integrity," and thought he would get along "splendidly."[48]

Hardly had the furor over the consular note died down than the High Commissioner again became embroiled in another diplomatic controversy. The Philippine government had allowed some 4,000 tons of reserve sugar to be shipped to China, in violation of the London Pact. In June, 1937, Mc-Nutt ordered that such sugar dumping must be stopped.[49] Immediately the sugarmen impugned the ruling, contending that such exports to Hong Kong did not violate the treaty. But the potentially explosive issue was soon quieted when the Philippine government ordered all future shipments suspended.[50] The ban on further exports to Hong Kong was generally well received in the Islands.[51] The matter ended when the United States State Department praised McNutt's quick action.[52]

In the meantime the High Commissioner aroused considerable opposition in the Philippines by a speech which he had delivered on democracy. He declared that democracy in the Philippines lacked substance, and was only a matter of form. "The establishment of a frontier post which flies the banner of freedom would be an empty victory unless there is complete, sincere adherence to democratic constitutional principles," he claimed. "Homage is not enough. Formal acceptance is not sufficient. Nothing short of the substance of democracy will satisfy those responsible for the Independence program or give validity to the enterprise," he believed.[53]

The Washington *Evening Star* expected that McNutt would soon be relieved of his Philippine duties because of his "unwise" statements, including the one on democracy, "which the Filipinos choose to interpret as an aspersion on their brand of democracy." It was felt that such utterances had impaired his usefulness in the Islands.[54]

About this time, several suggestions were being made for McNutt's future political activities. One was that he leave his Manila post and run for the United States Senate to succeed Frederick Van Nuys, who had refused to play ball with the

Administration, especially in Roosevelt's threat to purge the Supreme Court. It was rumored that President Roosevelt was behind the plan, and had already chosen Woodring as McNutt's successor in the diplomatic post. But McNutt himself was silent on the report.[55]

Another rumor was that McNutt would be offered the presidency of Indiana University. William Lowe Bryan had given up the post several months previously, and Herman B Wells, dean of the School of Business Administration, was named acting president. At the same time, however, McNutt was being seriously discussed as a strong contender for the 1940 Democratic nomination for the Presidency of the United States, especially if Roosevelt did not seek a third term.

Senator Sherman Minton characterized McNutt as "a natural," because he gave Indiana "the best administration Indiana ever had. He put more legislation on the books of Indiana for labor and the farmer than anybody ever did in the history of the state and he demonstrated his executive ability. He has acquaintances all over the United States. There isn't a crossroad that doesn't have someone that knows him. He's a great campaigner, too. There isn't a better one in the country. His views are substantially the views of the New Deal."[56] Minton was thus the first of McNutt's close associates to "nominate" him so boldly.

But McNutt's name had already begun to appear in the list of possibilities among the Democratic hopefuls for the nomination in 1940. As early as the previous December, his name was seventh on the list in the Gallup poll, following those of James A. Farley, George H. Earle, Henry A. Wallace, John Nance Garner, Herbert H. Lehman, and Cordell Hull. In April, McNutt was in fourth place, behind Farley, Earle, and Frank Murphy. In August, however, following the

Philippine episodes, McNutt was tied for eighth place with Wallace.[57]

Meanwhile, a "McNutt-for-President-in-1940" club was organized in Indiana, although at first it remained somewhat inactive. Yet many of McNutt's strongest backers, such as Frank McHale and Senator Minton insisted that the High Commissioner would soon resign his post and actively work for the nomination.

Thus it appeared that McNutt's hat would soon be thrown into the presidential ring, thereby risking the resentment of President Roosevelt. He would be the first active candidate on the 1940 Democratic scene. The audacity of the maneuver shocked some of the older politicians, who regarded any potential candidate for a presidential nomination who announced two years in advance of the nominating campaign as one seeking political suicide. The hand of every other candidate, and also of his followers, would be raised to hurl bricks, they argued.[58]

Early in 1938 McNutt returned to Washington to report to the President on conditions in the Far East. He had built up quite a reputation and had done the job that was expected of him. It is true that Farley and President Roosevelt thought that by sending him to the Philippines they would get rid of him. But he was so far-sighted that he surprised them, particularly in his knowledge of what was going to happen in the South Pacific, and especially in Asia. When he returned to the United States, he spoke in San Francisco, Los Angeles, and several other western cities, and predicted the unrest concerning both Japan and China. He considered it unthinkable that anyone should wage war against the Asiatic countries, because with their enormous population, "It would be like putting your fist in a bucket of water—you would displace the water until you removed your fist, and then it would level off."

McNutt's speeches on his way to Washington for his big reception and report to the President caused the people of the Far West and the Rocky Mountain area to want him as the champion of their rights. This was evidenced later in the 1940 convention in Chicago, when the Rocky Mountain states rallied 85 per cent of their vote in a caucus of eleven of these states for McNutt, just a half hour before he made his decision to withdraw his candidacy.

His visit to Washington was the climax of a triumphal trip across the continent, with receptions in Denver and his own home capital, Indianapolis. By the time the entourage had arrived in Washington, McNutt's campaign managers had come to the conclusion that he was "the people's choice" for the nomination. Frank McHale said, on arriving, "The time to throw in your chips is when the cards are running your way."[59] McNutt and his friends were going on the theory that President Roosevelt would not be a candidate for a third term, nor would he accept the nomination if his followers should tender it. Roosevelt himself, however, remained silent on the McNutt boom.

McNutt insisted that he was not a candidate for the Presidency or any other political office. When asked if he would accept the vice-presidential nomination in the event he failed to receive the nomination for President in 1940, he said, "Heavens and earth, that's two years off and as a matter of fact I am not a candidate for any office." When asked if he were in favor of a third term for President Roosevelt, he answered, "That's a question the President will have to answer for himself."[60] It seemed that whether the administration liked it or not, the McNutt boom was under way.

The Washington visit was used by his friends as an opportunity to throw his hat into the Presidential ring. A huge reception was arranged in his honor at the Mayflower Hotel on February 23. Some three thousand people were invited to the party, including all the Democratic members of both the House and Senate, Cabinet officials, major department heads, diplomats, high army and navy officers, Washington newspaper correspondents, Governor M. Clifford Townsend and other Indiana officials, and leading Democrats from throughout the country. Frank McHale, the new Democratic National Committeeman and McNutt's campaign manager, had worked out the details of the party with Senator Minton. Minton was quite frank to admit that the purpose of the affair was to give everyone an opportunity to meet "Indiana's Presidential candidate in 1940."[61]

The McNutt reception was one of the most elaborate functions of its kind ever held in Washington. The Indiana vanguard took over thirty-three suites at the Mayflower Hotel. It was estimated that the affair cost $5,000, although the Mc-Nutt forces called it "just a little party in Paul's honor by a group of his friends." When asked if the "Two Percent Club" were paying for the party, Frank McHale said, "No, that would be a dumb thing to do. No, there would be a lot of criticism if that sort of story came out. This party is being paid for by a group of Paul's friends."[62]

The Chinese Room of the hotel, with its oriental decorations, was the scene of the major activity during the reception. But hard or even soft liquors did not flow in this room. The initiated, or those experienced in such receptions, found their way across the hall to the Presidential dining room where punch, "perhaps wine and perhaps some stronger stuff," was distributed to all well-wishers. Two rooms were set aside for the press, both with superb bar facilities. One writer commented, "A hasty search of the records yesterday disclosed no precedent of any sort for the present reception. There have been many different and many tremendous parties in Washington, but none like this, where a Presidential bandwagon, newly painted, with at least 4,000 seats on it and any number of handholds for last-minute jumpers, has gone on view more than two years before the nominating convention."[63]

The menu was described as including "two massive eight-layer cakes, 18 inches in diameter, one bearing the seal of the United States in delicate frosting and the other the seal of Indiana; five symbolic displays, depicting the Washington Monument, Mount Vernon, a lighthouse, a yacht, and a pagoda; baskets of sweets, ranging from mints to chocolates; strawberry tarts (full pie size); three kinds of cakes—gateaux diplomate, gateaux mille feuille, and gateaux St. Honoree; patisserie Viennoise; and mignardises, which are specially created small cakes (cookie size) of a most exotic taste and appearance—Buffet delice Diana; croute au chaud; hot meat snaps; four kinds of canapes; caviar, smoked salmon, anchovy and pate de foie gras; petite cherry tomatoes stuffed with chicken salad; vol au vent fin de siecle (pastry shells stuffed with chicken); three kinds of mousse—Smithfield ham, sweetbreads and pheasant; gelatine of capon with salad Santa Maria; and hothouse-grape salad. There were Maryland biscuits with deviled ham; deviled eggs, sandwiches de luxe; fresh strawberries, and three kinds of doughnuts; stuffed celery, olives, nuts and fruits; four great urns of tea and coffee. The tables were decorated with tall red, white and blue candles in silver candelabra and great baskets filled with creamy-tan giant gladiola, rare black-purple Japanese iris, deep red roses, pussy willow, ferns and smilax."[64]

Everyone of importance in Washington had been invited to the McNutt party, except the New Dealers,[65] and the White House was not represented at the reception. There was a chilling response from President Roosevelt's official family. Most of the members of the President's cabinet pointedly turned down the invitations, with excuses which in some instances were little short of facetious. James Farley was fishing in Florida; Labor Secretary Frances Perkins was tied up in a conference on the employment of older persons; Secretary of the Treasury Henry Morganthau, Jr., was detained on his New York farm or occupied with monetary matters; Secretary of the Interior Harold Ickes was too busy; Secretary of Agriculture Henry A. Wallace was on a speaking engagement in California; and Secretary of State Cordell Hull was visiting old friends in Tennessee. Vice President John Nance Garner had a policy of attending only four annual functions and the McNutt party was not one of the four.[66]

The New York *Times* reported it to be "one of the most sumptuous, not to say elaborate, fetes ever staged in Washington," and added that perhaps McNutt's statement about not being a candidate for public office should not be taken too seriously.[67]

But there were no immediate direct results from the gala reception. Washington seemed to take a calm attitude toward the so-called McNutt boom. As for President Roosevelt, he appeared not at all disturbed by the potential challenge to his own possible candidacy in 1940. The day following the reception, McNutt made his official report to the President on conditions in the Philippines and the Far East. He predicted a bright economic future for the Islands, but doubted that the Filipinos wanted immediate independence. Because of Japanese threats at aggression, he felt that it would be unwise to hasten Philippine independence.[68]

The following month, High Commissioner McNutt returned to his post in Manila, leaving the political pot boiling on the home front. Democratic ranks in Indiana were especially split because of the controversy raised by Senator Van Nuys in his attack on President Roosevelt's 1937 proposal to "pack" the United States Supreme Court. Although the Senator had generally supported other New Deal measures, the administration now looked upon him unfavorably and decided to replace him in the Senate. Governor Townsend publicly censured Van Nuys for not supporting the President, and declared that the party would not renominate him. There was even the suggestion made by some that the Republicans should embrace Van Nuys and nominate him as their candidate.[69]

It was quite clear that Senator Van Nuys could not win renomination against the opposition of Governor Townsend and the Democratic machine, which had been built up by former Governor McNutt and which had become a highly effective device in controlling the patronage, especially through the Two Percent Club. The purpose of the latter was to secure the active political cooperation of the state and local elective and appointive officials. If the Republicans were to be defeated in 1938, the use of such methods was absolutely necessary. And it began to appear that the Democrats, because of the split in their ranks, would lose the senatorial election.

Senator Van Nuys defied the Democratic state machine, and even threatened to run as an independent. This would, of course, divide the party even further, and would make it impotent in 1940, when it was hoped that McNutt would be a Presidential candidate. A united party was therefore imperative in these critical years. After the Republicans had nominated Raymond E. Willis as its candidate for senator, the Democrats decided not to purge Van Nuys, and he was therefore nominated by acclamation.[70]

Lieutenant Governor Henry F. Schricker, who seemed to

have been the state administration's first choice, agreed to drop out of the race for the sake of party harmony, although he had previously supported Van Nuys' stand against the court-packing proposal.[71]

Writing in the New York *World Telegram* on July 7, 1938, Raymond Clapper observed that it was a fortunate thing for the Democrats to heal the party split, otherwise there would have been a pretty good chance of a Republican victory in November. "That would be a fine kettle of fish for former Governor Paul McNutt who expects to come back from the Philippines next winter to begin his campaign for the 1940 Democratic Presidential nomination. Loss of a Senate seat hardly provides the most effective springboard for a presidential campaign. Therefore all is forgiven and Senator Fred Van Nuys is coming back to the McNutt fold. The fatted calf is being made ready for the returning prodigal."[72]

In commenting on this apparent about-face, TIME magazine believed it was not the result of any change in New Deal feeling: "It was ordered in spite of Franklin Roosevelt by Paul McNutt. After a series of 10,000-mile telephone calls, High Commissioner McNutt decided that his own ambitions were more important than the President's urge. Defeat through division . . . would weaken his machine. Van Nuys' charges of scandal might sully the fair McNutt name. The renomination of Frederick Van Nuys became an incident in the plans of McNutt for 1940."[73]

In a typed article, dated July 12, 1938, entitled "The Washington Merry-Go-Round," by Drew Pearson and Robert S. Allen, McNutt was said to have had "no more liking for Van Nuys than the White House has. In fact, almost up to the very last moment he [McNutt] was seriously debating whether to run against him. During McNutt's visit to Washington last winter he told Roosevelt to leave the matter entirely to him, that 'the state organization would take care of Van Nuys.' That is why Roosevelt and Farley had made no move to insure that someone was put in the field against Van Nuys. They confidently depended on McNutt.

"What upset the applecart was the Republicans. McNutt *et al.* had based their plans on the expectation that the Republicans would nominate either former Senator Jim Watson or one of his henchmen. . . . But the Republicans didn't go for Watson or one of his lieutenants. Instead they named Raymond Willis, a highly respected small-town publisher. For McNutt this completely changed the political picture. It meant that Willis would get the solid Republican ballot, leaving Van Nuys and the McNutt candidate splitting the Democratic vote. And Willis' election would have been a crushing blow to McNutt's prestige. It would have meant no more buzzing for his presidential bee. So as between helping Roosevelt and safeguarding the McNutt presidential boom, McNutt lined up for McNutt. He welcomed Van Nuys home."[74]

As a result of the apparent harmony within the Democratic ranks, Van Nuys was reelected on November 8, 1938, although by less than 5,000 votes over Willis. But the Republican vote was larger than at any election since 1932, while the Democratic vote was smaller than in 1932 and 1936, thus making the Democratic margin of victory the smallest since 1932. The Republicans won the office of secretary of state by 1,061 votes out of a total of 1,559,465, although the Democrats won the other state offices. The Republicans won seven of the twelve Congressional seats. The Democrats retained their control of the state senate, but control of the state house of representatives was taken over by the Republicans by the narrow margin of fifty-one to forty-nine.[75]

The narrow success of the Democratic party in Indiana in 1938 indicated that McNutt's chances as Indiana's favorite son for the presidential nomination in 1940 were somewhat impaired, although his friends insisted that careful planning during the next two years would restore the Indiana Democratic machine to something like its former power and enable it to function effectively in McNutt's behalf when the Democratic national convention met to select its candidate for the next presidential election. Some of McNutt's Washington advisers believed he should resign from his Philippine post and return to Indiana to patch up the Democratic state machine and, incidentally, reestablish himself.

In the meantime Frank McHale, Indiana national committeeman, announced the establishment of a nation-wide organization to finance McNutt's forthcoming campaign for the presidential nomination. Frank McKinney was named by McHale to build up the financial organization, which was to be separate from the "McNutt-for-President-in-1940" groups whose purpose was to obtain the delegations of various states pledged to support McNutt. According to McKinney, subtreasurers for the finance group were to be named in each county, and the organization was to spread into other states. Foundations for campaign organizations had already been laid in New York, New Jersey, Michigan, Illinois, Colorado and California.[76]

The growing significance of Paul V. McNutt as a leading contender for the Democratic Presidential nomination in 1940 was beginning to be felt throughout the country. An interesting character sketch, not too flattering, written by Joseph H. Friend, appeared in *The Nation* on July 23, 1938. Entitled "Watch Paul McNutt," the article declared that "the longer one scrutinizes McNutt's record the more dangerous seem his aspirations—in more than one sense. He is far more than a clothes-horse with a classic profile and a gift of oratory, professing pious devotion to the President and the New Deal. . . .

He has administrative ability of a high order, self-discipline, great physical energy. He can be flatteringly affable and sharply arrogant. He is shrewd, and knows his political timing, though he has made one or two mistakes. He appears to have a sense of spectacle and a finger for the sensitive areas in the popular consciousness." After a lengthy and somewhat sarcastic review of McNutt's political career in Indiana, Friend predicted McNutt "will be a genuine danger in 1940—if Roosevelt does not run again."[77]

Like most presidential hopefuls, however, McNutt hesitated to set the course of his campaign until after President Roosevelt either had removed himself from consideration in 1940 or indicated his preference for a successor. Although McNutt's popularity had waned somewhat since he went to the Far East, his friends were convinced that his foreign assignment had helped rather than hindered his aspirations. He had escaped the bitter controversy over the Supreme Court bill, and had avoided any implication in the strife between industry and labor; he had made no pronouncement which might backfire.

When the year 1939 began there was much speculation as to whether McNutt would actively campaign for the nomination while still drawing his $18,000 per year salary as High Commissioner, or would resign his post. It was reported that President Roosevelt had advised McNutt to resign if he wanted to campaign, but this was not verified. While not opposing McNutt's presidential aspirations, Roosevelt was reported to have said that McNutt "could not temporize in view of the scrambled situation." Some political observers said that McNutt's candidacy had raised the possibility of a split in the Democratic party, pointing out that Roosevelt had frequently declared himself a liberal, and he could hardly afford to allow the mildly conservative McNutt to remain on the federal payroll while seeking an office for which Roosevelt himself might run again or might use his power to nominate a candidate who would carry the banner of liberalism.[78]

There was considerable feeling in the Philippines that McNutt was being rushed too much by his friends, who were letting their overenthusiasm run away with their judgment and were consequently doing McNutt more harm than good. Further, many Filipinos felt that McNutt was still vitally needed in the Philippines. His knowledge of the local situation and its relation to the broader problems of the Pacific area made him almost indispensable at that time. One editorial declared:

"We believe that the best interests of the public service would be served if Mr. McNutt's friends would refrain from attempting to stampede him into the United States political arena."[79]

But it became increasingly evident in the next few weeks that McNutt would soon resign his post and return to the United States. The Manila *Herald* editorialized that "Recent events related to United States High Commissioner McNutt . . . have placed the Filipino people at the point where . . . they realize all the more what a good man they are going to lose. . . . A substantial faction of the Democratic party is determined to launch him as the party's standard bearer in the next presidential election. No American, we believe, however great or humble and however poorly or well situated he might be, should refuse and can refuse such a call. However the profound sense of loss may hurt us, we cannot but say to the High Commissioner 'Go and may God bless you, for wherever you will be, we know that you are and will be a true and tried friend.' It is not exactly true, of course, that we are just now realizing how much of a loss the resignation of the High Commissioner will be to the country. . . . But in human emotions there is no pain or disappointment or hurt that cannot intensify itself when the tragedy impends."[80]

Julius C. Edelstein, writing in the Manila *Bulletin,* observed that the passing weeks brought no indication of any strong opposition to McNutt's possible candidacy. He wrote that "Even Ernest Lindley, foremost New Deal columnist, who is considered an outstanding authority on President Roosevelt's political philosophy, recently included McNutt among the list of favored candidates for the Democratic presidential nomination." Lindley indicated that "the Democratic party, in order to retain its appeal to the nation's youth, and to the spirit of advance and progress among voters of no distinct party allegiance, would be required to choose a candidate of youthful spirit and appeal." It was Lindley's belief that McNutt would hold out an inducement to youth. Edelstein felt that the inclusion of McNutt in the "youthful" group was considered a powerful advance by political observers, "especially when the classification is made by a political authority who is considered a spokesman for some New Deal elements." Edelstein believed that friends of McNutt saw this as an indication of decreasing animosity from the White House.[81]

On the second anniversary of McNutt's appointment as High Commissioner to the Philippines, an editorial appeared in the Manila *Bulletin* praising him for his accomplishments and reviewing his achievements. McNutt had come to the Philippines, said the editorial, "in a role unique under any flag. He has had to direct the growth of a young semi-independent country, making up by strength of character and the influence of personality for his lack of direct legal powers. The instances when he has actually exerted such an influence, by the very nature of his position, will probably remain state secrets for a long time. But that he has been influential as a personality not only in the government but also outside of it is indisputable.

"The prolonged country-wide discussion that he provoked by his single stricture on false democracy is an example of his influence. In his first July 4 address on the Luneta, he declared that a democracy can be so superficial that it has only form but not substance. Many of his listeners and many who read the reports of his speech in the newspapers and magazines inferred that the statement was an appraisal of Philippine democracy. Whatever it might have been, it ignited a consciousness of genuine democracy among the people so that thereafter they looked for the substance behind the forms.

"In some such way, within and outside the government, High Commissioner McNutt has exerted a salutary influence. He has performed with diplomacy what others would have taken legal authority to accomplish. In like manner he has set down the basic precedents in the new Philippine-American relationship with honor to his country and fairness to the Commonwealth. Not only has he carried out his task well; he has also made the task of his successors easier.

"Detached from America and overseeing the farthest outpost of democracy at the rim of a troubled Orient, he loomed in the horizon illumined by the fire of war a bigger man than ever. It was then that his admirers multiplied and his boom for the presidency gained momentum. It is reported that he may leave for America next month to report to President Roosevelt after which he will resign in order to campaign actively for the Democratic presidential nomination. We wish him luck. He has done well here, with both the American and Filipino peoples. In Washington he should do very well indeed."[82]

The following month Paul McNutt and his family left the Philippines for the States by way of China. Whether he would return to his post after reporting to President Roosevelt or not, still remained a moot question. Just before his departure he was awarded an honorary Doctor of Laws degree by the University of the Philippines. An editorial in the Manila *Herald* called this "one of those rare cases in which an institution honors itself by recognizing proven merit."

McNutt was cited as "one of the top-flight statesmen of America," who had "won recognition not only in this country and America but also in the entire Orient," and is "ranked among the leading possibilities for the Presidency of the United States." McNutt had "established the tradition of always giving his highest performance in every job and those he has served have also invariably given him their highest gift. . . . Having given of his best in the service of the American people, he may be awarded the highest recognition within the gift of the American people. . . . When this occurs we in the Philippines shall have the satisfaction of being able to say that we did not fail to recognize his proven merits because we responded in the same manner."[83]

On McNutt's departure from the Philippines the *Bulletin* wished him Godspeed and editorialized:

"Our desire to see him next in the White House is not self-seeking, although the Philippines would certainly bask in reflected glory as it did when William Howard Taft, who had part of his training here, was President. The main reason for our wish to see him President is the fact that he has completely won us with his charm, tact, sincerity, and intellectual honesty."

The editorial continued:

"Paul V. McNutt is an exception among American representatives here . . . the first representative here of American sovereignty who has won completely both the Filipinos and the Americans in the Philippines. He came here to fill what, in many ways, amounts to the hardest job under the American flag. He has had to watch the emergence of a young nation along lines set by the American Congress, and require adherence to these lines by virtue not of specific powers but of sheer personality and absolute fairness."[84]

The Philippines *Herald* stated in an editorial:

"The High Commissioner leaves these shores with the admiration of all Filipinos and Americans alike. If he can duplicate this non-partisan popularity in America, he will certainly be the next tenant of the White House."[85]

Another editorial, headed "McNutt Still Needed," expressed the feeling that it would be "to the best interests of the Philippines and American-Philippine relations that he should not resign at this time." He had "built prestige for his office from both the American and Philippine points of view." His record of service "would be notable even if he were leaving office today, but the need for a statesman of his caliber is not over. There is still much to be done, much that requires the background and information of the masterly strategy of a McNutt. By diligent work and judicious administration Mr. McNutt has built his office and himself up to such a point as to create an extraordinary demand for him in the office at a critical period such as the present. His grasp of the Philippine situation and the Far Eastern crisis is such as to argue strongly against his leaving office at this juncture."[86]

On the same day another paper declared that McNutt's services "have added luster to a name already bathed in the glamor of achievement." He had "won the hearts of the people . . . by the frankness and the charm with which he took them into his own heart." Two main forces had motivated his actions:

"first, his unflagging patriotism and devotion to his own land; . . . and second, his conviction that the ideals of his own people, ideals firmly grounded in unswerving devotion to God and country, had imposed an obligation on the people of actively fostering and preserving an infant nation which of its own choice had consecrated itself to those ideals."[87]

McNutt's two-year tenure was viewed as having been "of immense advantage." To the Philppines "it has brought a strengthening of the faith in democracy, and a revitalization of the belief that the nation can at need count on the strong support of powerful and devoted friends." To McNutt himself "it has brought new friendships, a new insight into world affairs, and greater experience to enrich a mind whose scope is all knowledge." And to the United States "it has brought the greatest gain of all—the rounding out of the mind and heart of one whom America can count among her greatest sons to the end that he may, when called, serve her most greatly."[88]

Ten thousand people, led by President Quezon, were on hand to give McNutt a stirring send-off. In fool-high letters atop a giant arch near the United States Navy Pier were written "Bon voyage Commissioner McNutt and family—with deep gratitude and appreciation of your good work—the Filipino people bid you Godspeed."

High Commissioner McNutt gave his parting message to the Philippine people over radio from the bridge of the U. S. Transport *Chaumont* just before sailing on May 11. McNutt said:

"Words are utterly inadequate to express the feelings which I have in leaving Manila and in leaving the Philippines. This is one of the happiest tours of service we have had, and we feel that we are leaving here many, many friends, and we shall always carry with us the happiest memories of these years spent here with you. And in the days which are ahead I wish for you and for all the people of the Philippines health, peace and prosperity. May God bless you and yours today and in the years to come."[89]

Shortly after his return to the United States, High Commissioner McNutt was invited to give an address before the Institute of Pacific Affairs at the University of Virginia at Charlottesville on July 7, 1939. He said in part:

"I have just come from the other side of what was once known, with some justification, as 'the good earth,' but what has earned in recent years the title 'the tragic earth.' . . . In this tormented, confused, deluded, bewildered, and bedevilled world today the prayer of every sane man is for peace, peace at home and with all peoples. . . . If we are to lead the way to peace we must practice peace at home. We do not find peace in the abstract. We find it by living and acting it. . . . I have come from one of the few other comparatively happy spots in the world, the Philippines, a happy place in an un-happy Orient—the one place out there where decency, de-mocracy, and peace reign; where the orderly processes of democracy have a chance to develop; where, and only where, the peculiar culture of America holds forth a torch of liberty and the love of fellow man."[90]

After briefly describing the historical development of United States-Philippines relations, McNutt concluded that "with good grace and speed we proceeded through participation and partnership to a fixed date, July 4, 1946, for absolute political international independence."[91] He then discussed the economic policy. "The Philippines were not at first brought into our own customs and tariff area," he said. "We did, however, grant Philippine goods the moderate ad-vantage of a 25 per cent discount on our import duties. This period, 1899 to 1909, may be termed a period of independent economy. . . . There was a slow but steady development based largely on indigenous economy. When 1909 came around . . . the policy of independent economy was changed to one of complementary economy. . . . The plan was to create an 'economic couple' between the motherland and the colony in such manner that both would prosper and neither be damaged. The arrangement was healthy. Both American and Filipino producers and laborers prospered."[92]

This policy of complementary economy was not continued for long. The period from 1913 to 1934 was termed one of competitive economy. Philippine industry and government revenue were directed into artificial trade channels, according to McNutt. "Today the Philippines are the only bright, prosperous spot in the Orient. Their people enjoy the highest wages and best standard of living in the Far East. The deadly tropical diseases—smallpox, cholera, bubonic plague—which long decimated the population, have been wiped out. Thousands of miles of good highways are maintained. Bridges have replaced bamboo rafts. The budget is balanced. Taxes are the lowest in the world. The reserve behind the currency is 100 per cent. The per capita national debt is less than $2. Schools and hospitals dot the jungle and plain. We built well in the Philippines. Our work is a monument to American idealism and enterprise—a living monument to 16,000,000 rescued from tyranny, rebellion, ignorance, poverty, and disease, and set upon the path of free government, peace, education, prosperity, and health. With all seriousness, no nation in the world can boast of so grand a monument."[93]

But the High Commissioner was not entirely optimistic. A problem had arisen, he claimed, "which we alone can solve. Politically we have brought the Islands through progressive steps to the verge of independence. Economically we brought the islands through progressive steps to almost complete dependence upon our markets. On one hand we sought to sever the ties, on the other we chained them ever closer to us." McNutt asserted the problem arose "from the insistent repeated requests of the Filipino leaders during the twenties and early thirties to fix an early date for independence, but for independence with a continuation, at least in part, and for a con-

siderable time, of economic protection we have granted them.
They also wanted neutralization or American military protection if they could get it."[94] It was his belief that there were
groups at home representing American producers and inves-
tors who found duty-free Philippine products in competition
with their own products quickly taking advantage of the
desire of the Filipino leaders. These groups brought pressure
to bear on general policy, and sought to obtain for the Philippines a fixed date of independence, but without economic
protection thereafter.

McNutt claimed that he had no quarrel with the lobbies
which, he said, were open and aboveboard and "behaved as
well or better than do most lobbyists." However, he felt that
there were offsetting American advantages "which were not
properly presented to the people." It was his opinion that
"if we accept the only common-sense interpretation of trade
between the two countries, 'purchasing what you need but
have not, and selling what you have but do not need,' the
trade between the United States and the Philippines as it has
developed under the free trade provisions can be shown to be
wholly normal and mutually advantageous."[95]

McNutt was convinced that the combination of Filipino
leaders interested in independence and American lobbyists
joined by sincere believers in self-determination at any cost,
and by a few isolationists, resulted in the Hare-Hawes-Cutting
Independence Act of 1932, "which sought to solve the problem of fixing the date of political independence 10 years later;
by providing immediate quota limits on duty-free Philippine
sugar, cocoanut oil, and cordage; providing for a 10-year-
period of transition under an autonomous Commonwealth;
providing for increases in duties on Philippine goods from 5
per cent in 1941 to 25 per cent in 1945; providing for 100 per
cent duties beginning at the moment of independence and

finally providing that the act should not become law until accepted by the Philippine legislature."[96]

As McNutt pointed out, the Hare-Hawes-Cutting Act had had rough going in the United States. It was vetoed by President Hoover, then repassed over his veto. When the act arrived in the Philippines, it had still rougher going. The Ninth Philippine Legislature met and rejected it. Many thought that was the end of it. But in 1933-34, other Filipino leaders came to the United States and tried to get a better bill, one that would be more protective to their economic interests and more clearly define the political powers of the Commonwealth government. But in this they were blocked, as no better terms were available. The act was then revived with no change in these respects, though it was renamed the Tydings-McDuffy Independence Act, and the clause providing for American military bases after independence was stricken out. The new act was then promptly accepted by the same Philippine legislature which had just previously rejected the former act. However, the resolution of acceptance carried a clause praying for future amendment of the economic terms of the act in accordance with the expressed view of the President of the United States that inequities in the act would be examined and corrected later.

In spite of technicalities, however, the Commonwealth was inaugurated, and sovereignty was not altered. On the second anniversary of the Commonwealth, President Manuel L. Quezon declared that "America's voluntary withdrawal from a country already under its lawful domain . . . stands as the beacon light pointing the way to a distressed humanity out of the threatening universal disaster. . . . Here is the admirable example of two peoples thrown together by the hands of destiny and agreeing between themselves in good will and with best wishes for one another to sever their political union that each may go its own way as God has willed that every people should. . . . On this day of our national rejoicing our first thought is of America and our grateful hearts go out to her in thanksgiving for her unfailing help, support and encouragement in our difficult task of nation building."[97]

But McNutt was not satisfied. He felt that the problem had been broadened. "Treaties concerning the Orient have been violated. Over the major part of the Orient famine and pestilence and bloodshed are raging. Our open-door policy has been more than seriously challenged. Our policy of freedom of the seas and freedom of the air is in the balance. And what of the Philippines? They have come to the crossing of the roads. The events of the last two years have given many thoughtful Filipino leaders an object lesson and food for thought. . . . Many have come to realize that independence, however attractive from a spiritual viewpoint, may mean a mere trade of sovereignties. They realize that the laws—the United States laws—excluding immigration could scarcely be enforced by an independent small nation in their quarter of the globe. The Philippines are sparsely populated, and they are surrounded with nations whose teeming millions are spilling over their national boundaries. An independent Philippines government thus faces a very real threat of racial extinction. Add to this the question of its ability to defend itself from foreign military aggression and the economic disaster attendant upon sudden loss of the American market and you have the picture."[98]

From the American viewpoint the picture was equally gloomy, thought McNutt. "If we withdraw from the Philippines we lose our voice in oriental diplomacy. We leave a barrier reef of islands from Kamchatka to Borneo—all practically within sight of each other—a barrier which will intervene between the United States and the continent of Asia.

In foreign hands this barrier will block our trade and intercourse with China. It will solve the claims of freedom of the seas and freedom of the air—solve them unfavorably to us and to our children. To us there comes a responsibility. It appears now in respect to the Philippine problem broadened to become a part of a greater Oriental problem. If we scuttle, if we run away, our monument will be destroyed. The things we counted on, our aspirations to point the way to a new benign colonialism, our handicraft will perish. Our grandchildren will read a history which will apply to us the epithet 'quitter'—a word which is just about the worst insult in the lexicon of a true American."[99]

The High Commissioner was convinced that he voiced the inherent desire of the United States to solve the Philippine problem in fairness to all, "just as we wish with fairness and justice to solve our domestic problems." On the political side, he believed that "our flag and sovereignty should remain, allowing to the Philippines every ounce of domestic autonomy they can absorb—holding in our hands foreign affairs, tariffs, immigration, currency, and public debt—scarcely more than marks of the necessary reservation of a dominion. . . . On the economic side, we should, from time to time, give the Philippines the best trade deal we can without injuring our domestic producers. We must admit the possibility of competition. . . Our aim should be to assist with capital and men, with good will and such preferences as we can afford, the return to a complementary and reciprocal economy between the United States and the Philippines."[100]

In regard to the problem of military protection, McNutt ventured to predict that "so long as our flag flies over the islands no foreign power will trespass, irrespective of the military forces stationed there. So long as our flag flies there, the Philippines will be the cornerstone of peaceful reconstruction in the Far East. . . . If our flag comes down, trouble will follow for at least a generation."[101]

In conclusion, McNutt declared that the Philippines were "an outpost of decency and peace—the only safe outpost for Christianity in the Orient." He asked the rhetorical question:

"Whenever have we not had outposts? Our entire history has been one of pushing the frontier; of setting distant points to be reached and distant aspirations to be achieved. Outposts have been the milestones of American progress. "Neither this American generation nor any other American generation should falter on its outward path. We cannot scuttle. We must not shirk. . . . We should proceed to a realistic re-examination of the needs of these people [the Filipinos] and the long-range interests of ourselves. . . . America will not impose her sovereignty by force upon any people. The enduring welfare and safety of both countries are to be the paramount consideration. It is my conviction that they are not far apart and that they can be harmonized—harmonized for the salvation of the Philippines, for the larger interests of America, and for the peace of the Pacific."[102]

So well had High Commissioner McNutt performed his duties during his two years of service that President Quezon could declare:

"To America we owe a special debt of gratitude. To her altruism and generosity we shall be indebted for our national independence. She has made us heir to her ideals of liberty and democracy and the beneficiaries of her civilization and culture. It should be our constant endeavor to preserve undiminished this invaluable inheritance as well as our friendly and cultural relations with her after we shall have become independent. . . . In our foreign policy, let our motto be: Justice and friendship for all!"[103]

In an earlier speech, read at the opening of the Second Philippine National Assembly on January 23, 1939, President Quezon had expressed publicly Filipino indebtedness to the High Commissioner for his cooperation with the Philippine

Government. He declared that it was "with a sense of great loss for our people and for me that I have heard of his contemplated return to the United States. If he should find it necessary to resign his present post, we would be deprived of a true friend and most able collaborator, one whom we need at this most critical period and who would be very hard to replace. But if he must leave us, we wish him to know that he takes with him our affection and gratitude, and our prayer that he may succeed in his future undertakings."[104]

By the middle of July, 1939, as had been predicted, Paul V. McNutt had resigned as High Commissioner to the Philippines. Proof of his service to the Commonwealth was indicated in a speech which President Quezon delivered before members of the National Assembly and broadcast over KZRM-Radio Manila and KZIB, September 5, 1939. He assured the government of the United States of Philippine loyalty and devotion "which have grown even deeper and stronger in the perspective of the many years of unselfish American endeavor to serve the best interests of the Filipino people. . . . Our loyalty to the United States is rooted in something more permanent, something more lasting, than legal or political relationship. Our loyalty is built on faith—faith in the sense of fairness and justice of the American people, faith in the great principles and ideals for which the Stars and Stripes proudly waves over land and sea, over a free and happy people. Our loyalty to the great American nation is but the fruit of her altruistic policy which has been characterized by justice and good will and by both moral and material assistance. That loyalty, I am sure, will outlive the sovereignty of the United States over our country, and will attest for all time the moral grandeur of America and the virtuality of her free institutions."[105]

At the time McNutt left office, his staff numbered thirty, exclusive of naval and military aides and other personnel loaned by the Army. In addition to the office staff, thirty employees, such as messengers, chauffeurs, and watchmen were on the office pay-roll, while nine house servants were carried on the discretionary fund.[106] His competent staff was in part responsible for the successful administration of his office, as they dealt with more diverse and important problems than is usually the case with public offices. But it was McNutt who made the final decisions, based upon his intimate and up-to-date knowledge of conditions throughout the Islands.

One outstanding authority on the Philippines, Joseph Ralston Hayden, in commenting on the office of High Commissioner, indicated some of the problems faced by McNutt. "He is far removed from his chief, the President of the United States, and isolated from official colleagues of comparable rank. The Philippine climate draws heavily upon his physical and nervous energy. There is a certain strain, too, in living and working among an alien people, no matter how hospitable and cooperative they may be."[107] The total appropriation for the office was about $160,000.[108]

Thus ended one more important and highly successful episode in the career of the Hoosier statesman, and the beginning of another. During the next eight years, McNutt was to render his greatest service to his country, and he almost received her highest elective honor.

Notes for Chapter 5

[1] Editorial, Syracuse, New York, *Post-Standard*, quoted in Manila *Bulletin*, April 27, 1937.

[2] McHale to author.

[3] Chicago *Tribune*, February 17, 1937.

[4] Editorial, Syracuse, New York, *Post-Standard*, quoted in Manila *Bulletin*, April 27, 1937.

[5] "The Philippines Today" in *Background*, U. S. Department of State, Office of Public Affairs, pamphlet, November 1951.

[6] *Ibid.*

7 Eufronio M. Alip, *Political and Cultural History of the Philippines* (1762-1947), Fifth Edition Revised, Manila, 1947, Vol. II, p. 220.

8 Pamphlet, "What Lies Ahead for the Philippines?" The American Historical Association for the War Department, 1945.

9 Joseph Ralston Hayden, *The Philippines: A Study in National Development* (New York, 1942, pp. xxvi-984), p. 815.

10 *Ibid.* p. 816.

11 *Ibid.*

12 Francis B. Sayre, "Freedom Comes to the Philippines" in *The Atlantic Monthly*, March, 1945, pp. 82-88.

13 Hayden, *The Philippines: A Study in National Development*, p. 779.

14 The Manila *Herald*, January 29, 1937. Clippings from the Manila papers cited below are found in the McNutt Collection, Lilly Library, Indiana University.

15 *Ibid.*

16 *Ibid.*

17 *The Philippines: A Study in National Development*, Joseph Ralston Haydon (Vice Governor of the Philippine Islands 1933-1935) New York 1942, (pp. xxvi-984), pp. 774-775.

18 Press statement of the President of the Philippines, *Messages of the President*, Vol. 2, Part 1, p. 444 quoted in Hayden, above, p. 775.

19 Manila *Tribune*, February 19, 1937.

20 Manila *Bulletin*, February 19, 1937.

21 *Ibid.*

22 Manila *Tribune*, February 19, 1937.

23 Manila *Bulletin*, February 19, 1937.

24 *Ibid.*

25 *President Quezon. His Biographical Sketch. Messages and Papers. A Record of the Progress and Achievements of the Philippine People.* Edited by Eulogio B. Roderiguez, Manila 1940, pp. 122-124.

26 *Ibid.*

27 *Ibid.*

28 *Ibid.*

29 Manila *Herald*, February 22, 1937.

30 *Ibid.* February 24, 1937. Also *Congressional Record*, February 23, 1937, p. 1857.

31 Manila *Bulletin*, April 26, 1936.

32 Philippines *Free Press*, May 1, 1937. Manila *Bulletin*, April 26, 1937. Manila *Herald*, April 27, 1937.

33 Manila *Bulletin*, April 26, 1937.

34 *Ibid.* April 27, 1937.

35 Manila *Herald*, April 27, 1937.

36 Manila *Tribune*, April 27, 1937.

37 Iloila *Times*, May 27, 1937.

38 Manila *Herald*, June 5, 1937, quoted from editorial page of New York *Sun*, May 24, 1937.

39 Manila *Tribune*, May 26, 1937.

[40] Manila *Tribune,* May 22 and 23, 1937.

[41] *The Philippines: A Study in National Development,* pp. 781-782.

[42] Manila *Herald,* May 18, 1937, by Salvador P. Lopez.

[43] Manila *Bulletin,* May 27, 1937, editorial by Juan F. Hilario.

[44] Manila *Herald Mid-Week Magazine,* May 26, 1937.

[45] Manila *Herald Tribune Mid-Week,* May 26, 1937, article by Eugenio E. Santos.

[46] Manila *Bulletin,* July 2, 1937, quoted from Brooklyn, New York, *Eagle.*

[47] Manila *Bulletin,* July 3, 1937, quoted from New York *Herald-Tribune.*

[48] Quoted in Manila *Tribune,* May 30, 1937.

[49] Manila *Tribune,* June 19, 1937.

[50] Manila *Herald,* June 19, 1937.

[51] Manila *Bulletin,* June 21, 1937.

[52] Manila *Herald,* July 8, 1937.

[53] New York *World Telegram,* July 12, 1937.

[54] Washington, D. C., *Evening Star,* July 14, 1937, article by H. R. Baukhage.

[55] Manila *Herald,* July 28, 1937. Manila *Bulletin,* July 29, 1937.

[56] Denver *Post,* August 25, 1937.

[57] *Rocky Mountain News,* August 29, 1937.

[58] Washington *Star,* February 23, 1938.

[59] *Ibid.*

[60] *Ibid.*

[61] New York *World Telegram,* February 2, 1938.

[62] Sidney Olson in Washington *Post,* February 23, 1938.

[63] *Ibid.*

[64] *Ibid.* February 24, 1938.

[65] New York *Herald Tribune,* February 24, 1938.

[66] Manila *Herald,* February 24, 1938.

[67] New York *Herald Tribune,* February 27, 1938.

[68] New York *Times,* February 24, 1938.

[69] Indianapolis *Times,* July 21, 1937 and September 29, 1937.

[70] *Ibid,* July 1, 5, 11, 12.

[71] Indianapolis *Sunday Star,* June 5, 1938.

[72] Raymond Clapper in New York *World Telegram,* July 7, 1938.

[73] Typed article, dated July 12, 1938, copyright by United Features Syndicate, Inc.

[74] *TIME* XXXII, July 25, 1938, pp. 10-11.

[75] Barnhart and Carmony, *Indiana, From Frontier to Industrial Commonwealth,* Vol. II, pp. 485-6.

[76] Newspaper article by John Ochiltree, no place, August 29, 1938.

[77] "Watch Paul McNutt" by Joseph H. Friend, *Nation,* July 23, 1938.

[78] Manila *Bulletin,* January 1, 1939.

[79] *Ibid.* February 6, 1939.

[80] Manila *Herald,* February 8, 1939.

81 Manila *Bulletin,* March 20, 1939.

82 *Ibid.*

83 Manila *Herald,* March 1, 1939.

84 *Bulletin,* May 10, 1939.

85 Manila *Herald,* May 10, 1939.

86 Manila *Bulletin,* May 11, 1939.

87 Manila *Tribune,* May 11, 1939.

88 *Ibid.*

89 Manila *Herald,* May 11, 1939.

90 *Congressional Record,* 76th Congress, First Session, Vol. 84, part 14, Appendix, July 13, 1939, to August 5, 1939, pp. 3203-4155, Extension of remarks of Hon. John W. Boehne, Jr., of Indiana.

91 *Ibid.*

92 *Ibid.*

93 *Ibid.*

94 *Ibid.*

95 *Ibid.*

96 *Ibid.*

97 Eulogio B. Rodriguez, ed., *President Quezon. His Biographical Sketch, Messages and Papers, A Record of the Progress and Achievements of the Philippine People,* Manila 1940, p. 156.

98 *Congressional Record,* see above 90.

99 *Ibid.*

100 *Ibid.*

101 *Ibid.*

102 *Ibid.*

103 Rodriguez, p. 239.

104 *Ibid.* p. 204.

105 *Ibid.* p. 260.

106 Figures from Joseph Ralston Hayden, *The Philippines, A Study in National Development,* New York 1942, (pp. xxvi-984), p. 779.

107 *Ibid.*

108 *Ibid.*

CHAPTER VI

A Good Soldier

In July, 1939, President Franklin D. Roosevelt appointed McNutt to head the newly formed Federal Security Agency, where he remained throughout the war. This post was considered one of the most important outside the Cabinet. The salary was only $12,000 as compared with the $18,000-plus of the Philippine job, but McNutt wanted to be nearer the center of the political arena, rather than on the periphery in Manila.

McNutt had been prepared somewhat for the appointment long before it was made. En route home from the Philippines in May he had received a letter from his administrative assistant, Wayne Coy, hinting that the President might want him to head one of the new agencies created by the Reorganization Act, either the Security Administration or the Federal Works Agency. Harry Hopkins, Coy wrote, did not think it advisable for McNutt to accept "unless it is offered you in such a way that you can't do otherwise. He points out that the time is so short, that it will be almost impossible to accomplish enough in one of these positions to contribute materially to your record as an Administrator. At any rate, it is a question that doesn't call for any answer until the President states his wishes."[1] Obviously Coy was referring to the Presidential nomination the following year.

Before being offered the Federal Security post, McNutt was again given serious consideration as president of Indiana University. Even before he had taken the Philippines position, he was mentioned as a possible head of the Hoosier institution. Some thought that an acting president should be appointed, so that the office could be held open for McNutt until he returned from the Orient. But the trustees finally appointed Herman B Wells as the successor to Dr. William Lowe Bryan.

McNutt had also been given consideration as a possibility for the presidency of Ohio State University. When he returned from the Philippines, the board of trustees asked him if he would be interested in the position, but he wrote them that he would be unable to accept, even if it should be offered to him, although he was deeply interested in education.

His appointment as Federal Security Administrator gave McNutt the responsibility of implementing the entire social security program. Various federal agencies concerned with the many welfare and relief activities were brought under his supervision. The Agency was authorized to administer all federal welfare laws through the Social Security Board, Office of Education, Public Health Service, National Youth Administration, Civilian Conservation Corps, and others. The Agency acted as an overall supervisory policy-making body in controlling the functions of its constituent bodies.

The Federal Security Agency was established on July 1, 1939, under the authority of the Reorganization Act of April 3, 1939. McNutt was therefore its first head. The Agency consisted of various bureaus which administered the programs authorized under the statute. These included the Bureau of

Old-Age and Survivors Insurance, Bureau of Public Assistance, Bureau of Employment Security, and the Bureau of Federal Credit Unions. The program was implemented through twelve regional offices in which were located 327 local field offices.

Under the Office of Education, research and experimentation were conducted. Publication of educational materials and their distribution to state and municipal educational institutions were among the services rendered.

The Public Health Service conducted research in the causes and prevention of disease, and published its reports for the use of hospitals and state and municipal departments of health. It also was charged with the responsibility of enforcing quarantine laws at ports of entry. It cooperated with state and local agencies in their public health programs, and provided hospitalization for certain types of patients under federal law. It established sanitary rules regarding shipment of animals and food in interstate commerce, and enforced federal laws forbidding the transportation of animals and people with certain designated diseases. The Surgeon-General of the United States was made responsible to the Federal Security Administrator.

While not at first a part of the Federal Security Agency, the National Youth Administration was absorbed into the Federal Works Agency in 1943, and thus came under McNutt's supervision. It had been created in 1935 to furnish part-time work for high-school and college students. Its main function was to relieve unemployment distress, raise wages by reducing the number of unemployed, assist families on public welfare rolls, and maintain educational standards through financial assistance to needy students. The Federal Works Agency had been established in 1939 to supervise the maintenance of public buildings, administer federal highway funds, and coordinate all federal housing activities. It included the Works Progress Administration, Public Works Administration, Bureau of Public Roads, United States Housing Authority, and other agencies. The Civilian Conservation Corps was set up to solve the unemployment problem of the early depression years. It involved a program of public works projects dealing with reforestation, flood and fire control, irrigation, etc. It was also absorbed into the Federal Works Agency in 1943.

As Federal Security Administrator, therefore, McNutt had an extremely important assignment. His friends felt that he was eminently qualified to handle the responsibilities in connection with the manifold duties the office entailed. He had demonstrated his administrative abilities while governor of Indiana and more recently as United States High Commissioner to the Philippines. President Roosevelt was complimented on his choice for the job, and McNutt was congratulated on his acceptance of the nomination.

McNutt's personal friend, General Douglas MacArthur, congratulated him on his appointment. Writing from the Philippines, he said he could not refrain "from telling you I regard it as one of the smartest things you ever did. This insures you at least the benevolence and probably the active support of the dominant wing of your party, and does it in a way that should not lose you the support of those who recognize the conservative caution of your liberalism. In addition it furnishes a perfect sounding board for the exposition of your views on practically all the burning internal questions of the day. All you needed was such a chance to sell yourself to the people at large. It will prove perhaps the most vital decision of your life."[2]

Political enemies of McNutt, however, considered the appointment full of political dynamite. Some felt that this would turn out to be one more stepping-stone to the realization of higher political ambitions—the presidency. Others believed that McNutt was not qualified for so responsible a position, in view of certain factors in connection with the governorship and the commissionership. And even some who were not his political enemies—indeed some of his friends—feared that President Roosevelt was purposely giving McNutt enough rope in an exceedingly unpopular task so that he would eventually commit political suicide.

When the President's nomination went before the Senate on July 12, 1939, Senator Styles Bridges, Republican from New Hampshire, introduced a resolution which read in part:

"Whereas Paul V. McNutt, as Governor of the State of Indiana was alleged to have been instrumental in forming the so-called Two Percent Club made up of state employees and officeholders of that State, whereby the said employees and officeholders were required to contribute 2 percent of their salaries for political purposes" . . . resolved "That it is the sense of the Senate that Paul V. McNutt shall not be permitted, while serving as Federal Security Administrator, to establish a so-called Two Percent Club of employees of the above-named agencies for the purpose of assessing their salaries for political purposes."[3]

Senator Bridges then asked for unanimous consent that the resolution be considered and acted upon immediately. Senator Barkley moved, however, that the resolution be laid on the table. This was agreed to. Senator Bridges then declared that inasmuch as "the Democratic members of the Senate have therefore gone on record as favoring the Two Percent Club of Indiana as established by Mr. McNutt, then Governor of Indiana," he thought "it very appropriate before he is put in charge of one of the most important agencies of the Government, that the people of the country have some knowledge of the Two Percent Club of Indiana, what it is, what it stands for, and Mr. McNutt's connection with it."[4]

Senator Bridges continued:

"I have known Mr. McNutt for a number of years. He served as Governor of Indiana during the time I had the privilege of serving as Governor of New Hampshire. I think he is a nice fellow. I have nothing personally against him. He is a handsome man. He has many fine qualities. But the Two Percent Club that is so closely associated with Mr. McNutt and Mr. McNutt's history and political life smells. It not only smells but its odor could be described by even a stronger term."

He then described the Two Percent Club which he called "one of the most brazen political acts ever put across in this nation." According to various estimates, he said, the assessment which was put on all state employees "for the benefit of the Democratic Party" raised somewhere "around $300,000 a year."[5]

The reason for offering the resolution at this time, said Senator Bridges, was "to call attention to this situation."[6] He referred back to 1932, when McNutt belonged to the "Stop Roosevelt" movement. According to Senator Bridges, McNutt was working against the nomination of Roosevelt at Chicago. "Mr. Farley, by his very astute methods, secured some support for Mr. Roosevelt in Indiana; but I am given to understand that there has always been a sort of distant feeling between Mr. Roosevelt and Mr. McNutt, and particularly has there been a strong feeling between Mr. Farley and Mr. McNutt. Now Mr. McNutt comes home in all his grandeur and is appointed to a new post, one of the best jobs in the Government.

"There is a great question in my mind and in the minds of the people of the country, whether Mr. McNutt has been taken in by the New Deal and President Roosevelt, or whether he has swallowed the New Deal. I do not know which is the case. There is some question of the New Deal's interest in McNutt's political future, because Mr. McNutt no doubt is going forward with his campaign for the Presidency, at the same time being entrusted with the care of the youthful citizens of our country and many of the unfortunate citizens of our country in the various agencies. He will have a two-fold job to make himself the nominee of his party for President and to administer this new agency."[7]

Bridges then read from an article by Joseph Alsop and Robert Kintner which appeared in the Washington *Evening Star*:

"The Two Percent Clubs, a feature of the McNutt machine's ironclad Indiana dictatorship . . . are simple, if rather brutal, institutions. Pretty nearly everyone who wants to keep a job with the State of Indiana has got to belong to them. Their chief function is the collection of 2 percent of the salary of everyone with a government job. The Two Percent Clubs have locals, chiefly consisting of a sharp-eyed treasurer, in all the large agencies of the State Government. Every payday the treasurers collect their 2 percent and turn it over to the treasury chest of the McNutt machine. Thus the funds of the taxpayers of Indiana were really the source most heavily drawn on [for the McNutt political program]."[8]

According to Alsop and Kintner, McNutt's governorship "was notable for three things. The 2-percent clubs were established. The Governor exhibited a curious fondness for marching the National Guard about the State, declaring martial law at the drop of a picket sign in labor disputes. And a McNutt-conceived reorganization of the State Government was put through, which brought the State of Indiana as tightly under McNutt's control as Louisiana ever was under Long's. These three things led Norman Thomas to describe the new Presidential candidate as the Hoosier Hitler."[9]

Senator Bridges then reviewed McNutt's activities while High Commissioner to the Philippines. He criticized him for the "toast" episode, and explained his point in objecting to him. He declared that he liked "the gentleman personally; I have no objection of a personal nature to him, but I do think that a man who has been associated with the Two Percent Club in Indiana, one of the most brazen samples of political racketeering I know of in the entire Nation, should not go unchallenged when he is appointed to head one of the great governmental agencies of this country, where he will have under his charge the young and the old and the unfortunate of the Nation." He concluded with the hope that, based upon his past record, the nomination of McNutt would not be confirmed by the Senate.[10]

Senator Sherman Minton of Indiana then spoke in behalf of McNutt's appointment. He admitted that the Two Percent Club was established by the Democratic organization and employees voluntarily, but not by McNutt, "to help defray the expenses of the Democratic organization of the State of Indiana," and they were "proud" and "glad" to pay it. No one was fired because he did not contribute, Minton said. He himself, as a member of the state administration then, paid his assessment voluntarily and gladly, he claimed, although not everyone paid. The judges "never would pay," and he knew "that certain others in the Statehouse never did pay."[11]

Bridges then asked Minton if the Two Percent Clubs were political in character, and Minton admitted they were "a Democratic organization, and the purpose of it is to keep the Republicans out of power in Indiana, and may God prosper it." Bridges then asked: "Is it not more to keep the McNutt machine in power than to keep the Republicans out of power?" Minton answered that the two were "synonymous, and as long as the McNutt crowd has been in power in Indiana, we have managed to keep the Republicans wandering in the wilderness and I hope we will continue to do so." Minton believed the methods used by both the Republicans and Democrats in raising money to finance their political campaigns were "honest, honorable, and straightforward." The nomination of McNutt was finally confirmed.[12]

But Senator Bridges did not cease his attacks on McNutt. On July 24 he presented before the Senate "a very interesting publication which is called the Indiana Unemployment Compensation Advisor . . . the official publication of the Indiana Unemployment Compensation department, division, or commission, or whatever it may be called, which is a unit of the Social Security Commission, which is a unit of the Federal Security Agency, which is headed by Paul V. McNutt."[13]

On the cover of this publication was a picture of McNutt with the caption "Paul V. McNutt Again 'The Boss'." Below the picture were set forth "the stepping stones of Mr. McNutt's career." And at the top there was a picture of the capitol and the White House in Washington, and the date "1941." On the first page inside the cover was an editorial entitled "Congratulations, Paul! Good Picking, Mr. President!" The editorial began with the words:

"Congratulations to Paul V. McNutt and to the millions of Americans who will be benefited by his appointment as head of the newly established Federal Security Agency. Congratulations to President Franklin D. Roosevelt for securing Paul V. McNutt to head the most enduring, humane, and far-reaching program of his administration."[14]

The editorial continued:

"In the Federal Security Agency, approximately 40,000,000 people are covered by the old-age insurance and approximately 28,000,000 by unemployment compensation. In the social security program, which also includes old-age assistance, aid to dependent children, aid to the blind, and aid to crippled children, McNutt will find himself very much at home."[15]

Bridges was able to have the entire article printed in the *Record* as a part of his remarks. It traced the history of social security legislation in Indiana from 1936, when Governor McNutt called a special session of the General Assembly to dovetail state action with the Federal Social Security Act. The legislature followed McNutt's suggestions in adopting various laws. He had studied every detail of this far-reaching program, and the Indiana laws, "written with his personal help and passed under his leadership, have been outstanding in the country. Neither the law nor its administration has been attacked either by Indiana agencies or by the Federal Government—something that can be said of few other states," according to the pamphlet.[16]

The editorial continues:

"The National Youth Administration and the Civilian Conservation Corps, embracing close to a million of the underprivileged youth of America, can expect enlightened leadership from McNutt. . . . The Federal Public Health Service which will fall within his jurisdiction needs only to look at the outstanding health department he established in Indiana to be reassured of the future success of this Federal Agency. The Office of Education . . . is indeed fortunate to have McNutt, one of America's outstanding educators, one thoroughly familiar with its needs and problems, at its helm."[17]

"The responsibilities of McNutt's new position are terrific. . . . The coordination of . . . [all the agencies] is a man-sized job. . . . Paul V. McNutt has demonstrated repeatedly in his unusual career his leadership, administrative ability, and integrity in the long list of organizations he has headed. . . . Indiana is proud of McNutt's record. Indiana has been his home, and Indiana has profited most from his civic and governmental leadership. Now the Nation is to be the recipient of his public service." The article was signed by Clarence A. Jackson.[18]

Senator Bridges made one final comment. "I merely want to point out at this time that the parade has started; politics is on the march in the Federal Security Administration. His [McNutt's] own unit in Indiana is the first one coming to the foreground. . . . The official publication of a State unit, which is a branch of a Federal agency, marks the stepping stones up to 1941, when, in their opinion and by their prediction, Mr. McNutt will step up to further honors. On that point I do not agree with them; but I merely point out that it is very clear that the old traditions still hold; the Two Percent Club is apparently functioning in another way, and Mr. McNutt is certainly starting his campaign without loss of time."[19]

Perhaps the best objective view of the whole matter was expressed in an article written by Richard L. Strout which appeared in the *Christian Science Monitor* and was included in the *Appendix* to the *Congressional Record* by Senator Sherman. It stated:

"Sooner or later Americans must do some hard thinking about the organization of political parties. It is one of the most fundamental problems in the United States. We are in the main proud of the party system and committed to its perpetuation, though it finds no mention in the Constitution. But how should these parties be organized, and above all, how financed? This question is raised by two recent news events: the national attention given to Paul V. McNutt, who, as Governor of Indiana, organized the 'Two Percent Club,' which was a frank salary assessment on state officeholders, and the passage of the Hatch bill, which forbids political activity by an army of Federal workers.[20]

"Parties have to have money to win elections. How shall they get it? Reformers have been unrealistic about this whole matter. Many of them have preferred not to look behind the scenes. We know that one way of keeping parties together is by the patronage. Most of us agree it is a bad way. The Hatch bill may do a good deal to end it, if (and it is quite an if) it can be enforced. Another way is by party war chests raised by gifts. Is this a good way? Reformers decry the McNutt scheme of making every employee pay 2 percent of his salary. This writer believes it is a vicious system. But there is danger of being smug about it; after all the McNutt scheme was brutally frank, it was relatively open and aboveboard, it dragged the forbidden subject into the air. Is it worse to have a party financed and held tight together by that method, or by secret political contributions of special interests in return for favors made after the election? This is an uncomfortable but a very real question, and it demands a reply. . . . Nobody can deny that at present money has to be raised. The question is, Shall it be by '2 percent clubs,' by contributions from the wealthy, by patronage, or by some other means as yet unexplored in America?"[21]

In the meantime, evidence that McNutt was seriously interested in becoming a Presidential candidate in 1940 continued to grow. Washington newspapers broke out in a rash of page-one stories about Indiana's "favorite son." While these stories were generally friendly, every columnist had his own profound conclusions. Only Joseph Alsop continued his scoffing barrage. It seemed that most of the columnists were convinced during the summer of 1939 that there were "just two genuine, gilt-edged candidates for the Democratic Presidential nomination in 1940—President Roosevelt and his newly appointed Federal Security Administrator."[22]

At least one writer felt that Roosevelt and McNutt were each depending on the other for support in the 1940 convention, whenever it was decided who should be chosen as the nominee. It was possible that the picture might change before the following June, "but the McNutt-Roosevelt alliance has, for the present at least, left Jim Farley and Jack Garner like a couple of side dishes that nobody ordered."[23] The writers were generally highly complimentary of the McNutt appointment. Ernest K. Lindley, President Roosevelt's biographer and noted pro-New Deal columnist, believed that the maximum meaning of the appointment was that Roosevelt "looks upon McNutt as a possible heir and wants to look him over at close range and try him out in a difficult job before making up his mind about McNutt's qualifications." Historian Mark Sullivan wrote that Roosevelt had appointed McNutt for "his outstanding qualification for the job."[24]

Republicans generally, however, feared that if McNutt were a candidate their chances for return to power would be lessened. They granted that he had real possibilities and was an aggressive campaigner. His physical appearance and vigor were among his dominant assets. His public-speaking ability was widely acclaimed. His radio voice was the equal of Roosevelt's, and his personality was just as dynamic, although at times he was criticized for his dictatorial and autocratic tactics.

Just before McNutt resigned the Philippine post, he received a letter from Wayne Coy, his administrative assistant in Manila, informing him that Harry Hopkins had expressed the opinion that the President had made no decision as to running for a third term or whom he might support in the event he did not run. Hopkins believed that Roosevelt did not want to run for a third term, "provided he could find someone who could carry out his program and who would be strong enough as a candidate in the convention to prevent control of the convention getting into the hands of the conservatives of the Party."[25]

Most of the so-called "inner circle," according to Coy, were advocating that the President run for a third term. Hopkins had told Coy that among that group were some people "who are not friendly to you, although there has been a marked increase in interest in your campaign in recent months." Coy thought the "present problem confronting the inner circle is the activity of Farley who is definitely campaigning for delegates for Farley. They are as much against him as they are against Garner and Clark." Hopkins had offered to give McNutt assistance in his campaign "in a way that would keep you available." Hopkins said that McNutt should assume that he was "just as friendly to Roosevelt as anyone, and that newspaper reports to the contrary should not be any matter of concern." He thought it important that McNutt "work on this assumption, offer no apologies, nor make any moves to make it appear at the present time that the White House had given you encouragement, either directly or indirectly." Coy was confident that in Hopkins "we will have the influence of the person closest to the President. Whatever is done in the campaign must be done with this relationship in mind."[26]

An interesting biographical sketch and summary of McNutt's political philosophy was submitted about this time by McNutt's secretary in reply to a request from a student in Georgia. The statement read:

"Mr. McNutt's candidacy is based upon the philosophy of a moderate liberal. He has supported the Roosevelt administration faithfully but has not been identified with the group of extreme reformers. He is friendly with all factions of the party, being on good terms with most of the advisers of the administration and with the more conservative groups in the party. His thorough understanding of public administration, his ability to get on well with his associates and with those who serve under him, and his extensive and sound knowledge of national economy, are calculated, it is thought, to appeal to the substantial business interests of the country. His demonstrated humanitarian interests should appeal to the liberal leaders. His experience and his extensive knowledge of foreign affairs, acquired in the Philippines, is calculated to inspire confidence with respect to our international relations."

The statement continued:

"He believes in a strong national defense policy and in an adequate army and navy and air force; but he is passionately devoted to the principle of keeping America out of foreign wars. He is not a national isolationist and he appreciates the importance of America's foreign trade for our internal prosperity. He believes that adequate military and naval defenses and frank dealing with foreign powers will enable the country to participate in world commerce without serious danger of war."[27]

There were at this time two major stumbling blocks in the way of McNutt's candidacy. One was Vice President John Nance Garner, who was a real factor to be reckoned with. He showed no interest in McNutt's candidacy. The other was James A. Farley, the Postmaster General, who undoubtedly would be a strong influence in the pre-convention situation. He was frankly and definitely against McNutt. He was quoted as having said that "if McNutt is nominated, it will be over my dead body."[28]

Farley had been opposed to McNutt ever since the Hoosier governor had failed to board the Roosevelt bandwagon at the Chicago Convention in 1932 until the nomination was inevitable. At that time the key to Roosevelt's nomination rested in the three states of Indiana, Ohio, and Illinois. Farley believed that if two of these states, or even one of them, could be induced to vote solidly for Roosevelt, his nomination would be practically assured. Farley had hurried to Indiana for a last-minute pep talk with the Hoosier leaders just before the state convention. He wanted the state's thirty National Convention votes. He urged a delegation pledged to Roosevelt, and promised to reward them in return. He even offered the chairmanship of the committee on permanent organization at the Chicago convention to McNutt, but the latter refused to work for an instructed delegation.[29] As a result, Indiana's vote in the convention was split, and Farley never forgave McNutt for his non-cooperation.

Years later, in referring to the Chicago convention of 1932, Farley said, "I sat down to work. There was much to do. We had to hold our delegates. The opposition was predicting we were about to fold our delegates and steal away. Paul McNutt said the Roosevelt vote was disappointing, otherwise Indiana would have led the bandwagon."[30] After McNutt had given up the governorship in 1937 and Roosevelt was considering him for the Philippine post, Farley attended a testimonial in his, Farley's honor. During the dinner the President, Vice President Garner, and Farley chatted between courses. One exchange involved McNutt and his impending appointment. According to Farley, Roosevelt had said he was not so sure that he would make the appointment, "because McNutt is inclined to be dictatorial in his attitude and he might not be the right fellow to send out there. Maybe he ought to go on the Maritime Commission."[31]

Garner answered: "I don't know him very well, but I know he is a candidate for the Presidency in 1940, and it might not be a bad idea to send him out there." The President smiled thoughtfully. Farley asked, "Do you think the Philippines will be far enough?" The President laughed and answered, "Yes, yes."[32]

Later, in a frank and intimate discussion between Roosevelt and Farley as to the possibilities of various members of the Cabinet and others for the 1940 Presidential nomination, the President asked Farley about McNutt. He replied:

"I think McNutt has a lot of ability, but he's ambitious and we can't be sure of him. I have told you many times before that he prevented you from getting the vote of Indiana in 1932."[33]

In referring to Roosevelt's purges of senators and others for their opposition to his Supreme Court packing scheme, Farley claims that the President asked him what he thought of running McNutt for the Senate against Frederick Van Nuys. Farley said:

"Boss, there's no use going into that again. McNutt was responsible for having the Indiana delegation vote against every Roosevelt proposal in the convention. Why, if he had had his way, you wouldn't be here today."

Roosevelt counseled, "Now, now, Jim, I know Paul is a hot presidential candidate, but so is Tydings [Senator Millard Tydings of Delaware]." Farley replied, "McNutt's a red-hot candidate, but I don't think he can be nominated. He won't have any candidates with him but the Indiana delegation."[34]

On July 6, 1939, McNutt went to see Farley to talk about the number of candidates for 1940 if the President did not run. Farley told him that there was nothing to do until the President made known his intentions around the first of the year. McNutt agreed. A few days later McNutt was named Federal Security Administrator. While the announcement occasioned no little surprise in official circles, it was no surprise to Farley, "because I saw in the move an adroit maneuver to silence Paul's campaign for the nomination. As a member of the President's official family of near-Cabinet rank, he was bound not to campaign unless he had the blessing of the President."[35]

Frank McHale, a Democratic leader from Indiana, wrote Farley in March, 1939, inquiring as to Farley's intentions. He was assuming, he said, that the President would not be a candidate, and he wanted to be the first to advise him of

McNutt's possible candidacy. If Farley were not to be a candidate, McHale assured him that he would be "greatly appreciative of your advice and suggestions and will welcome your friendly attitude toward Paul's candidacy. I am sincerely convinced that all Democrats can support him without sacrifice of their essential principles."[36]

At the same time McHale wrote in a similar vein to Garner:

"I have no authentic information that you will be an opponent of former Governor Paul V. McNutt for the Presidential nomination. If you should be, then I am quite sure that the rivalry will be a friendly one. . . . If you are a candidate, you will grant us, I am sure, a friendly rivalry."[37]

In July Farley had a conference with Roosevelt at Hyde Park, when they discussed presidential possibilities. When he brought up the name of McNutt, the President "slowly turned down the thumb of his right hand."[38]

In December Farley and Secretary Harold Ickes had lunch to talk over the candidacy of McNutt, which was apparently distressing the Secretary, who "could not see McNutt for first place, or for Vice President in the event the President tried for a third term." According to Farley, "Ickes was bitter in his references to McNutt, and held the latter's selection for either place would be 'a terrible thing,' and 'the worst thing in the world that could happen to the country.' "[39]

Shortly afterward, Farley had a half-hour conference with the President. He found him "chuckling over clippings of editorials taking McNutt's presidential candidacy over the jumps." The President observed that "Paul seems to be getting into trouble in a lot of places. He's getting a general razzing around the country." Farley commented "I hate to say 'I told you so,' " to which Roosevelt replied, with a laugh, "Well, he's getting a lot of experience in running, even if he isn't getting any place."[40]

Toward the end of December, Vice President Garner became a candidate for the 1940 nomination. Shortly afterwards, Farley visited Harry Hopkins, Secretary of Commerce, in his Georgetown home. In a jesting way he told Hopkins that he was managing Garner's campaign, but was wondering whether he should shift to McNutt. Hopkins remarked that McNutt was at the bottom of his list, to which Farley replied with a laugh, "You are quite complimentary, because he isn't even on mine." Hopkins thought McNutt "had no business going around telling people he had the Boss's blessing. He hasn't had a kind word."[41]

A week later Farley reported to the President that he had called a meeting of the Democratic National Committee for February 15, 1940, to select a convention site. The President approved. "By the way, Jim," he said, "rumors are reaching me that Senator Wheeler and your friend McNutt are giving the impression that the administration is for their candidacy." Farley countered with "I thought McNutt was your friend." The President laughed and said "Yes, just as close a friend as Burt Wheeler."[42]

Early in 1940, Farley himself became a candidate. Ernest K. Lindley had published an article purporting to be the answer to the third-term riddle. According to Farley, "the article said the President had declared he would not run again unless Britain were overrun by the Nazis, that Cordell Hull was his choice for his successor, that the Vice Presidency lay between Jackson, McNutt, and Wheeler, and, finally, that I was not a sound vice-presidential candidate because of my religion."[43]

In the meantime, the "McNutt-for-President" drive gained momentum. His Indiana friends, especially Frank McHale, who thought Farley was "not unfriendly," were extremely active in his behalf. An intensive mail drive was instituted, with hundreds of letters going out each day to party workers in every state appealing for their support. Practically every person who had been mentioned as a possible candidate for the nomination had been included on the mailing list, including Farley, Garner, Senator Bennett Champ Clark of Missouri, and Senator Wheeler of Montana.[44]

A concerted effort was made to prove that McNutt and the majority of Indiana Democrats were really New Dealers and were not all opposed to Roosevelt's policies. It was felt that such a gesture to the President would be helpful to McNutt's candidacy. The McNutt boosters would prefer to have Roosevelt's support rather than his opposition, although the President had given no indication that he was friendly to McNutt, who had been described as a middle-of-the-road progressive. But the McNutt promoters believed that the Hoosier leader would at least be acceptable, as national standard-bearer, to the President.[45]

However, some of McNutt's friends believed that he would quit the race, if there were any indication that Roosevelt would be a candidate for a third term. This view was expressed by Senator Minton in June, 1939, although McHale refused to share it. "Our whole campaign is based on the assumption President Roosevelt is not going to be a candidate," he said. But "if the President becomes a candidate, we will be for the President, and that includes McNutt." McHale made this statement:

"We have no authentic information that either President Roosevelt or Vice President Garner are actually candidates for the presidential nomination next year. Therefore we are following out the mandate of the Democrats of Indiana as expressed in the platform of their state convention in 1938 wherein they place Paul V. McNutt before the people of the country as a candidate for the nomination for President of the United States in 1940."[46]

Some observers saw in the Minton statement a play to the Roosevelt liberals in order for him to become their candidate in the event Roosevelt ultimately eliminated himself. Others thought it favored a postponement of the McNutt candidacy from 1940 to 1944. In such a case McNutt's friends might have been looking beyond 1940 in seeking Roosevelt's support for their favorite son. At any rate Minton's pronouncement, if it truly expressed the views of McNutt, indicated that the Democratic leaders were ready to align themselves with the Roosevelt liberals as against the Garner conservatives.

Yet there was increasing evidence that Roosevelt was making plans to again be a candidate in 1940. He was faced with the difficulty of implementing some of his domestic policies because of an uncooperative Congress where the conservative wing of the party was particularly strong, and these rebuffs from the Capitol seemed to act as an incentive to Roosevelt to run again, rather than to surrender to the conservatives. Many of his own party had combined with the Republicans in opposition to the New Deal program. The list of New Dealers available for the nomination was being considerably reduced. Even the number of Democratic governors acceptable to the New Deal inner circle had been reduced to nothing.[47]

While McNutt was en route home from the Philippines in June, 1939, he indicated he would not be a candidate should Roosevelt decide to run again. His friends, he said, had begun his campaign for the nomination entirely on the assumption that the President would not be a candidate.[48] He put the race squarely up to Roosevelt, but promised to support the third-term candidacy if Roosevelt decided to run.[49]

This position, however, was bitterly criticized by some of

NcNutt's detractors. Joseph Alsop and Robert Kintner, two of the leading columnists of the day, wrote:

"If cynical opportunism and shameless pushing can capture the Presidency of the United States, then Paul V. McNutt will be the next occupant of the White House. The recent McNutt announcement, that his Indiana organization will go along if the President is a candidate for a third term, is only one more step on the way. Since it is iron-clad as well as malodorous, the NcNutt organization may be expected to fulfill its fuehrer's promise if he really tells it to do so."[50]

The columnists continued:

"The report is that McHale has concentrated on getting second-choice promises from the bosses, presumably on the theory that there will be a deadlocked convention. . . . But McNutt, who looks as though he were born to ride a white horse and was once called the 'Hoosier Hitler' by Norman Thomas, regards himself as a man of destiny. . . . The McNutt people are planning a heavy speaking program for their leader and, between speeches, he will probably assist the over-burdened McHale in the great search for delegates. Possibly, in the end, all this pushing and grabbing will turn out to have been wise. On the whole, however, even the extreme shrinking violet type of candidacy is less unappetizing."[51]

Two other columnists wrote in a similar vein. Drew Pearson and Robert S. Allen charged that "it was not unnatural for McNutt to be the first among the motley crew of Democrats now plodding toward 1940 to make it absolutely clear that he was a candidate for President of the United States. He has never deviated from that goal since." They felt he was wise in being out of the country during the internecine warfare that had been raging within the Democratic Party. The "purge," they believed, never bothered him. He was also wise enough not to stay away too long, only to return "and find the cards stacked against him." He had "carefully timed himself to get home one year before next year's convention, with twelve months in which to corral delegates."[52]

The chief factors that McNutt had to reckon with, according to Pearson and Allen, were Roosevelt and Farley. "Either one could probably spike him," they said. McNutt had frankly asked Roosevelt a year previously for an opinion on his candidacy, they claimed, and his friends reported that Roosevelt replied that he wasn't indicating any preferences for the 1940 nomination. "But," he added, "I am keeping a list of people I'm against. And you're not on that list." Jim Farley, however, would be "a tougher obstacle," in the opinion of the two columnists. "For he does not like McNutt, and makes no bones about it." They concluded with the assertion that Mc-Nutt was "playing a cagey game. Briefly, it is to play ball with all candidates in the hope of being their second choice if they can't make the grade themselves. Naturally, it all depends on whether Roosevelt is in the picture."[53]

Another columnist, Ernest K. Lindley, predicted that Mc-Nutt would have a sizable block of delegates "and probably some second and third choice support from other delegates. His vow of loyalty to his chief and declaration that he will not be a candidate if the President wants a third term has softened the hostility of the New Deal crowd and quickened their curiosity. They are beginning to ask each other whether Mc-Nutt might 'do' if the President doesn't run again and if, as now seems probable, they are unable to nominate anyone from their own intimate circle."[54]

Meanwhile McNutt had virtually admitted his candidacy, although not officially. When asked if the efforts which were being made to bring about his nomination would cease with his appointment to the Federal Security post, he said, "I see no reason for them to stop." The efforts on his behalf were "with my knowledge." He was pleased with reports from his headquarters, but "loyalty has always meant much to me. I am loyal to the man who is my chief." He declared that he was in sympathy with New Deal principles. But he claimed that he had never given any consideration to the possibility of the vice presidency, either with Roosevelt or anyone else.[55]

The Democrats, of course, were running in the dark, until President Roosevelt officially made up his mind whether or not he would be a candidate to succeed himself. There was general belief among McNutt's supporters that only with the assistance and blessing of Roosevelt could any Democrat attain the presidential nomination and election in 1940. This was probably responsible for the flat declaration by McNutt that he would withdraw from the race if the President ran again. This announcement no doubt made McNutt some friends among the New Dealers, but not in the die-hard, anti-third-term Democratic circles. It was the opinion of at least one commentator that "if the President . . . does not become a candidate, Mr. McNutt is one of those aspirants who must be reckoned with. He is not just an 'also ran,' at this stage of the game. He is probably the most attractive candidate personally that has offered himself."[56]

Another columnist evaluated McNutt as follows:

"Paul is no joke. He's got a full face and profile so good it would almost get him a Hollywood rating. And, while that's almost enough these days, he smiles well, can fish if he has to, likes to ride in engine cabs, takes the microphone in stride and would probably be willing to feed hot dogs to a King and Queen. When a man has these qualifications he is a standout in American politics. Find a candidate who is like that and who can also lead a swing orchestra and you have a man who is unbeatable for the presidency."[57]

After McNutt was appointed Federal Security Administrator, Raymond Clapper wrote that this was a break for McNutt. It was a recognition of Roosevelt's "great confidence in him, which is bound to have considerable political meaning read into it, as Mr. Roosevelt out of his long experience

knows." The post was "one of the most important administration assignments in the Government, requiring large executive ability and imaginative talent." It was an "ideal job for
a presidential aspirant, because it reaches out to touch the
American people with many friendly fingers." It was "of more
public importance than most of the Cabinet places and carries
the opportunity to do a large constructive job. No aspirant
for the presidency could have a better springboard than it
offers to demonstrate large-scale executive ability."[58]

It was Clapper's belief that "this development pulls some
of the props from under the widespread belief that Mr. Roosevelt intends to seek a third term, although it does not necessarily eliminate that possibility, because Mr. McNutt is publicly committed to withdraw if the President desires to run.
Meantime it has the effect of bringing him under the Administration wing and keeping him fenced off from outside alliances
with anti-Roosevelt groups. The most natural inference is that
President Roosevelt has decided to give Mr. McNutt some
rope and it is now up to Paul whether he makes it into a
noose or a lariat."[59]

Lyle C. Wilson, writing in the Columbus, Ohio, *Citizen*,
declared that the new Roosevelt-McNutt "alliance" mystified
politicians. He gave as one explanation that Roosevelt was
"reaching out for all the support possible in his forthcoming
contest with the conservative Garner faction." McNutt would
achieve "one of his major objectives—the maintenance of good
relations with the New Deal." He was "aware that any
Democrat who has to fight the Administration for the nomination and then is unable to get Mr. Roosevelt's support in the
campaign would have small chance of election."[60]

This informal alliance between Roosevelt and McNutt, according to Wilson, "would commit neither to anything very
definite and would not demonstrate that the president was

[251]

determined upon a third term. But his minimum demand upon the 1940 convention doubtless will be the nomination of a candidate acceptable to him. It is beginning to appear that McNutt is determined to be in the category of those acceptable to Roosevelt and that the President is content with that arrangement. McNutt also is avoiding a break with the Garner conservatives."[61]

McNutt's appointment continued to be the political sensation of the era. Some observers felt that the Hoosier had been "laid away in lavendar, or at least so effectively taken into camp that no longer was he regarded 'as a thorn in the side of the third termers.' "[62] He was "fully aware of the rich opportunity for adding to his public stature." On the purely personal side, "the pulchritudinous man from Manila has plenty on the ball. He is almost disturbingly good-looking, has a smile and style amazingly like that of Roosevelt, a billion-dollar platform manner and radio voice—and a wife famed throughout Hoosierland for her beauty and charm."[68]

Other observers believed that the appointment now opened the way for McNutt as the Number Two man on the ticket with Roosevelt, through the elimination of Henry Wallace and Harry Hopkins. It was the view of many that such a Roosevelt-McNutt team would be elected in 1940, and McNutt would be in a leading position for 1944.[64] Mark Sullivan, dean of Washington correspondents, admitted that the "ticklish job" now put McNutt's future in Roosevelt's hand. The President "can now almost guarantee whether McNutt will become a leading candidate or a negligible one." Sullivan reported that Roosevelt "criticized the newspapers for seeking a political motive in the appointment," for the fact was that McNutt was chosen "because of his outstanding qualifications for the job." The President, he said, was "irked by newsmen," and insisted that "believe it or not, some things are done without political motive."[65]

An editorial in the Detroit *Free Press*, headed "Oh What a Spot!" said:

"What a lovely spot for a man to be in, if he happens to want to build up a nice well-mannered, well-oiled national campaign machine! Do you wonder why Mr. Roosevelt put him there? If you do, you are not alone. Everybody else does too. And nobody, except the President and the Administrator, knows the precise answer."[66]

Raymond Clapper called the appointment a jolt to the New Dealers, who were upset by the McNutt choice. "Probably not in the entire history of this administration have the New Dealers received such a jolt. . . . The extent and intensity of this feeling can only be suggested because nobody wants to talk for publication." There was "mixed astonishment, bewilderment, and dismay if not despair." He claimed that "some feel betrayed. Others hope that in time some explanation or subsequent development may make the affair seem less foreboding than it appears to them now." Clapper admitted that McNutt was "a very able man," and his opponents "would feel better if he were a fumbler and hang himself." He was viewed even by his enemies as determined and highly competent, "but one whom they distrust."[67]

The Detroit *Free Press* published an editorial on July 29 which characterized the appointment of McNutt as "bad for the country." It described McNutt as "a hardboiled professional politician, anti-labor and pro-jingo, whose only claim to the presidency is his desire for it," who was put in a place "where he can wield tremendous influence over a group of the most important public agencies in the country, and the ones from which politics should be most firmly kept out. Of all the public men in the United States, McNutt is nearly the last to deserve a job like this. What possible political motive could the President have that would justify him in playing ducks and drakes with the Social Security Board and its allied agencies in this way?"[68]

The St. Louis *Post Dispatch* feared that Roosevelt by his appointment of McNutt had "a bear by the tail." If he regarded McNutt "as someone to be killed off, he certainly would not have put him in charge of the Federal Security Agency. . . . That would be disposing of a Captain of Infantry by giving him a Field Marshal's baton." There was no question as to McNutt's gifts "as a politician and as an administrator, but there is little in his career to suggest that he is motivated by anything but burning personal ambition which he has served by ruthless methods—or that he subscribes to anything but a philosophy of force. . . . The probability is that, as far as McNutt is concerned, Mr. Roosevelt will find himself sooner or later in the excruciating dilemma of the man who had a bear by the tail. . . . For there is an atmosphere of Fascism about the ex-Governor of Indiana, the martial outline of a man on horseback to whom it might be dangerous to entrust the 'new instruments of public power' forged during the two Roosevelt administrations."[69]

Shortly after his appointment, McNutt addressed the national convention of Young Democrats at Pittsburgh. Roosevelt had given his approval before the appointment was officially announced, but it was now considered as significant. The non-political subject was listed as "The Liberalization of Youth."[70] But the delegates put on a well-staged demonstration, with a parade and a ten-minute ovation. The banners of nearly a score of states were carried around the convention hall amid terrific din of yelling and shouting. In his speech, McNutt called for the continuance of an active, dynamic "modern liberalism," with the preservation of the people's civil liberties, the correction of abuses "which have threatened our economic and social safety," and a "determination to accelerate and fortify the nation's economic machine." He demanded that the social security system be "strengthened and enlarged."[71]

Following the Pittsburgh address, McNutt made no more public political speeches until just before the 1940 convention. But his supporters were extremely active in his behalf, either for the Presidency if Roosevelt decided not to run, or for the Vice Presidency if he did. Calling McNutt the "Heir Presumptious," Raymond P. Brandt wrote in the Washington *Star* that he was decidedly a candidate "on the make," and he would be a force to be reckoned with at the 1940 convention "whether Roosevelt actively or passively seeks the nomination or is merely content to exercise his power of selection of successor."[72]

As the 1940 convention approached, there were some handicaps which McNutt had to overcome, and not the least of these were some of the labels which were attached to him. One was the name "Boob McNutt," which had originally been used by the cartoonist Rube Goldberg for one of his comic-strip characters. Someone asked McNutt about his feelings in regard to the name, and he simply replied:

"Why, I feel very grateful to Mr. Goldberg. I had never met him until just the other night, and I learned that he had withdrawn the comic strip, after years of profitable existence, because he felt my political opponents might try to capitalize on it."[73]

Another unfortunate label which his enemies used was "dictator." When asked about it, McNutt replied that it was "an old story the Republicans started against me out in Indiana in our last campaign. It always works out that if a man is willing to carry the load and assume the leadership of his party, he is called a dictator. If his party controls the legislature, or the Congress, and follows through with the enactment of his policies, it is called a 'rubber-stamp.' A man has to expect to be called names in public life. He has to take that as part of the game. Not only the man himself but his family. Some of the things his family has to endure are all but insufferable. This very fact prevents many fine, capable men from entering public service. In the end, the most a man can expect is the self-satisfaction of having done a good job for his state or nation."[74]

In spite of these apparent handicaps, Paul McNutt continued to win friends and influence people in behalf of his potential candidacy. Even Raymond Clapper began to give some evidence of his increasing friendliness toward McNutt. He asked the question "what does the McNutt candidacy mean?" and his own answer was that "the Administration has one acceptable alternative, and can no longer stand on the ground that Mr. Roosevelt is the only man available for 1940."[75]

Clapper insisted this was not a blurb for McNutt. "The facts are plain," he said. "I know plenty of people in Washington who are opposed to Mr. McNutt, but none who argued that he is not of Presidential stature. . . . He satisfies the requirement that the candidate be a practical politician with adequate 'it.' . . . His utterances are down the liberal track in conformity with Administration requirements. . . . Whatever others may think of Paul McNutt, the White House will have to do a fast handspring to rule him out as unacceptable, after the build-up it has given him."[76]

In the meantime, the Administration conducted a very thorough investigation in every corner of Indiana to try to determine if there were any evidence of tax evasion or fraud on the part of McNutt. A month after McNutt was appointed

Federal Security Administrator, Washington sent a squad of sixty Internal Revenue agents into the state, and for seven months these investigators toured Indiana with a fine-tooth comb, talking literally to hundreds of people, friends and enemies of McNutt, asking them for proof of irregularities. They went into every town where he had made a speech as governor to see if he had accepted speaking fees which were not reported on his income tax. In the little town of Rising Sun, where McNutt, while governor, had dedicated a civic building, they asked the judge who handled the ceremony if the governor had been paid for the speech. The judge made an affidavit saying that not only had no fee been paid but that Governor McNutt would have been insulted if one had been offered.

There were all sorts of ugly but unfounded rumors in connection with the investigation and the newspapers devoted much space to it. American Legion records were scrutinized and the contents of McNutt's private safe box, the key of which he had voluntarily given the revenue agents, were examined. The agents even questioned McNutt's insurance broker to ascertain how much McNutt was paying in life insurance premiums.

The Roosevelt administration remained silent about the investigation and further silence on the part of Washington officials was inexcusable as a matter of common decency. Clapper called the investigation a method of crucifying McNutt, and he deplored the "despicable tactics" use in this "slow-motion political assassination."[77]

Ernest K. Lindley also bitterly assailed what he called "the McNutt Inquisition." Whether it was planned as "a smearing exercise" or not, the highly publicized Federal income tax investigation of McNutt and his Hoosier political aides "is about the most merciless job on record of smearing a

Presidential candidate," he charged. "The reputation of a penniless saint could not survive this kind of inquisition." Lindley believed that McNutt's personal finances had received "such an X-raying as probably no other Presidential candidate has ever had to endure." McNutt's friends were confident, he said, "that nothing can be found—because there is nothing to be found—to reflect upon his financial integrity." He concluded that even some of his bitterest enemies in Indiana "would be flabbergasted if anything were uncovered to indicate that McNutt had been in politics for money."[78]

An editorial in the Indianapolis *Times* declared:

"Whether you do or don't like Mr. McNutt as an individual or as a Presidential candidate, you can hardly fail to agree that he is getting a dirty deal. . . . If internal revenue agents can be used in this way to accomplish the political ruin of Paul McNutt, they can be used to punish any citizen the Administration does not like. And the evidence is plentiful that they have been so used."[79]

While the investigations were nearing their end without any proof of irregularities, the McNutt band wagon was rolling along under the auspices of a widespread organization with eastern headquarters at Eighty Broadway, New York City. Oscar R. Ewing, a native Hoosier, was the eastern manager. On March 16, 1940, the organization reproduced and sent out articles favoring McNutt's candidacy. One of these articles, written by Frederic William Wile, appeared in the Washington *Star* for March 4. "If Roosevelt puts away the crown, McNutt is the best Democratic bet. His other elements of eligibility aside, and they're neither few nor unimpressive, pivotal Indiana's entry is the only Democrat seriously in the running, with his party's traditional gubernatorial background as a prerequisite to the presidential nomination. . . . It is the fashion of the hour, inspired mainly by ultra-New Dealers and overzealous third-termites, to scoff at McNutt's chances. That is mostly wishful thinking. He is very much in the running and insiders know it."[80]

Another article, written by G. Gould Lincoln in the Washington *Star*, claimed that the McNutt supporters "have become increasingly active. They have what amounts to a national organization in the field—skipping states only which have favorite son candidates for the Democratic presidential nomination, as, for example, Texas, Tennessee, and New York. Far from dropping the McNutt campaign, . . . the McNutt managers are combing the country for delegates to the Democratic National Convention . . . pledged to McNutt for second choice to Roosevelt. In other words, the McNutt managers are saying again and again 'Paul McNutt will not run if the President is a candidate, but if he is not, and we believe the President will not seek a third term, then promise to vote for McNutt.' "[81]

According to Gould, the McNutt managers claimed they were getting many promises of delegates on this basis. If Roosevelt were out of the race, McNutt was the only real candidate. They would not be diverted to any other candidate, even if he were to have the backing of Roosevelt himself. Of course the McNutt forces hoped the President would in the end give his support to McNutt. Gould believed that "no other Democratic aspirant for the Democratic presidential nomination has so wide-spread an organization as that now working for McNutt—not even Vice President Garner, nor Farley. Hull none whatever. Wheeler very little."[82]

During the next three months, nevertheless, the world situation had become so critical that the feeling was increasing that Roosevelt was considering himself indispensable, and would therefore seek a third term, in spite of heavy opposition even within his own party. Yet he had made no public statement as to his intentions. Most of the potential candidates for the nomination were waiting impatiently for him to declare himself one way or the other.

Early in May, McNutt took a three-week leave of absence with the approval of President Roosevelt. His speaking tour covered states from Michigan to California. He discussed not only the welfare programs under the Federal Security Administration, but also political questions which were expected to figure in the national presidential campaign. He later made a short tour through the Deep South. On these two trips he visited only states which did not have favorite-son candidates. On more than one occasion he declared that his own candidacy was predicated on the condition that President Roosevelt would not be a candidate for a third term. He reiterated his previous statement that if the President ran, he would support him.

Meanwhile the President had become increasingly interested in the 1940 convention, and he apparently saw his possible successor in every man of any consequence in the country. Rather than grooming someone for the nomination, as the time approached he became more and more critical of these would-be candidates. According to Farley, Roosevelt could not see Garner under any circumstances—"he was too conservative." He didn't want Hull because he was too slow—"thought things over too long." He could not have Farley because Farley was a Catholic and that would not be wise. Because of all this, in 1939 Farley wrote in his diary:

"I am satisfied in my own mind that the President will not be a candidate for reelection, but *might be willing to listen to argument*. I don't know if he has anyone in mind definitely to succeed him. If he had to make a selection at the moment I believe he would select Harry Hopkins, Robert Jackson, or Frank Murphy in the order named."[83]

Farley's maneuvers in the months preceding the convention are interesting. While it is doubtful he had any idea that he could be nominated for the presidency, he did have some hopes that he could secure the second spot on the ticket. As early as 1939 he had written:

"There isn't any doubt in my mind if I assist in bringing about Garner's or Hull's nomination, I can have second place with either man if I want it."

It was his opinion that "the leaders of the party with few exceptions do not want Roosevelt to run for a third term." They were "sick of Wallace, Hopkins, Corcoran and the rest and did not relish the idea of a bitter campaign defending a third term candidacy." Farley noted that Roosevelt was irritated whenever certain names were mentioned as his successor. The President was angry that McNutt should even permit his name to be discussed for the presidency, and called it bad taste for a member of his administration to place himself in this position, unless he resigned.[84]

In June, 1939, Garner told Farley that under no circumstances would he support a third term. Farley agreed and confided: "The two of us can pull together to stop Roosevelt."

Soon afterwards Roosevelt invited Farley to Hyde Park to discuss the 1940 campaign and potential candidates. Roosevelt mentioned the third term, and in a low voice said, "I am going to tell you something I have never told another living soul. Of course I will not run for a third term, but I don't want you to pass this on to anyone because it would make my position difficult if the fact were known prematurely." Farley agreed to remain silent. The President then asked Farley to choose a candidate who was sympathetic with the New Deal program. But it is questionable that Farley believed Roosevelt was really telling the truth about his intentions.[85]

As the war in Europe spread, Roosevelt was becoming

more convinced that he should seek a third term. At a dinner party at the White House, he said to Farley's wife that he was having a terrible time because people were trying to make him run and he didn't want to. She replied, "Well, you're the President, aren't you? All you have to do is to tell them you won't run." He looked very much surprised and turned away. From then on Farley knew Roosevelt would run again, even though he was laying his plans for a "draft."

According to John F. Flynn, "the whole story is a chapter of duplicity, in which Roosevelt, who had definitely decided to run if he could make it, was putting on before Farley the pose that he didn't want to run, . . . while all the New Deal agents, with his full knowledge and approval, were scouring the country for delegates and Roosevelt was using every artifice and pressure he could command to kill off every possible contender for the nomination. Saved now by the war from the disaster which overtook his administration in 1938 . . . he could now rise out of the ashes of a mere New Deal leader to become a modern St. Michael brandishing his sword against Hitler and all the forces of evil throughout the world."[86]

On May 31, McNutt officially dropped out of the presidential race, and appealed to the country to draft Roosevelt for a third term. "It is my sincere hope," he stated, "that he will accept the renomination for the Presidency." As to the matter of the no-third-term precedent, it "becomes insignificant in view of the danger to our security, and the hopes or desires of any individual must be subordinated to the national interests," he said. He felt there were "able men in both parties who are capable of directing the affairs of the nation under ordinary circumstances. But the emergency which faces us is so critical that it requires the strong leadership, and wealth of experience in world affairs, that the President alone can provide."[87]

"At every cost," McNutt continued, "America must maintain a unity and solidarity which will enable us to throw our entire strength into the task of preparing to face a hostile world. The country is behind the President and his foreign policy. It believes that in his leadership lies the best hope of peace. I am confident that I express the sentiment of a large majority of our citizens in saying that I want Franklin Roosevelt as the next President of the United States."[88]

Thus the McNutt-for-President drive came to an end. McNutt now considered himself in front-running for the vice presidential nomination, although the field was crowded with no less than a score of contenders. And any man who sought the nomination would have to secure the approval of Roosevelt himself. Those who were being considered included Hull, Garner, Jesse Jones, James Byrnes, William O. Douglas, Robert H. Jackson, Louis Johnson, Sam Rayburn, Scott Lucas, Speaker Bankhead, Henry Wallace, and McNutt. Bankhead was finally discarded by Roosevelt because he was too old and in poor health, as was Jones.[89]

In a conference with Farley at Hyde Park on July 7, Roosevelt said flatly that he would not take Garner or Rayburn, and he summarily disposed of Byrnes. After the President's reference to Byrnes, Farley said facetiously that he had a nominee for him in McNutt "which moved him to laughter and the exclamation, 'We did a good job by bringing him into the administration, didn't we?' "[90]

In his memoirs, Farley reported a telephone conversation which he had with Roosevelt over who should be nominated. The President said he was for Wallace, but Farley claims he tried to get him to accept Bankhead or Barkley or Jones. Farley was opposed to Wallace, but Roosevelt said, "I am committed." When Farley suggested "Why not Paul McNutt?" Roosevelt laughed and replied: "Apparently you still have your sense of humor." And Farley answered, "If I ever lost that, there will be no point to my being around the convention."[91]

The major question in the minds of most of the delegates on the eve of the Democratic National convention in Chicago was who would be nominated to succeed Roosevelt, but some of the leading delegates felt certain that Roosevelt would be nominated for a third term. The prologue to this event was supplied by the European situation, and Roosevelt had well-laid plans to be "drafted." Although he apparently had not confided fully in many of his closest political friends, several of them, including Ickes, Hopkins, Wallace, and Jackson were a part of the inner White House circle and they had been carrying on a behind-the-scenes campaign "without hindrance from the President and knew, without being told, that they were operating in accordance with his wishes."[92]

According to Flynn, Roosevelt had declared as early as August, 1939, at a meeting of the Young Democrats that "if the nominee were a conservative or one who just gave lip-service to the New Deal," Roosevelt "could not offer active support to the ticket and indicated what kind of candidate he would support."[93] Arthur Krock in the New York *Times* said "his description of the ideal candidate seemed like a self-portrait." And soon after that, Mayor Kelly of Chicago told the same group "they must not take 'no' from Roosevelt."[94] By December, 1939, Vice President Garner was convinced that Roosevelt would be a candidate. Garner was unalterably opposed to a third term and declared his own candidacy as a public protest.

When Farley visited Roosevelt at Hyde Park two weeks before the convention, he was greeted by the President's mother, who said she was upset at the report Farley was resigning as national committee chairman to go into business.

"You know," she said, "I would hate to think of Franklin running for the presidency if you were not around. I would like you to be sure to help my boy." The President's wife also met Farley and said she was shocked at the thought of his not directing the campaign for her husband. Apparently Roosevelt's own household believed he would be the candidate.[95]

Flynn claims that after luncheon, Roosevelt explained to Farley why he had failed earlier to declare he would not be a candidate. The reason he gave was that to have done so "would have nullified his position in the world and handicapped the efforts of this country to be of constructive service in the world crisis." Probably Roosevelt was putting on a carefully studied act with Farley. The President "shook his head dolefully" and said: "I still don't want to run for the Presidency." He repeated, *I don't want to run, and I am going to tell the convention so.*"[96]

Roosevelt then suggested to Farley several ways in which he would do this, but Farley told him that by waiting so long he had "killed off every other candidate and that the leaders were afraid to be against him lest they suffer punishment and that if he didn't want to run he should do what General Sherman did many years ago—issue a statement saying: 'I will not run if nominated and will not serve if elected.'"

Roosevelt was not prepared for this reply. "He fell into a reverie for a moment, explained to Farley that if nominated and elected he could not in these times refuse to take the inaugural oath even if he knew he would be dead in thirty days. That ended the subject so far as Farley was concerned. He knew that Roosevelt was going to be nominated and run."[97]

Miss Frances Perkins, Secretary of Labor, was never sure just when the President decided to run. She claimed, however, that those responsible for the campaign knew around March or April that he would be willing "if it could be han-

dled properly" but they were pledged to absolute secrecy.
Harry Hopkins had been selected to take charge of Roosevelt's headquarters and "to make all the decisions in Chicago
and have a private wire to the White House." Cordell Hull in
his *Memoirs* states that Roosevelt, during all this time, had
been urging him to run for the presidency, but Hull had insisted that he did not want it.[98] These were the same tactics
which Roosevelt had used with McNutt. While he kept urging McNutt to run, at the same time Roosevelt was planning
to seek a third term.[99]

In a somewhat sombre mood, the Democratic National
Convention opened in Chicago on July 15. Vice President
John Garner had refused to attend. Most of the delegates
were mere pawns in the hands of the leaders, who themselves were puppets acting at the President's command, and
who did not know what was transpiring. Edward J. Flynn,
who succeeded Farley as national chairman, declared that the
convention "was not a cheerful gathering," and that the political leaders "thought a mistake was being made, that never
before had the third-term issue really been brought to a test.
. . . I think it is only fair to say that the majority of the delegates in Chicago were not enthusiastic for the renomination
of the President."[100]

Frank McHale gives some very interesting personal observations about the 1940 convention. He claims that Farley,
who was then national chairman, had by this time broken
with Roosevelt, and had become a candidate himself for the
Presidency of the United States. He had covered some twenty-
eight states in his travels. McHale had visited about thirty-
one in behalf of McNutt. In the presence of Frank McKinney
in the Biltmore Hotel in New York City, he had told Farley
as he had told McNutt in summation of his observations
and conclusions after traveling over the country that in his

opinion when they went to Chicago that President Roosevelt could stand on one side of the street and Farley, Garner, McNutt, Byrd, and other would-be candidates and leaders of the Democratic Party could stand on the other side of the street and Roosevelt could say to the delegates as they came in, "Those who want to vote with me come on this side," and McHale said the result would be that "we would be standing over there by ourselves with just a few friends around"; that as far as he was concerned, the President was bigger than the party.

McHale had observed one thing about the delegates coming to the convention. Although they respected Roosevelt, and his leadership ability had a great appeal to them, they would not let him name the crown prince, and particularly they would not permit him to name Harry Hopkins, Wallace, or Senator Byrnes, and that the delegates wanted to express themselves and have somebody in there who was speaking for the Democratic Party and who would have the Democratic organization in mind.

Farley tried to tell McHale that his thinking was absurd, that he had the organization and that he had made Roosevelt. McHale smiled and told Farley that "if it had not been for Roosevelt, Farley would still be the fight commissioner of the State of New York, and the nation would never have heard of him and that he had reflected glory by reason of his association." What McHale had said proved true at the convention.[101]

Harry Hopkins, who was Roosevelt's campaign manager, was very much in evidence. He was in constant communication with the President and reported to him by direct wire every move made in the convention. His headquarters were in Suite 3089 of the Blackstone Hotel, with a private line to the White House. This telephone was in the bathroom, the only place where privacy could be assured![102] Senator Alben Barkley, who was named permanent chairman of the convention, concluded his speech with the announcement:

"And now, my friends, I have an additional statement to make on behalf of the President of the United States. . . . The President has never had and has not today any desire or purpose to continue in the office of the President, to be a candidate for that office or to be nominated by the convention for that office. He [the President] wishes in all earnestness and sincerity to make it clear that all the delegates to this convention are free to vote for any candidate."[103]

There was no mention of the President's not being willing to run, or asking the delegates to select another candidate and thereby taking himself out of the contest. Barkley's meaning was obviously clear. Roosevelt was in the race for the nomination.

Mrs. Roosevelt claims that she had never questioned the President about his political intentions. The very fact that she "had never wanted him to be in Washington" made her doubly careful not to intimate that she had "the slightest preference concerning his decision on the subject." Many people around him worried, she wrote, "some because they were afraid he would run, others because they were afraid he wouldn't; and the atmosphere as they came and went was sometimes tense. People on both sides came to me about it, but I refused to say anything, for a man is entitled to plan his own life, particularly in matters as serious as this."[104]

"I had . . . every evidence to believe that he did not want to run again," Mrs. Roosevelt continues. "However, as time went on, more and more people came to me saying that he must run, that the threat of war was just over the horizon and no one else who might be nominated and elected had the prestige and the knowledge to carry on through a crisis."

She had been deeply troubled by the fact that "I saw no one actually being prepared to take Franklin's place, and on several occasions I asked him if he did not think he should make a definite effort to prepare someone. Franklin always smiled and said he thought people had to prepare themselves, that all he could do was to give them opportunities and see how they worked out." She felt that "he, without intending to do so, dominated the people around him and so long as he was in the picture, it was very hard for anyone else to rise to a position of prominence. Finally, however, I came to realize that, after all, this was something that people had had to do many times before and that no man could hand another more than opportunity."

Mrs. Roosevelt explained, however, that she "did not mean that Franklin did not think seriously about a successor, for he did, fully agreeing that anyone had a right to aspire to the office of president." In spite of Harry Hopkins' bad health, "Franklin encouraged his ambitions till his illness proved too great a barrier. I think he finally decided that Secretary Hull would be the wisest choice. In domestic matters they had not always agreed; but the future, it seemed, would take knowledge of and experience in foreign affairs, and here Mr. Hull was preeminent. Besides, he knew Congress, and people respected his character and integrity.

"I heard many other people discussed as possible candidates, their virtues and failings clearly set forth—not always by my husband—but as the time for the convention drew nearer, I could see that it was going to be extremely difficult to have anyone else nominated. First, the Democratic party had not found anyone else it thought could keep it in office, and second, serious-minded people were worried about the war."

Before the convention actually opened, said Mrs. Roosevelt, "it was evident that Franklin was going to be nominated and would run; I think he had been persuaded that if he were nominated, he could not refuse. I believe he did not honestly want the nomination. If he had not been nominated, he would have been completely satisfied and would have lived his life very happily; and yet when you are in the center of world affairs, there is something so fascinating about it that you can hardly see how you are going to live any other way. In his mind, I think, there was a great seesaw on one end, the weariness which had already begun, and the desire to be at home and his own master; on the other end, the overwhelming interest which was the culmination of a lifetime of preparation and work, and the desire to see and to have a hand in the affairs of the world in that critical period."

Finally Mrs. Roosevelt said to the President: "You have made up your mind you will not go to the convention even if you are nominated but that you will speak over the radio, and that means, I hope, I do not have to go?" Roosevelt replied very firmly that it was his definite intention that neither of them should go. Mrs. Roosevelt told him in that case she would go to Hyde Park "and stay at my cottage and get the big house ready so that when the convention was over, he could come up for a time."[105]

Roosevelt's personal disinclination to be a third-term candidate was also mentioned by Robert E. Sherwood in his *Roosevelt and Hopkins: An Intimate History*. He speaks also of Mrs. Roosevelt's "strong opposition" to a third term. According to Sherwood, Roosevelt had told Hopkins "that there were financial reasons for his wish to return to private life—that his mother was digging into capital to keep the place at Hyde Park going."[106]

Various descriptions have been given as to how the Roosevelt managers manipulated the convention. As reported by John Flynn:

"Ed Kelly had been entrusted with the job of managing the demonstrations. On the floor . . . over the heads of each delegation, stood the standards of the states with the states' names on them. Kelly had prepared a collection of duplicate standards and a bunch of choice spirits, well-muscled, from the stockyards and other districts of Chicago, were mobilized off in the shadows. Loud speakers were distributed around the hall, the wires of which led down into the bowels of the Chicago Stadium under the earth where there was stationed Chicago's Commissioner of Sewers. As Barkley finished the message, it took a moment for the delegates to get it, but only a moment. In that moment, the Voice of the Sewers went into action and from out of the loud speakers all over the floor burst the voice 'We Want Roosevelt.' It continued: 'Pennsylvania Wants Roosevelt! Virginia Wants Roosevelt! New York Wants Roosevelt! Massachusetts Wants Roosevelt!' and so on through the states. And as the Voice boomed, the goons emerged from the shadows with the fake standards of the states and began parading around the hall. The delegates, now shouting and cheering, fell in, except certain delegations which resented the appearance of the fraudulent standards of their own states marching around the floor. A number of fights were set off as attempts were made to grab these standards, but the marching goons with their spurious banners started filing by the platform in front of the smiling Senator Barkley who had really just nominated Roosevelt for the presidency, and as each standard went by, Barkley leaned over and kissed it. It was really all over then and the delegates, by their quick translation of Roosevelt's false declaimer, registered their understanding of the man perfectly.

"The next problem confronting the managers of the 'draft' was how to put it over. They didn't want to have Roosevelt formally nominated. That might present him with the necessity of refusing. Their first scheme was to have some delegate rise on the first roll-call, when Alabama was called, and move to dispense with the roll-call and nominate Roosevelt by acclamation. But Farley ruled that out on the ground that it would be a violation of the rules and furthermore, looking rather significantly at the proposers, he said 'If you do that it won't be necessary to have an election.' Various other plans were suggested. Finally they were compelled to have a formal nomination which was made by Senator Lister Hill of Alabama.

". . . Farley . . . went through to the bitter end. He was nominated by Carter Glass, now a venerable patriarch of the party, who was hooted and booted [sic] as he made the nominating speech. Ed Flynn had tried to get Farley to withdraw. Farley refused. He said: 'Don't get the impression that I am running for the presidency. Everyone knows the President has the votes but what they are trying to do is to put on an act to make it appear to the world that this is a unanimous draft. I am determined to let the people know I am opposed to a third term and this is the only way I can do it.' "[107]

As a result of all this maneuvering Roosevelt was nominated on July 17 without any serious opposition. He received 946½ votes on the roll-call ballot, while Farley was given 72½, Garner 61, Tydings 9½, and Hull 6. At the end of the roll-call, before the vote was announced, Farley moved to make it unanimous. And so the President was "drafted" by the Democrats.

Then came the real fireworks of the convention—the nomination of the vice presidential candidate. As has been pointed out previously, there were a number of possibilities, such as Senator Bankhead, Speaker Rayburn, Jesse Jones, Paul McNutt, and many others. Each felt that if this were an "open" convention, he might have a chance, but their hopes were soon dashed.

Just before Frances Perkins, the Secretary of Labor, left Washington for Chicago, she had discussed possible candidates with Roosevelt, who registered his disapproval of each. When she asked him if he thought Henry Wallace would be acceptable, he said it was his belief that Wallace would strengthen the ticket, and as he was not an isolationist he would be a good man if anything happened to the President during the European crisis.[108] When Miss Perkins arrived at the convention, however, she found that nobody knew who Roosevelt wanted on the ticket with him, and the contest became pretty bitter. The delegates were in a black mood and the feeling was sour, she claims. Bob Allen, of the columnist team of Pearson and Allen, came to her in great excitement to say that the situation was terrible. "It will end in a terrific rise of Roosevelt haters," Allen said, and he wanted her to call Roosevelt and urge him to come to Chicago.[109]

When Miss Perkins called Roosevelt and told him about the bitterness, the confusion, and the near fights, she urged him to come to Chicago and use his personal influence by addressing the delegates personally. But he refused, and suggested Mrs. Roosevelt should go in his place, which she did. Miss Perkins urged Roosevelt to make up his mind about his vice-presidential choice and thus settle the controversy. When he asked her about Wallace she said she saw no signs of a Wallace campaign. After some hesitation the President then told her:

"Yes, I think it had better be Wallace. I think I'll stick to that."

He then told her to pass the word to Harry Hopkins. When Hopkins got the news he was surprised and called the President for verification, and then announced to the press that Wallace was the President's choice.[110]

Mrs. Roosevelt gave a rather vivid description of her part in the convention. When the proceedings began, she was at Hyde Park. "Life was going very placidly," she wrote, "when suddenly one day the telephone rang. Frances Perkins was on the wire. She said:

'Things look black here; the temper of the convention is very ugly. The President should come to Chicago if he wants

Mr. Wallace nominated; but if he won't come, I think you should come.'

"I told her I thought it utter nonsense for me to go, but I thought she ought to tell my husband her feeling and that he ought to go if anyone went. I felt there was nothing I could do. Miss Perkins rang off, saying she would talk to Franklin. When she called him, he told her he was not going to the convention, but that if he were nominated he wanted Henry Wallace as his running mate."[111]

According to Mrs. Roosevelt, Frances Perkins called her again the next day and told her that the President had indicated he would be quite willing to have his wife go to the convention if Miss Perkins "felt it was essential." Mrs. Roosevelt replied to Miss Perkins, "Franklin may be willing, but how do I know how Jim Farley feels about it? I certainly am not going out there unless he invites me. I know there is bad feeling because Harry Hopkins has been more or less running things and perhaps has not been very tactful, and I am not going to add to the hard feelings."

Miss Perkins then wanted to know whether Mrs. Roosevelt would go if Farley asked her to, and she replied, "I should have to ask my husband first." When Miss Perkins finished talking, Mrs. Roosevelt called the President and reported the conversation and asked what he wanted her to do. He said:

"It might be very nice for you to go, but I do not think it is in the least necessary."

She then asked him:

"If Jim Farley asks me to go, do you think it would be wise?"

The President replied:

"Yes, I think it would be."

Mrs. Roosevelt then waited, and later in the morning the

telephone rang and Jim Farley asked her to come to the convention.[112]

Mrs. Roosevelt was met at the airport by Farley, and they drove into Chicago alone. En route he told her that the President had not talked to him since the convention opened and had never told him who was his choice for vice president. She was "horrified to realize that things had come to this pass between these two men, because I always had a feeling of real friendship for Jim Farley. I listened while he told me why he thought that Jesse Jones or William B. Bankhead or Paul McNutt, or some other candidates, should get the nomination."

Farley was advised by Mrs. Roosevelt that before anything happened, he should talk to her husband. She then went directly to the hotel where Farley had his offices and called her husband and told him what Farley had said. She also told him she had just learned he had not talked to Farley and suggested he do so and tell him how he felt. Farley then telephoned the President, who told him Wallace was the person he wanted on the ticket with him. Farley argued with him "rather half-heartedly," but Roosevelt insisted on Wallace. Mrs. Roosevelt believed that the President "evidently felt at that time that Wallace could be trusted to carry out our policies on foreign affairs if by chance he, Wallace, found himself hurled into the presidency. Franklin's feeling then was so strong that he was willing to insist on his running mate and thereby give him a chance to prove his ability." It was then that Farley told Roosevelt:

"You're the boss. If you say so I will do all I can to nominate Wallace, but I will have to work fast."

Farley then turned to Mrs. Roosevelt and said he would have to get hold of Elliott Roosevelt, because he was about to second the nomination of Jesse Jones; "that Paul McNutt was strong, too," and they would have to get to Convention Hall as quickly as possible. They drove there and Mrs. Roosevelt went to her seat immediately, "got hold of Franklin, junior, and told him to find Elliott, because I was most anxious that he should not nominate anyone and so appear to be in opposition to his father's desires. Elliott came over and we talked for a minute; and I found that Jim Farley had already reached him with the information, so he did no nominating."[113]

According to James F. Byrnes, President Roosevelt had told him shortly after his nomination that Harry Hopkins had been conferring with labor leaders, especially Philip Murray of the CIO and William Green of the AFL, both of whom favored Henry Wallace for the vice presidential nomination. Byrnes had expressed doubt about the wisdom of this decision, and again urged that Hull or Barkley be selected instead. But the President was certain Wallace was his choice, as this would ensure the support of labor and the farmers. Byrnes finally yielded to the President's demand, and reluctantly said he would go along with Wallace. He requested Roosevelt to delay making his choice known until he, Byrnes, had conveyed the decision to the committee. The members of the committee were not very enthusiastic about Wallace, but agreed to accept him if the President could not be dissuaded.[114]

After reporting back to the President, Byrnes said he went to his room, "worn out by the long hours in conference with the Platform Committee." His rest was cut very short, "because some of the delegates were immediately up in arms when they learned of Mr. Roosevelt's preference for Wallace. Speaker Bankhead, who had been a more or less active candidate, began to receive additional pledges of support. Paul McNutt was being urged to get into the race." Byrnes was kept busy refusing to allow delegates from various states to place his name in nomination. By the time the convention was called to order that evening, the insurrection against Wallace was so great that Byrnes "telephoned the President again to inform him that there would be several nominations and a real fight." The President replied that he had already received similar reports. He was seriously offended, he said, and declared that "traditionally the nominee for Vice President had been named by the nominee for President; and that if there was such a lack of confidence in him that Wallace was rejected, he would not accept the nomination for President." Roosevelt told Byrnes that he could so inform the delegates.[115]

As soon as the delegates heard Roosevelt's decision on Wallace, bedlam broke loose. Flynn reports the reaction of some of the leaders of the convention:

"Ickes said it was a damned outrage. Jesse Jones was sore. The other candidates were indignant. The delegates didn't want Wallace and they were ugly about it. Ed Kelly called the White House and urged the nomination of Byrnes but the President objected. A lot of the leaders wanted to fight it out but one by one the candidates withdrew in disgust. As Wallace was nominated, the delegates booed and booed every time his name was mentioned. Ed Flynn took the floor and told the delegates that the President wanted Wallace. Senator Lucas said the same thing in a speech and both were greeted with boos."[116]

When Mrs. Roosevelt arrived at the convention, she was introduced by Farley. She made a gracious speech to the delegates, who received her with respect. But she privately agreed that the nomination of Wallace was a mistake. Elliott Roosevelt also appeared at the convention and voiced his opposition to Wallace, telling Farley he preferred Jones. Mrs. Roosevelt telephoned the President and told him she agreed with Farley that Wallace "just won't do." Roosevelt then asked that Farley be put on the phone, and told him:

"I've given my word to Wallace. What do you do when you give your word?"

Farley answered:

"I keep it."[117]

The convention was now in a state of pandemonium, if not on the edge of rebellion. Roosevelt had not yet given his word whether he would "consent" to be "drafted," although he was already preparing the draft of the speech he would deliver over the radio accepting the nomination. The White House announced that he would not make any statement or deliver any address until after the vice presidential candidate had been chosen.[118]

Then the convention proceeded to ballot for the vice presidential nominee. The floor and the galleries were in an uproar, with both delegates and spectators adding to the confusion. It was virtually impossible for order to be maintained; boos and catcalls almost drowned out the pleas from the rostrum. The hall was filled with people having either fake tickets, or none at all. One by one the leading contenders were nominated, including Wallace, Bankhead, McNutt, Farley, Lucas, Jones, and Barkley.

While the seconding speeches were being made, Byrnes went to the floor to visit delegation leaders to whom he repeated Roosevelt's statement. Many of these leaders were opposed to Wallace, and there was considerable doubt regarding their support of him.[119]

McNutt appeared to be the people's choice. His managers claimed that he had promises of enough votes to bring about his nomination, probably on the second ballot. He had received the assurances of Harry Hopkins that on any list of acceptable running mates which the President might submit, his name would be included. But word finally reached Mc-Nutt that the President was requesting him to step aside in favor of Wallace. He was called to Hopkins' suite at the Blackstone Hotel and informed of the President's decision, and was asked to second Wallace's nomination. McNutt telephoned the White House, and when he was satisfied that this was the President's wish, he acquiesced. McNutt's supporters were furious, and felt that they had better than an even chance to nominate their man, even in the face of the President's request for nomination of Wallace. McNutt remained adamant, and begged them to help him make good his pledge to support Wallace. His Indiana friends finally and reluctantly accepted his decision, which was a most difficult one for McNutt to make. Yet he had previously gone on record that he would abide by the President's wishes, and he was a man who refused to go back on his promise.[120]

Some of McNutt's friends in other states, however, refused to withdraw their support, and his name was placed in nomination. The hall immediately was rocked with a tremendous burst of applause which was the first that could be recognized as spontaneous. The ovation which McNutt received when he strode forward to the rostrum, shaking his head firmly after he had been presented by Oklahoma, to withdraw his name and second that of Wallace, was the heartiest and most spontaneous of the convention. The demonstration went forward under its own enthusiasm, without the aid of the organ and bands, in spite of the efforts of the chairman and McNutt himself to stop the demonstration. Finally McNutt, after considerable difficulty, was introduced to the audience. This was a signal for renewed and greater cheering. He wanted the opportunity of withdrawing his name, but the audience refused to let him speak, and implored him to remain in the race.

The demonstration continued for several more minutes. At last the chairman was able to quiet the convention with a plea to hear McNutt, reminding the audience that the entire nation was listening by radio. Standing at the lectern, tall and bronzed, with the perspiration streaming over his handsome features, McNutt started to address the convention. He was immediately interrupted by renewed cheering and shouts, whistling, and ringing of bells. This continued for twenty minutes, until finally the audience had become sufficiently quiet for him to announce that he would withdraw from the race. The sentence declaring his intention was all but lost in the din of objection that was raised.

Finally a semblance of quiet was obtained and McNutt spoke:

"I want to express my eternal gratitude for the thousands of true and loyal friends who have accorded me such loyal support. I would be ungrateful were I not to give some expression of appreciation. The state of Indiana, from whence I am proud to come, believes our party is destined to be the vehicle by which the processes of liberal government are to be preserved. In taking that responsibility, it is, above everything, necessary that we remain a united party. Our party stands on the record of the last seven years. It goes to the people under the leadership of the greatest peacetime President in the history of the nation.[121]

"America needs strong, logical, liberal and stable leaders in the kind of world in which we live today," he said. "We cannot take chances now. A nation gets only one chance these days. If it makes a mistake it is lost. We must have leaders who will keep this country safe and free. We have such a leader in Franklin Delano Roosevelt. He is my Commander-in-Chief. I follow his wishes, and I am here to support his choice for Vice President of the United States. . . . I therefore ask emphatically that my name be withdrawn and I pledge my enthusiastic support to the nominee who is being selected on this historic occasion."

Mrs. Roosevelt rose and shook hands with McNutt as he withdrew.[122] The crowd yelled its disapproval of McNutt's statement, as he gravely nodded his head and went to the rear of the jammed platform.[123] The day was his forty-ninth birthday.

McNutt and his managers were confident that he would have been nominated for vice president if there had been no interference from the White House. Commenting on his action earlier in the day in releasing his delegates as soon as the presidential wish was made known, McNutt said:

"And I had the votes to be nominated on the second ballot."[124]

When Frank McHale sent word to various state delegations releasing their votes, gloom spread over the palatial Indiana-McNutt headquarters in the Boulevard Room of the Stevens Hotel which was gaily decorated with flags, streamers, and huge pictures. The room was just inside the Michigan Boulevard entrance of the hotel. It contained over 8,000 square feet of floor space reached by one easy flight of stairs from the lobby. Its ceilings were thirty feet high. These were the largest and most impressive headquarters of any delegation. The room was dominated by a huge portrait of Roosevelt, sixteen by twenty-four feet, the largest in Chicago.[125]

One leader referred to the treatment of McNutt by Roosevelt as "cruel." Privately it was now admitted that McNutt was given the Social Security job to bottle him up. Had he made an independent campaign, some of the Hoosiers believed he could have obtained enough votes to even block a third-term nomination for Roosevelt. There was special resentment because the President had permitted McNutt and other leaders in his administration to stick their necks out by becoming candidates for either of the two highest offices on the ticket. The collapse of the McNutt aspirations brought about by the presidential edict brought an end to a campaign that had cost a fortune. One trustworthy estimate was in excess of $200,000.[126]

Actually, McHale places this figure around $240,000. He claims that almost fifty percent of it was given by Republicans and independent voters who had confidence in McNutt. One of the shrewd tactics McNutt had used when he was governor, was to appoint outstanding Republicans rather than mugwumps as minority members of various committees. Naturally he gained the support of many Republicans, because as he often stated, there was nothing being done in his administration that required a mugwump to cover up; that he wanted the laws administered fairly and impartially; and the only thing he believed in was that the minor jobs and the majority chairmanships should be held by Democrats, because he was a Jefferson-Jackson Democrat.

According to Frank McHale, many Republicans worked for McNutt's candidacy. Will Hays of Sullivan, Indiana, former Republican state and national chairman and postmaster general under Harding, and currently head of the moving picture industry, was a good example of many Republicans interested in McNutt's candidacy. When McHale called him and asked for a fifteen-minute appointment concerning McNutt, he replied, "If you are going to talk about McNutt, I want three hours with you instead of fifteen minutes, because I am an American first, Republican second, and always a Hoosier."

When McHale arrived at Hays' office, the latter outlined a strategy for the conduct of McNutt's campaign. He had files on the individuals who molded public opinion in cities and towns of 5,000 or more throughout the United States, including their political and religious affiliation and their businesses. These he made available to the McNutt organization, but he stated that being a Republican he would have to support the Republican ticket.

When Secretary Wallace was nominated, the convention hall was filled with prolonged boos and catcalls and shouts of derision. Administration leaders readily admitted that they were in for a battle in their efforts to obtain Wallace's nomination. Nevertheless, they claimed that they had enough votes to do so. "It looks like we've got a fight on our hands," said Senator Claude Pepper of Florida after circulating among the delegations. "This might be an indirect stop-Roosevelt fight put on by those discontented persons who failed to do it directly." This statement was the result of word from the White House that Roosevelt would have to revise the address he had prepared for delivery to the convention by radio if some one other than Wallace were chosen. In fact, word had spread through the delegations that unless the convention chose Wallace, Roosevelt would refuse the nomination for first place on the ticket.[127]

Mrs. Roosevelt describes the balloting:

"Franklin, junior, and I kept tallies on the roll calls, and for awhile Mr. Wallace did not do very well. The convention was decidedly out of order; the galleries were packed with special groups favoring different candidates, and confusion was rampant. Word began to get around, however, that Mr. Wallace was to be the candidate. Mrs. Wallace sat beside me. I doubt if she had ever tried to follow a roll-call before. She looked very unhappy and asked: 'Why do you suppose they are so opposed to Henry?' I did not have time to explain that probably most of the people had been sent in purposely to demonstrate for someone else."[128]

Meanwhile, during the balloting, Hopkins was feverishly telephoning the White House almost every minute. The President's radio resounded with the din of discord from the con vention. But the rebellion failed to stop Wallace's nomination, and Roosevelt could relax for the first time since the convention opened. He was now able to dictate his acceptance speech.[129]

When the convention opened, Wallace had only a handful of personal votes, but in the balloting which followed he received the nomination of the convention, although there was no enthusiasm for the candidate. In fact, there was serious opposition to the President's choice. The feeling was so cool that Wallace was never even allowed to deliver the speech of acceptance which he had prepared. After he was sure of the outcome, Byrnes started to leave the convention hall to notify the President that he could relax, that Wallace would be nominated. He passed Wallace on the way out, and told him not to worry, that he would be chosen by the convention. Wallace asked Byrnes if he thought he should make a speech of thanks to the delegates. Byrnes replied that he "had witnessed the temper of the delegates and reminded him that the proceedings were being broadcast to millions by radio; that if the galleries should again boo him as they had when his name was presented, it would be very unfortunate." Wallace took Byrnes' advice to let well enough alone and did not ask for recognition.[130]

In describing the convention one reporter commented:

"Few convention annals contain such evidence of undisguised bossism. The pandemonium that raged during the balloting was more than protest against the selection of a former Republican as Roosevelt's running-mate. It was resentment of undemocratic dictation. The White House escaped the ignominy of having its wishes flouted, but the rancor created by the whole Wallace incident will ramify into the campaign and flare to Democratic disadvantage right up to election day—this, despite the personable and intellectual qualities with which the Secretary of Agriculture is endowed."[131]

The columnist continued:

"The significance of Paul McNutt's feat in almost stampeding the Chicago convention . . . is not underestimated. Had the Roosevelt high command failed to put over Wallace in the nick of time, McNutt might have run away with the prize on a succeeding ballot. His ovation, while trying to obtain the convention's attention long enough to renounce the nomination, was the most genuine demonstration of the week. Its echoes are not destined to die out. Already there's talk of 'McNutt for President in 1944.' . . . He is expected to be active on the stump for Roosevelt and Wallace."[132]

In reviewing the work of the Chicago convention, the Gary *Post Tribune* editorialized:

"Even among those who are opposed to him politically, Paul V. McNutt must have won a measure of admiration by his conduct at the Democratic convention in Chicago. There must have been real temptation, in the face of the ovation such as McNutt received, to permit his delegates to vote their will. The former Indiana governor might have been nominated, or, failing that, might have blocked the choice of Secretary Wallace and enabled Speaker Bankhead to win the Vice-presidential choice. Certainly he could have caused serious difficulty for the Wallace forces if he had been a little less positive in renunciation of his candidacy. McNutt could not have been blamed if he had tossed a wrench into the machinery that was electing Wallace. His own candidacy, for the presidency or the vice presidency, had been battered about with little mercy by the Roosevelt forces. He had withstood some severe blows during the last year or so. In a position to strike back, he could hardly be blamed if he had done so."[133]

The editorial continued:

"Instead the Hoosier shouted down the cheers in his own behalf and swung most of his delegates to the Wallace column. The reason for his action? He realized the nomination would be 'impossible,' as he expressed it himself, if he won it. Rejection of Wallace, after the president had expressed his preference, would have done far more harm to the party than any defections because of the selection of the agriculture secretary, a former Republican. So McNutt fought his way to the platform and halted probably as honestly enthusiastic a demonstration as the Chicago stadium saw last week. It may be the last time he will be cheered by a Democratic national convention. It is four more years till 1944; it will be difficult to keep a presidential boom alive that long. But he had a job to do . . . and he did it in soldierly fashion."[134]

As a result of his self-sacrifice, McNutt emerged from the convention in high favor with the White House. He could have had almost any post in the Administration he wanted, including the chairmanship of the Democratic National Convention or the Postmaster Generalship. His loyalty to Roosevelt had an impact that "wipes the slate clean of all real or imagined black marks." Many felt that he could now point his political star toward 1944, or "trophies nearer at hand." Or perhaps the President was "reserving other bouquets for Mc-Nutt." There was some speculation that he would not remain long as Federal Security Administrator.[135]

Writing in the Washington *Star* Jay Franklin said:

"When the heat was turned on, when McNutt could have secured his heart's desire, when he could even have profited personally from the situation, he stood like a stonewall, like a great rock in a weary desert of sweating, shouting, confused men. Revenge was his, if he had wanted it—and there was ample precedent before his eyes in the spectacle of the President's former friends trying to knife the party. He took the greater and the simpler course and is entitled to the respect of all Americans, regardless of party, who believe that public office is more than a game of hot hands for the boodle. . . . It is a pleasure to offer this tribute to one who remained cool while lesser men were trying to fry their fish on the hot political pavements."[136]

Soon after the convention adjourned, President Roosevelt telephoned McNutt to tell him personally that he was a good soldier who had performed his duty and had put loyalty to his commander-in-chief above all personal considerations.[137]

According to McHale, President Roosevelt called McNutt and said, "Paul, you were like a Minuteman of Concord to-night. You stood there against all the odds and I shall never forget this and four years from now, I'll help to reward you for what you did for me and the party tonight."

The next day, McHale said, he and Mrs. McHale and Paul and Mrs. McNutt were having dinner. Mrs. McNutt asked McHale what he thought of Paul's chances four years hence. McHale said, "If Paul wants to know, I will tell him. He never would be considered a serious candidate because many of the men who fought for him had wanted him to go down fighting." But McNutt believed that the President had the right to choose his running mate, and therefore it was only right that he should withdraw. Yet he never really recovered from the shock that he had received at the convention. It was his greatest disappointment, although he had endeared him-self and ingratiated himself into the esteem and confidence of all citizens alike, but particularly in the Democratic party.

McNutt's withdrawal from the race had won almost universal approval. Hundreds of telegrams and letters poured into headquarters praising him for his action. "There is no question but that McNutt is a much bigger man today in the eyes of the Democrats and the people of the nation for his unselfish action," commented McHale.[138]

Meanwhile the Republicans in their convention had nominated another Hoosier, Wendell L. Willkie, as their standard-bearer, with Charles L. McNary of Oregon, the Senate minority leader, as his running mate. During the campaign which followed, Roosevelt made very few speeches at first, but spent most of his time with the domestic and foreign problems which faced his administration. He did, however, make several tours throughout the country and contacted many voters. He made five major speeches in the campaign, in which he stressed New Deal reforms and the necessity for experience in the Presidency. The major portion of campaign speaking, however, was done by McNutt, who was tremendously popular with the Democratic politicians. While his speeches received little national publicity, they created a great and generally favorable mass of local publicity, and the urgent demands for his services at political rallies were several times greater than he was able to fill.[139] Roosevelt and Wallace won the election with 27.2 million votes to Willkie's and McNary's 22.3 million. The electoral college gave the Democrats 449 votes to 82 for the Republicans.

Notes for Chapter 6

1 Letter from Wayne Coy to McNutt, May 19, 1939. McNutt Collection.

2 Letter from Douglas MacArthur, Manila, to McNutt, July 12, 1939. McNutt Collection.

3 *Congressional Record*, Senate, July 12, 1939, p. 8927 ff., 76th Congress, First session, Vol. 84, Part 8, Washington, 1939.

4 *Ibid.*

5 *Ibid.*

6 *Ibid.*

7 *Ibid.*

8 *Ibid.*

9 *Ibid.*

10 *Ibid.*

11 *Ibid.*

12 *Ibid.*

13 *Congressional Record*, July 24, 1939, p. 9802 ff.

14 *Ibid.*

15 *Ibid.*

16 *Ibid.*

17 *Ibid.*

18 *Ibid.*

19 *Ibid.*

20 *Appendix* to the *Congressional Record*, Vol 84, Part 14, 76th Congress.

21 First Session, p. 3621, July 27, 1939.

22 Indianapolis *Times*, July 15, 1939, article by Daniel Kidney.

23 *Ibid.*

24 *Ibid.*

25 Letter to McNutt from Wayne Coy, May 19, 1939. McNutt Collection.

26 *Ibid.*

27 Letter from McNutt's secretary to William A. Dunlap, student chairman, Senior Forum, Darlington School, Rome, Georgia, April 11, 1940.

28 Quoted by Everett C. Watkins in the Indianapolis *Star,* April 10, 1939.

29 As reported in the Indianapolis *Star,* July 16, 1938.

30 *Jim Farley's Story, The Roosevelt Years,* by James A. Farley, New York, 1948 (pp. x-388), p. 23.

31 *Ibid.* p. 71.

32 *Ibid.*

33 *Ibid.* p. 115.

34 *Ibid.*

35 *Ibid.* p. 170.

36 Frank McHale to Farley, March 29, 1939. McNutt Collection.

37 McHale to Garner, March 29, 1939.

38 *Jim Farley's Story, The Roosevelt Years,* p. 185.

39 *Ibid.* p. 214.

40 *Ibid.* p. 215.

41 *Ibid.* p. 219.

42 *Ibid.*

43 *Ibid.*

44 Indianapolis *News,* May 18, 1939.

45 Indianapolis *Star,* May 26, 1939.

46 Indianapolis *News,* June 13, 1939.

47 Washington, D. C., *Daily News,* June 19, 1939.

48 *Ibid.*

49 New York *Times,* June 19, 1939.

50 Joseph Alsop and Robert Kintner in "The Capital Parade," June 22, 1939, no place.

51 *Ibid.*

52 Drew Pearson and Robert S. Allen in San Francisco *Chronicle,* June 26, 1939.

53 *Ibid.*

54 Ernest K. Lindley in Washington *Post,* July 5, 1939.

55 As reported by J. Gould Lincoln in the Washington *Evening Star,* July 6, 1939.

56 *Ibid.* July 8, 1939.

57 Dave Boone in the New York *Sun,* July 8, 1939.

58 Raymond Clapper in the Washington, D. C., *Daily News,* July 10, 1939.

59 *Ibid.*

60 Lyle C. Wilson in the Columbus, Ohio, *Citizen,* July 11, 1939.

61 *Ibid.*

62 Frederic William Wile in the Washington, D. C., *Star,* July 12, 1939.

63 *Ibid.*

64 George D. Riley in Washington *Times-Herald,* July 12, 1939.

65 Mark Sullivan in the Washington *Post,* July 13, 1939.

66 Editorial in the Detroit *Free Press,* July 14, 1939.

67 Raymond Clapper in New York *World-Telegram,* July 14, 1939.

68 Editorial, Detroit *Free Press,* July 29, 1939.

69 St. Louis *Post Dispatch,* August 20, 1939.

70 Indianapolis *Star,* July 29, 1939.

71 Pittsburgh *Post Gazette,* August 12, 1939.

72 Raymond P. Brandt in the *Washington Star,* November 26, 1939.

73 Reported by Robert R. Mullen in the *Christian Science Monitor,* January 16, 1940.

74 Reported by W. B. Ragsdale in the Flint, Michigan, *Journal,* January 25, 1940.

75 The Los Angeles *Times,* January 28, 1940.

76 *Ibid.*

77 Raymond Clapper in Washington, D. C., *Daily News,* March 13, 1940.

78 Ernest K. Lindley in the Washington *Post,* March 20, 1940.

79 Indianapolis *Times,* March 15, 1940.

80 Frederic William Wile in Washington *Star,* March 4, 1940.

81 G. Gould Lincoln in Washington *Star,* March 7, 1940.

82 *Ibid.*

83 Quoted in John T. Flynn, *The Roosevelt Myth,* New York, 1948 (pp. x-438) p. 179.

84 *Ibid.*

85 *Ibid.* p. 181.

86 *Ibid.* p. 182. As early as March, the Gallup poll, asking the question: "If Roosevelt is not a candidate, whom would you like to see elected President in 1940?" got the following response from Democrats: Garner, 42%; Hull, 10%; Farley, 10%; Hopkins, 8%; McNutt 5%; no opinion, 25%. *Garner of Texas: A Personal History,* Bascom N. Timmons, New York 1948 (294 pp.), p. 253.

87 New York *Herald Tribune,* May 31, 1940; also New York *Times,* May 31, 1940.

88 *Ibid.*

89 *Ibid.*

90 *Jim Farley's Story, The Roosevelt Years,* p. 256.

91 *Ibid.* p. 300.

92 Flynn, *The Roosevelt Myth,* p. 209.

93 *Ibid.*

94 Quoted in *Ibid.*

95 *Ibid.*

96 *Ibid.* p. 210.

97 *Ibid.*

98 *Ibid.* p. 211.

99 Personal interview of author with Mrs. Watson in her home in Brookline, Massachusetts, February 2, 1963.

100 Quoted in Flynn, p. 212. Taken from Edward J. Flynn, *You're the Boss*, pp. 156-7.

101 McHale to author.

102 Robert E. Sherwood, *Roosevelt and Hopkins: An Intimate History*, p. 172.

103 Quoted in Flynn, *The Roosevelt Myth*, p. 214.

104 Eleanor Roosevelt, *This I Remember* (Harpers 1949, pp. x-387), p. 212 ff.

105 *Ibid.*

106 Robert E. Sherwood, *Roosevelt and Hopkins: An Interpretation* (Rev. Ed. New York: Harpers 1950, xix-1002), p. 94.

107 Flynn, *The Roosevelt Myth*, pp. 215-6.

108 Frances Perkins, *The Roosevelt I Knew*, pp. 130-134.

109 Quoted by Flynn, *The Roosevelt Myth*, p. 216-7.

110 *Ibid.*

111 Eleanor Roosevelt, *This I Remember*, pp. 214-17.

112 *Ibid.*

113 *Ibid.*

114 *All in One Lifetime*, James F. Byrnes (New York 1958, 432 pp), p. 124.

115 *Ibid.*

116 Flynn, *The Roosevelt Myth*,

117 *Ibid.* Quoted from *Jim Farley's Story*, p. 300.

118 *Ibid.* p. 218.

119 *All in One Lifetime*, p. 125.

120 Ernest K. Lindley in Washington *Post*, July 22, 1940.

121 Indianapolis *Star*, July 19, 1940.

122 *Ibid.*

123 Typewritten article in Mrs. Watson's scrapbook.

124 Maurice Early in Indianapolis *Star*, July 19, 1940.

125 Indianapolis *Star*, July 19, 1940.

126 *Ibid.*

127 Typewritten article in Mrs. Watson's scrapbook.

128 Eleanor Roosevelt, *This I Remember*, p. 218.

129 Sherwood, p. 179.

130 Typewritten article in Mrs. Watson's scrapbook.

131 Frederic William Wile in Washington *Star*, July 23, 1940.

132 *Ibid.*

133 Editorial, Gary, Indiana, *Post Tribune*, July 23, 1940.

134 *Ibid.*

135 Robert C. Albright in Washington *Post*, July 28, 1940.

136 Jay Franklin in Washington *Star*, July 30, 1940.

137 Daniel M. Kidney in Indianapolis *Times*, July 19, 1940.

138 *Hoosier Sentinel*, July 26, 1940.

139 Ernest K. Lindley in Washington *Post*, October 25, 1940.

CHAPTER VII

The Call of Duty

There is no doubt that Paul V. McNutt's decision to re-nounce the Vice Presidential nomination in 1940 had far-reaching consequences, not only for the United States, but for the history of the world as well. By his loyalty to his party and his chief, he had stopped the rising popular tide which might have swept him into that office. And the critical years ahead might have been influenced by policies quite different from those of the Roosevelt-Wallace or even the Roosevelt-Truman administrations. But that is in the realm of specu-lation. McNutt had made his decision to put party devotion and loyalty before his personal ambition, and he was willing to continue to serve his country in the job to which he had been appointed the previous year—Federal Security Adminis-trator.

President Roosevelt was fully aware of the importance of McNutt's decision and did not hesitate to express his appre-ciation. Shortly after the Democratic National Convention had adjourned, McNutt received a letter from the President, in which Roosevelt extended his "sincere thanks for all that you did" at Chicago. "All the people with whom you worked during the Convention have the same feeling that I have—that you came out of the Convention with colors high. The ovation which you received was a tremendous tribute and I know must have thrilled you as it did all of us who heard it. I hope I shall see you very soon—I want to talk with you about many things," wrote the President.[1]

McNutt's loyalty and devotion to his party and its candidates contributed much to their success in November. Throughout the entire campaign, he worked tirelessly in behalf of the Roosevelt-Wallace ticket. He spoke extensively in many parts of the country and supported the Democratic platform wholeheartedly. In spite of his disappointment at the Chicago convention, he was still a loyal Democrat and did everything he could to enhance the cause of his party and its ultimate victory in November.

President Roosevelt was not unappreciative of the contributions which his Federal Security Administrator had made toward the winning of the election. Before the end of November, the President sent McNutt another personal note telling him again "how very much I appreciate all that you did during the campaign. I know of your untiring efforts and the many speeches you made even though the newspapers did not mention them. I am grateful to you for your fine loyalty and cooperation at all times," the President wrote. Apparently Roosevelt felt a keen sense of obligation for the services which McNutt had rendered in behalf of his election to a third term, unless he were not telling the truth as to his real feelings.

Naturally, there was much speculation as to the possibility that Roosevelt was actually grooming McNutt for the Presidential nomination in 1944, even though that date was still a long way off. And of course much could happen in the next four years. The war in Europe was growing in intensity. The

Axis Powers were increasing their tyranny and aggression. The United States was becoming "The Great Arsenal of Democracy." And it was becoming more difficult for Roosevelt to keep the country on the road of neutrality. Yet the government continued to maintain a semblance of neutrality for more than a year following Roosevelt's reelection.

In the meantime, the United States was increasing her aid to the enemies of Germany, Italy, and Japan, using methods of questionable neutrality. We had abandoned our traditional policy of isolationism and non-involvement, and we had begun to prepare ourselves for defense, if not for actual participation as a belligerent. As the arsenal of democracy, the United States stepped up its program of production of war materials in 1940 and 1941. The Selective Service Act had become law. The Destroyer-Base Deal had been put into effect, and a program of Lend-Lease was instituted. Hemispheric solidarity was now realized, and America was recognized as the moral leader of the world against Axis tyranny and oppression.

In December, 1940, President Roosevelt appointed McNutt to the very important task of coordinating the entire health, medical welfare, and nutrition and recreational aspects of the national defense program. This was in addition to his duties as Federal Security Administrator, which office he held until the end of the war.

On July 16, 1941, Harold D. Smith, Director of the Bureau of the Budget, sent a memorandum to President Roosevelt submitting for his approval an executive order which established the Office of Defense Health and Welfare Services to be directed by the Federal Security Administrator. The order transferred the activities of the Federal Security Administrator as coordinator of health, welfare, and related defense activities from an organization status dependent upon the

Council of National Defense to the Office of Emergency Management in a position coordinate with the other defense agencies. The order also provided for establishment of a health and medical committee under the new office. The President sent a memo to Dr. McIntyre on the same day, inquiring about this order, and again, on September 1, 1941, the President asked Dr. McIntyre to let him know if the order should be signed. Dr. McIntyre recommended signing the order, by memo, on September 3, and it was signed by the President the same day. McNutt remained as director of this program until 1943.

In 1941, President Roosevelt appointed McNutt chairman of the very important War Manpower Commission, and he continued in this position until 1945. At the same time, he was a member of the War Production Board and the Economic Stabilization Board. So important were these appointments considered that many believed the President was not only rewarding McNutt for his political cooperation, but was also placing him in a very strategic area concerned with the defense effort.[3] Apparently Roosevelt was completely satisfied with the past performances of his Federal Security Administrator.

In these several positions, McNutt occupied a unique vantage point where he was required to take a wide view of the activities and problems associated with defense. In a speech which he made before the Annual Conference of State and Territorial Health Officers with the United States Public Health Service in Washington on April 29, 1941, he likened defense to a wedge. At the apex was the soldier, who had to have "the paraphernalia of man and, as the living unit necessary to the business, he must be fed and clothed and kept in good health." The military authorities, he said, "are primarily responsible for the details of his existence. They are respon sible for safeguarding his health in the limited areas over which they have jurisdiction."

But a good part of the soldier's time, said McNutt, "is spent in the surrounding civil communities." Even the briefest of times, he said, could be significant, "since one can pick up infection very fast." The duty of the public health officials was to facilitate the relationship between the civil and military authorities. According to McNutt, the traditional public health services had the job of solving the public health problems in environmental sanitation, food and milk sanitation, communicable disease control, and venereal disease control. This part of the work was pretty well in hand. Yet McNutt saw two or three problems of grave import which were not under control, and "we have scarcely faced the situations realistically."

One of these problems concerned the industrial worker, who was the responsibility of the public health agencies. In today's war, claimed McNutt, "industrial mobilization and expansion make possible military mobilization and expansion. In the speeding up of industry, our responsibilities in the field of industrial hygiene are multiplying. Able-bodied men are being mobilized into the Army, while women, young adults, and older men replace them in their jobs. These new workers make imperative increased provision for industrial hygiene activities. For all workers, new industrial processes create hazards which demand for their solution the skill of the hygienist, the toxologist, and the industrial engineer."

"Even in more peaceful days," McNutt continued, "we could not claim that we had more than started this work—and here we are in a crisis that affects industry profoundly." This was the peculiar responsibility of the health agencies, McNutt believed. The Public Health Service was throwing all the resources it could behind this work. But it was not only the occupational hazards with which health departments should concern themselves. Such programs "should provide for the worker at work, at home, and in the community. This complete consideration for the worker's health is in the pursuit of better national health through peaceful years. It is even more necessary as the efforts for defense take on momentum," said McNutt.

Another problem which greatly concerned McNutt was the old problem of medical care—what to do for those who needed a doctor and had no money—how to provide hospital care for those who lacked the financial "open sesame" to these institutions. In many small communities where industrial plants had expanded due to the defense program, the tax structure could not be expected to cope with the situation. Into such defense areas came large numbers of people who soon became the responsibility of the community, because of the abnormal situation. McNutt claimed that the national emergency was making the distribution of physicians and nurses "even more unequal than it has been. Something must be done to counteract the forces doing this unequalization. The supply of civilian medical and nursing personnel should be maintained and, if possible, increased," McNutt insisted. The inadequacy of hospital facilities was due to be aggravated by the emergency, he feared.

The third important problem in health defense, according to McNutt, was that of nutrition. He indicated that the President had already called the first national conference on nutrition, and it was expected that much would be accomplished as a result. McNutt gave assurances that it was the intention of the Federal Government "to put all that it can into the program of health," and he hoped that the states would "continue their rightful position as leaders in our joint enterprise."[4]

Until the United States actually entered the war as a belligerent, the major work of the health agencies was devoted to civilian activities. But after Pearl Harbor, the vigorous prosecution of the war took precedence over everything else. These health departments, like other civilian agencies, were forced to give up valuable personnel for service with the armed forces and on the field of combat. McNutt realized the gravity of the situation, and called upon the members of the health agencies to put forth a prodigious effort in the emergency.

One of the problems which had to be attacked immediately and vigorously was in the field of industrial hygiene. The world's attention was focussed on the combined man and machine power of the United States. It was McNutt's belief that "On our ability to fabricate and deliver the materials of war are based democracy's best hopes and the enemies' darkest fears. Whatever impedes production diminishes both our hopes and their fears. Any factor which steals the worker's time or saps his energy threatens our national security and gives aid and comfort to the enemy," he said.[5]

McNutt claimed that sickness and disability were such factors. The time lost annually to industry through illness and disability was appalling. McNutt estimated that "if this [time] were spent on the job instead of in the hospital or sick room, it would give us about 165,000 fighting tanks—40,000 more than the President has asked for during *both* years 1942 and 1943. It would enable us to send down the ways more than 50 new superdreadnoughts of the *North Carolina* class— a fleet large enough to protect our shores and also clear the sea lanes for any expeditionary forces we choose to dispatch."[6]

The Government had appointed experts to put our supply system on a sound wartime basis. But supplies alone were not enough. It was McNutt's belief that "strong, healthy men and women are needed to transform materials into fighting assets." This called for a sound wartime management of our human resources. It was the duty of the health agencies, said McNutt, "to see that people are fit to take their places at their machines, on the assembly lines, on the farms, or do a faster and more efficient job than ever before." It was the responsibility of the agencies, he said, "to transfer the largest possible proportion of this lost time from the debit to the credit side of the national ledger."[7]

McNutt mentioned the development of industrial hygiene as a public health activity as one of the many advances which had taken place in recent years. But it was his opinion that, "in view of the present crucial needs not enough effort as yet is devoted to this activity." He felt that considerably greater financial outlays must be made by the states themselves. "Of the $1,006,000 budgeted for industrial hygiene purposes by state and local agencies during the fiscal year 1942, approximately 64 per cent was contributed by the Federal Government and only 36 per cent was state and local funds. On this basis, the states are not yet doing their share," he said.[8]

Money, however, was not all that was needed. It was McNutt's belief that "wisdom, initiative, and sustained effort will be required in greater measure than ever before." He estimated that in less than a year there would be 10,000,000 more persons engaged in war industry than there were at the end of 1941. Many of these new war workers would have to be drawn from the older age groups, the women of the country, and those whose physical condition was poor. "The time has come," said McNutt, "when we should launch a rehabilitation program in order to utilize the potential labor power of the physically handicapped. As the labor supply approaches the depletion point, the only way to step up production will be to increase the efficiency of the individual worker." Yet

McNutt was aware that longer hours and increased working speed would tax the workers' strength and resistance; mental stresses would become increasingly severe; and nutrition would be impaired, especially if America "has to become the granary as well as the arsenal of democracy." To all these growing tasks and problems would be added "those pertaining to extra-cantonment health and sanitation, large-scale migration of workers, and the complicated duties of civilian defense," McNutt advised.[9]

As Director of the Defense Health and Welfare Services, McNutt felt a keen responsibility in attempting to solve all these problems as an aid to winning the war. There was a universal acceptance of the basic importance of health in practically all aspects of civil welfare. Yet it was McNutt's belief that many health departments were severely handicapped by outworn customs and traditions. This had to be changed, he was convinced, if we were to win the war. "We must realize that business as usual is out. Inertia and solicitude for special interests cannot be tolerated in our health agencies today," he said.[10]

According to McNutt, failure to be more aggressive and to expand activities in conformity with needs "cannot in many instances be attributed to lack of funds." He cited the fact that since the passage of the Social Security Act in 1935, the Federal Government had been making substantial grants to the states "in order to help them finance their health programs." As a result, a framework of organization had been set up which allowed a very wide latitude of operations. Yet the states had failed to develop many of the essential services. McNutt felt that the reluctance of the states to undertake these necessary functions was especially inappropriate at such a crucial time. "What is needed today," he said, "are operating agencies which will step in and do the most urgent tasks, regardless of tradition and custom."[11]

This was the point McNutt was making: in the development of the civilian defense program, the Office of Civilian Defense looked to existing agencies for actual operation. But he questioned whether state and local health departments had come forward and assumed their rightful dynamic roles in the program. The part played by community health agencies left much to be desired, in his opinion. The health departments were in a position to give material assistance to the federal agencies in planning and implementing his program, but many remained cautiously on the sidelines while others showed themselves to be activated more by special pleading than by true civic needs. Because of these conditions, a coordinating agency, the Office of Defense Health and Welfare Services had been established to build teamwork and cooperation for national salvation.

A rather unusual function fell under the jurisdiction of McNutt as director of the Office of Defense Health and Welfare Services. On February 6, 1942, Harold D. Smith, Director of the Bureau of the Budget, sent a memorandum to President Roosevelt for his signature, designating certain areas of the west coast in which the presence of enemy aliens would be prohibited, and advising that the government was faced with the task of removing and distributing into other localities enemy aliens living in prohibited areas. This duty was assigned to McNutt, and the work was to be done in coordination with the Department of Justice. The secretary of the treasury was authorized to allot $500,000 to the Federal Security Administrator for this purpose, the President approving the recommendation.[12]

On the same day, the President allocated $5,000,000 to McNutt's agency to provide temporary aid necessitated by enemy action to civilians, other than enemy aliens, residing in the United States, who were disabled or who were dependents of civilians who were killed, disabled, interned, or reported missing, or who were otherwise in need of assistance or services. The President wrote McNutt asking him to assume such responsibility.[13]

But this was just one of many on McNutt's long list of war services. He was directly or indirectly connected with every aspect of the federal government's many programs for prosecuting the war. One of the most serious phases of the entire period from 1940 to 1945 was that concerned with labor. As the defense industries increased production, the amount of labor difficulties increased, and strikes resulted. The supply of jobs now equalled the labor supply, and unsatisfactory labor conditions became the basis for much resentment. The strikes which resulted adversely affected the production of vitally needed materials.

An eleven-man National Defense Mediation Board was established by executive order on March 19, 1941, for the purpose of resolving labor disputes in defense industries. The Board was set up within the Office of Production Management, since it was to be a part of the defense setup. The latter had emerged in January, 1941, with William Knudsen as Director General and Sidney Hillman as Associate Director.[14] But the Board had no legal authority to enforce its decisions and was reduced to general conciliatory and mediation efforts, in attempting to compromise the claims of labor and management in such disputes.

There was much friction and tension during the first year of the existence of the Office of Production Management. In 1942, it was merged with the War Production Board, with Donald Nelson as director, with authority to mobilize the nation's resources for a total war effort. This board was the principal agency in the field of production and supply. It functioned throughout the war, and was not terminated until October, 1945.

At the beginning of the war, labor used its unique advantage to secure its demands through strikes, which crippled the war effort. Yet the proportion of man-hours lost in proportion to the man-hours worked was kept at a minimum. It was estimated that this ratio ran throughout the war period at something like two-tenths to four-tenths of one per cent. A month during which the proportion rose to six-tenths of one per cent was regarded as a bad one.[15] This good record was undoubtedly due to the passage of the Smith-Connally Anti-Strike Act of 1942, which was passed over President Roosevelt's veto. Its main objective was the prevention and reduction of strikes. The act broadened presidential power to seize plants where interference with war production was threatened by a labor disturbance. It also made illegal the instigation of strikes in plants seized by the government. Labor unions were now made liable for damage suits for failure to give notice of intention to strike in war industries.

This bill was severely denounced by labor leaders and others throughout the country, but such objection did not seem to bother President Roosevelt. Although he also was opposed to it, as was expressed in his veto message, he felt it his duty to enforce the act. To those who protested against it, he always replied:

"If it it isn't any good, as you say, it will be abandoned. Congress is entitled to make an experiment. Do the best you can to carry on."[16]

After Pearl Harbor, there were many people throughout the country who began to raise questions about the inequity of men being drafted under the compulsory act, while there was no similar draft of manpower for industrial service. Many felt that the two war services should be treated equally, and that there should be a universal draft for labor, similar to the English system. There is no doubt that the flow of labor supply was unequal; there were numerous complaints of high labor turnover and unregulated migration of labor into districts already plagued with unemployment and housing problems. Other objections were based on racial discrimination and other unfortunate hiring practices.

President Roosevelt was finally induced to create, by executive order, a nine-man War Manpower Commission on April 18, 1942, for the more effective utilization of manpower resources. Paul McNutt was named its chairman. Immediately, labor voiced its opposition to the program, which it was feared might lead to a conscription of labor. The Army and Navy were in favor of such conscription because it would provide a means of solving the problems of their contractors for a steady, competent, regulated, docile labor supply.

The authority which the executive order had given to McNutt in the field of manpower has been described by some as dictatorial. But actually his authority was extremely limited, and he was not able to exercise any broadly effective leadership. Secretary of War Henry L. Stimson and McNutt were good personal friends, but they did not always agree on the manpower problem, and there was continual friction, especially in regard to the mobilization of civilian labor.[17]

The Secretary of Labor, Frances Perkins, had opposed the establishment of the War Manpower Commission on the ground that "it was bound to create an enormous institution of government, many of whose functions would be in competition with activities of existing agencies; that it was unnecessary, and that it established a foolish and dangerous control on human beings; that the regulations would probably be more confusing than helpful; and that all we needed to handle the free flow of manpower into the war industries was to revive and release the Employment Service, giving it an independent status or attaching it either to the Labor Department or the War Production Board."[18]

It was quite apparent that Miss Perkins was very reluctant to give McNutt jurisdiction over so important a program, much preferring to have it in her department. President Roosevelt was obviously confused and disturbed by the attitude of some of his advisers on the matter, but the War Manpower Commission was finally set up and McNutt was appointed its director, thereby assuming the most extensive power over the American people ever held by any individual except the President. This Commission included representatives from every agency of the government with any interest in manpower, such as the War Production Board, the Labor Department, the Army and the Navy, the Social Security Board, the Civil Service Board, the Selective Service Board, and numerous others.

The need for such authority as that given to the War Manpower Commission was imperative. When the rearmament program was first begun in the summer of 1940, there was a sizable backlog of unemployment upon which to draw. The armed forces did not drain men from industry in any large numbers. But after December, 1941, these withdrawals were greatly increased. Industry speeded up its conversion to a war footing. As a result, millions of workers transferred to war jobs. Women began to enter the labor field. Men with special skills were in great demand.

Immediately after its formation, the War Manpower Commission took steps to estimate the total manpower requirements for industry in relation to military, agricultural and civilian needs. It also made provision for the more orderly recruitment and placement of workers, and instituted a system of vocational training for new workers.

Soon after the creation of the War Manpower Commission, President Roosevelt wrote to Mayor Fiorello H. LaGuardia of New York City in reply to the mayor's transmittal report of facilities available in New York City for war production. The President had asked McNutt to call together representatives to discuss this matter with LaGuardia and Governor Herbert H. Lehman, and to ascertain what specific steps could be taken to meet the current problems of unemployment in New York City. The President admitted that the solution of this problem would not be an easy one. He knew that the several federal agencies concerned with war production and procurement were fully aware of the importance of more effective utilization of the production facilities and the labor supply of New York City in the war effort. He felt sure that the steps which were being planned would assist in alleviating the situation.[19]

During the first half year of its existence, the War Manpower Commission devoted much of its time to organization and coordination. Twelve regional offices covering the entire country were set up. A program of voluntary cooperation of labor and management was the basis of procedure. Considerable progress was made toward the realization of the objectives of the Commission, but it was soon evident that the scope of its authority had to be broadened if it was to deal effectively with the many ramifications of the whole manpower situation.

Therefore, on September 17, 1942, the President placed under the direction of the chairman the United States Employment Service, the National Youth Administration, the Apprentice Training Service and the Training-Within-Industry Service which had been operating under other agencies. On

December 5, the Selective Service System was made an integral part of the War Manpower Commission and all voluntary enlistments were prohibited.

There was also the question as to the part agriculture would play in the war. Governor Dwight H. Green of Illinois wrote President Roosevelt on October 8, 1942, urging the formation of a program that would make manpower available to agriculture. Green's letter was referred by the President to McNutt, who replied to the governor that this problem had been receiving his careful study and attention for some time. The War Manpower Commission, the Agriculture Department, and the Selective Service System were all conscious of the growing shortage of farm labor, due principally to inductions into the armed forces and migrations in an effort to find jobs elsewhere.[20]

While the military program was stepping up its tempo, there were increased demands for manpower by industry and the armed services, with the result that the labor market tightened considerably. In August, 1943, fathers began to be drafted into the armed forces, with deferments for certain types of skilled workers who were vitally needed in war jobs.[21]

The War Manpower Commission ultimately served its purpose without resort to labor conscription, for which President Roosevelt was grateful. But nine months after Pearl Harbor, Fowler V. Harper, Deputy Commissioner, reported that production efforts were definitely being restricted by manpower shortages. Such shortages of male labor existed in thirty-five important production areas; and in eighty-one others, shortages of male labor were anticipated in the near future. In only forty-four labor market areas was the labor supply adequate to meet the current and expected demands. Harper listed "Selective Service withdrawals, job shopping, pirating, inadequate housing and transportation, and the high cost of living in many war centers" as contributing to the rising turnover rates.[22]

Harper cited some of the current problems of manpower, such as those in the shipyards and in many of the major aircraft firms, due to housing shortages and labor turnover. He questioned whether voluntary and cooperative methods would be adequate to meet the problems. He insisted, however, that "if and when these methods cease to be adequate, the War Manpower Commission will be prepared with legislation which will make up the deficiencies of existing policies and procedures." But he sounded a note of warning about national service legislation. "It is not a simple matter," he warned. "We cannot, in America, get along with the simple order for the mobilization of manpower that characterizes less complicated societies with traditions less democratic than ours."[23]

Somewhat facetiously Harper illustrated this point by citing the order of the Emperor of Ethiopia when his nation was invaded by Fascist legions:

"All men 14 to 80 years report, bringing spears. Married men bring wives to cook and work. Single men bring any convenient woman. Men found at home will be shot."

This was simple, direct, and to the point, Harper said, but he also pointed out that Ethiopia lost the war.[24]

"If we in America enact into legislation a program for assigning men to industrial jobs and keeping them there," Harper advised, "we must include in the law those democratic safeguards which reflect the very issues for which we are fighting. The War Manpower Commission is not neglecting this problem. . . . And when the occasion calls, the War Manpower Commission will be ready."[25]

The position of women in the total war effort also was given serious consideration by the War Manpower Commis-

sion. Arthur S. Flemming raised the question whether or not
the government was using women to the fullest extent in the
war program. He felt that the government was really trying
to practice what it was preaching, but looking at the picture
realistically, he believed that the utilization of women in war
jobs was not being carried far enough. He also was of the
opinion that the physically handicapped and minority groups
were not being used sufficiently by the government. Pirating
from one job for the benefit of another was also condemned
by Flemming. "We have got to work out plans for the elimination of unnecessary pirating," he demanded.[26]

Flemming then discussed the problem of turnover, which
was seriously jeopardizing the war effort. "We are on a
treadmill insofar as the recruitment of personnel in the departmental service is concerned," he claimed, "and the same
thing is true in various parts of the field service." He did not
see how the government could continue to operate a system
of voluntary enlistment in industry along with a system of
selective service and training for the military.

According to Flemming, the chairman of the War Manpower Commission had issued a directive to the heads of all
departments and agencies of the Federal Government, telling
them under what conditions they could request deferment
of government employees. It was hoped that this document
would be a guide to industry also. The same principles were
to apply to the War Manpower Commission itself. The chairman had also issued a directive to the Civil Service Commission which gave him authority to transfer an individual from
one job to another for the best interests of the war program.
This was the first time in the history of the Federal Government, Flemming observed, "that anyone has had the right to
say to an employee, 'If you are going to continue to work for
the U. S. Government, then you are going to work in the X

Department instead of in the A Department,' and to add, 'Of course if you don't want to continue working for the government you have the privilege of getting out completely; but as long as you want to stay on the payroll of the U. S. Government, you must work in the job where, in the judgment of the Civil Service Commission, you can render the most effective service.' "[27]

Probably the most significant statement of the manpower problem was made by McNutt himself in a speech given before the Winter Personnel Conference of the American Management Association in Chicago in February, 1943. He referred to the executive order which was signed by President Roosevelt on December 5, 1942, for the purpose of promoting "the most effective mobilization and utilization of the national manpower and eliminating so far as possible waste of manpower due to disruptive recruitment and undue migration of workers." According to McNutt, this required that every man or woman physically able to render personal service in the war effort should have the opportunity to do several things:

"To serve in an essential industry; to engage in an endeavor which will utilize to the highest degree his or her particular abilities most needed in the war effort; to perform at his or her highest productive rate, and to continue to do so during the maximum working hours that are commensurate with good health and sustained effort."[28]

If these goals were to be effectively achieved, McNutt believed that three requirements would have to be met:

"1. Persons now engaged in essential activities must remain where they are unless they transfer to still more essential activities or to essential activities in greater need of their particular abilities; 2. Persons now employed or engaged in less essential activities must be relocated; 3. All persons must raise their productive efforts to the highest possible level."[29]

McNutt was convinced that it was the function and the

duty of the War Manpower Commission to take certain steps to facilitate these actions. "It must insure the mobilization of the national manpower, which, in general, involves the activities of registration, recruitment, training, and placement of people. And, in addition to that," he said, "the Commission must insure the utilization of manpower." This would involve the uses to which people are put once they are placed in essential industries, and the extent to which their skills and knowledge are made productive.

"We have at our command all the tools required for complete utilization of the human energy and ability needed to fill our armed forces, to operate our war industries and supporting activities, to maintain our civilian economy, and to win the war," he claimed. "There are, however, alarming signs that there is waste manpower: absenteeism, turnover, labor hoarding, undermanning, labor disorder, bad morale, individual frustration—all these exist to the extent that they are matters of great concern."[30]

McNutt then traced the history of American labor-management relations under voluntary cooperative efforts which, he said, had effected "the greatest productive combination yet known to men." He declared it was well established that "neither labor nor management can be compelled or driven effectively but that, given proper guidance and assistance, both can be led to increased effort in a common cause." He felt it would accomplish no good if the War Manpower Commission were to set up an agency to approach the manpower utilization question by saying to labor and management, "We will show you how, and you must comply." Such an approach, he thought, "would insult the intelligence of people who have literally spent their lives dealing with one phase or another of manpower utilization, and who know most about the problems which it involves. It would generate nothing but a well-justified feeling of resentment. It would amount to dangerous and unwarranted meddling during a time of crisis. It would defeat the very purpose it was designed to achieve."[31]

On the other hand, McNutt believed if the subject were approached sincerely, in the true light of the situation, with the attitude "We are here to learn from you your problems of manpower utilization, so that the War Manpower Commission may assist in their solution," the possibilities for constructive service and assistance would be unlimited.[32]

The work of the War Manpower Commission fell into the natural divisions of military recruitment, civilian recruitment, and training. To implement the program, three bureaus were established within the Commission: the Bureau of Selective Service, which served to take people from civilian activity into the armed forces; the Bureau of Placement, which took people from unemployment or less essential activities into essential activities or more essential ones; and the Bureau of Training, which prepared people for essential activities. "Manpower," said McNutt, "means nothing more nor nothing less than America itself. Manpower is America. We are utilizing manpower to win this war. We are making use of all America's resources. This problem and this program of manpower utilization are indeed a problem and a program of 'human engineering.' . . . [It is] America herself, geared to battle strength, waging this war for human freedom with all her skill and with all her might."[33]

In general, American labor was one of the most patriotic groups during the war. This was true of both labor unions and labor in general. The war emergency required of labor a new kind of responsibility. From its ranks emerged men who were capable of heading up some of the most important aspects of the government program. The war years showed that "the labor movement in America had come of age." The tremendous war production program, which Donald M. Nelson, chairman of the War Production Board, called "the biggest job in all history," could never have been accomplished so quickly and efficiently as it was, had labor been more selfish or less patriotic.[34] Not only did the government have to provide intelligent direction and control from its top officials, but a much more important task was to make it possible for the energy and general know-how of America to operate without too much difficulty. It was Nelson's belief that "America's reliance on democracy and on its tradition of free, unfettered enterprise never justified itself so brilliantly as it did in the war."[35]

Yet there were times when labor took advantage of the situation and impeded the war effort with serious strikes and manpower difficulties. Frances Perkins, as Secretary of Labor, was in a very vulnerable position, and many people questioned her ability to handle the situation. Even President Roosevelt thought at one time that it might be helpful if he should replace her with a man. While he had real affection for Miss Perkins personally, still he was coming to believe that continued labor troubles might have an adverse effect on the elections which were coming up in 1944. Even though he had always believed in the principle of merging independent agencies in the established departments of the government, he had already created two independent agencies, the War Manpower Commission to handle manpower problems, and the War Labor Board, to take care of wages and salaries. These should have been placed in the Labor Department, but Roosevelt was reluctant to entrust Miss Perkins with such far-reaching responsibilities.

James F. Byrnes, head of the Office of War Mobilization, told the President that Miss Perkins "was doing as good a job as could be done by any woman, but that her job was one for a tough, two-fisted man at any time, and now it was almost impossible." Roosevelt replied that he had long been holding a letter of resignation from Miss Perkins, which he could accept at any time. Byrnes expressed the opinion that the appointment of a man "would help at this particular time," to which the President replied, "All right, Jimmy, you get the man." The next day, Byrnes suggested to Roosevelt that he "appoint Miss Perkins head of a bureau having jurisdiction over education, relief programs, health and the Children's Bureau; transfer Ickes to the Department of Labor, placing War Manpower duties in that department; and make McNutt Secretary of the Interior." Byrnes told the President that Mc-Nutt was "a good administrator and he knows the West," which obviously was a requirement for the Interior Department. The President seemed to favor the idea at first, but a few days later, after a conference with Philip Murray, president of the C.I.O., he changed his mind, and Perkins, Ickes, and McNutt retained their respective positions.[36]

Agitation for a national service law was urged as early as 1942. In July of that year a sub-committee of the War Manpower Commission submitted a report favoring such legislation, but other agencies of the administration opposed it. Such a bill was introduced in Congress in February, 1943, by Senator Warren Austin and Representative James Wadsworth, both Republicans, but they were not supported by the White House at that time. President Roosevelt realized the political difficulties involved, and was reluctant to push such legislation. He was supported in his position by most of his administration, and particularly those members representing labor and progressive groups.[37]

It was at this time that President Roosevelt received a note from McNutt, enclosing some suggestions for a speech that the President was preparing on the armed services problem. Our total supply of manpower and womanpower was sufficient for all our needs, McNutt said. The problem was one of allocation and administration. "It will require total mobilization of our citizens and far-reaching sacrifices by all," he stated. "And by total mobilization I do not mean everyone but you. We believe we have the administrative machinery and the operating plans to perform this overwhelming task." The President had conferred maximum authority upon McNutt, who kept him constantly advised as to the manner and method of exercising that authority. The program which McNutt had outlined was sufficient, provided it was accompanied by the uncompromising and unqualified cooperation of everyone.

McNutt continued his suggestions:

"In mobilizing for total war we are doing what no other great nation in the war has been able to do; we are mobilizing civilian manpower by voluntary methods, by the cooperation of management and labor, individually and collectively. And so far we have succeeded. But more difficult days lie ahead. Manpower shortages are spreading while manpower demands grow. The problems are becoming more and more difficult. We are going to keep on solving them by voluntary means just as long as the cooperation of management and labor, with each other and with their Government, makes it possible."

But McNutt suggested the President make a further assurance:

"I am prepared at any time to recommend to the Congress measures, full and complete, to insure by law the orderly execution of manpower policies. Months of careful thought and planning have gone into the preparation of plans for national service. Its full implications for the lives of every citizen have been considered. Such measures will necessarily impose heavy restrictions upon the normal peace-time freedom of industrial enterprise and individual activities, but I am convinced that the American people are prepared to make the full measure of sacrifice necessary to complete victory."[38]

As the war continued, labor difficulties increased, as was predicted; and there were growing demands for industrial conscription, especially when the railroad workers threatened to strike. Secretaries Stimson and Knox as well as other leaders believed that a national service law was necessary, and early in 1944 they submitted to the President a formal recommendation that the crucial manpower situation required the prompt enactment of such a law, even though there was bitter opposition to the plan in Congress and in the labor unions. On January 11, Roosevelt sent a message to Congress calling for a national service law "to prevent strikes" and make available for essential war service "every able-bodied adult in the nation."

He described such legislation as the only truly democratic method of organizing manpower.[39] "Disunity at home—bickering, self-seeking partisanship, stoppage of work, inflation, business as usual, politics as usual, luxury as usual—these are the influences which can undermine the morale of the brave men ready to die at the front for us here," the President said.[40]

Apparently Roosevelt had not discussed his intentions with any of his leading advisers who were responsible for manpower, as it was a complete surprise to them, even though some favored such legislation. According to Byrnes, McNutt was enraged "because he was taken by surprise at what was being done in his own shop. Why, he demanded, had the chairman of the Manpower Commission not been consulted?"[41] It is doubtful, of course, whether Roosevelt really expected the recommendation to be enacted by Congress, which it was not, but at least it was a warning of what might happen if the labor situation became any more critical.

Fortunately, the war was nearing its end by this time and such a national service law was no longer needed. War production was tapering off. Employment in the war industries had been declining for some time. Less than a week after the President's speech, McNutt's War Manpower Commission announced that it did not expect any further increases in the munitions industries' manpower. By this time even McNutt was opposed to the legislation as being unnecessary, although he later gave his endorsement with the wry comment that "he was bound to go along with the boss."[42] But Secretary Stimson continued to push the idea, in spite of the easing off of war production. The invasion of Europe was still months away, but the government had already begun to make plans for reconversion to peacetime pursuits.

While the manpower draft was being debated, Brigadier-General Lewis B. Hershey, Director of Selective Service, announced that he had instructed all local draft boards to review occupational deferments for all men of military age. This announcement embarrassed McNutt, who was at that very moment speaking in Des Moines about the benefits that had been derived from occupational deferments. Needless to say, McNutt was shocked by this new turn of events. Donald Nelson was equally embarrassed. The new policy resulted eventually in production deficiencies due to a shortage of manpower. By the end of 1944, the Truman Committee had examined the situation and found the new draft policy had actually "created temporary surpluses in the armed forces and corresponding shortages in war production."[43]

Meanwhile, the reconversion program had gone into effect, as scheduled, on August 15. It was not put into actual operation, however, because James Byrnes, head of the Office of War Mobilization, had ordered that the War Manpower Commission should take special steps to provide labor for war factories. This order took final authority over any increase in civilian production out of the hands of the War Production

Board and placed it in the hands of the War Manpower Commission. It required that any local War Manpower Commission official had to prove the need for increased civilian production. In effect, it gave the Commission power to prevent any increase in civilian production.[44]

McNutt's duties as chairman of the War Manpower Commission were extremely burdensome at times, especially when his work was hampered so often by appearances before congressional committees. James F. Byrnes related a typical situation which occurred when he was Director of War Mobilization. He and Donald Nelson, along with McNutt, had been requested to appear before a Senate committee. The three waited for over an hour, and no Senator had made an appearance. Finally, after a further short wait, one of the young lawyers present "said that the chairman and members of the committee were very busy and would be delayed, but he would start the inquiry." After the meeting, as Byrnes was leaving, McNutt told him "that it seemed he spent a good part of each day in committee hearings." Of course each was reluctant to ignore a request that was signed by the chairman of a congressional committee.[45]

During the war, McNutt made an extremely strong appeal to women to do their part in the war effort, and he was gratified with the results. He was firmly convinced that the path to victory would have been much harder and stonier if it had not been for the contributions of women in every phase of the conflict. In 1943, there were over six million more women working in industry than when the rearmament program first began in June, 1940. A great many of these women were taking the places of men who had gone into the armed services. But McNutt appealed for even more women workers who were willing to do their full share, especially in those communities where there was an acute labor shortage. In one popular appeal, he stated:

"We must have full womanpower, as well as our full manpower, behind the war effort. And every woman who *takes* a job and *stays* on the job is doing just that much to promote a quicker Victory and to bring our men in uniform back sooner to their homes."[46]

McNutt was also appreciative of the part which the Negro played in the civilian labor program during the war. He was once asked if he believed the position of the Negro would be permanently improved as a result of this contribution, and he replied that he thought there was every likelihood this would be true. He based his confidence on several factors. The proportion of Negroes employed in war industries had steadily increased. At the outset of the war there was a very definite prejudice against Negroes on the part of most employers, but this prejudice was progressively broken down.

Much of this Negro employment was due, of course, to the tight manpower situation. But a great deal of it was due to the unremitting efforts of the government and the Fair Employment Practices Committee. It was certainly the policy of McNutt and the War Manpower Commission to urge the use of Negro workers to the highest degree possible. Furthermore, the Negro generally proved himself a steady, efficient, and dependable worker. Many employers found that their prewar prejudice had no foundation in fact, and they intended to keep a large number of Negro workers on their post-war payrolls. It was McNutt's sincere belief and hope that the occupational advances which were made by the Negro during the war would be maintained in the post-war period.[47]

The work of the War Manpower Commission aroused favorable and unfavorable comments, quite naturally, from both management and labor. In some communities, management and labor were able to sit down around the council table and develop a truly effective manpower program. Out of these experiences emerged a practical approach basic to the solution of any critical war manpower problem, whether local or national in character. It was sometimes difficult for McNutt to understand why one community, given a problem, could set in motion democratic processes of self-analysis, while another community with a comparable problem found its efforts to achieve these results were paralyzed by prejudice and unreasoning emotion.

One illustration of a community's opposition appeared in an editorial in the Detroit *Free Press* of November 30, 1943. The editorial asked "why a man totally unfit to head the War Manpower Commission in these critical days of shortages in factories and on farms is retained in a position where he had made confusion worse confounded? One can hardly blame a man, for not having more brains than nature gave him and certainly not for floundering about in a job in which he is given neither adequate authority nor a clear-cut policy to administer. As soon as the War Manpower Commission was organized, a subordinate announced that a plan for drafting labor was virtually complete. When organized labor let out a shriek, this was declared to have been 'premature.'

"The retention of Mr. McNutt as head of WMC and of Madam Perkins as head of the Labor Department is symbolic of Administrative ineptitude all along the home front. The whip of criticism should not be applied to these obvious incompetents, who are doing the best they can, but rather to those in higher authority, who keep them in posts they are not big enough to fill. There's where incompetency begins."[48]

This editorial infuriated McNutt, who replied that the writer was so eager to arouse political prejudice that he misstated some of the fundamental facts about the war manpower program. McNutt claimed that it was not "organized labor" that "let out a shriek." He put the blame on Frederick Crawford, president of the National Association of Manufacturers, and Eric Johnston, president of the United States Chamber of Commerce. McNutt charged that the editorial writer was so intent upon making a class issue of manpower administration, and throwing the whole matter into politics, that a simple matter of accuracy did not deter or bother him. McNutt concluded that this type of editorial writing "represents the kind of prejudice and frenzy that has made Detroit's manpower problem difficult to deal with."[49]

On March 28, 1944, McNutt appeared before the Costello Committee of the House Military Affairs Committee, and warned that "the difficulty of replacing men going rapidly into military service may require stronger measures to transfer 4-F's into essential civilian work." McNutt explained that "the Selective Service system will not be drafting any *more* men than originally anticipated but it will be drafting *different* men." He said that the Army would make heavy inroads into the "cream" of the manpower supply and into essential war production and supporting activities "which have been so far afforded some measure of protection." He reported that "manpower utilization up to the present had been a success," and that "critical labor-shortage problems in industrial areas have been solved and labor turnover has been reduced."[50]

Another problem which interfered with the full effectiveness of the war effort on the home front was the interdepartmental rivalry, bickering, and jealousy, due largely to overlapping functions and clashes of personality. On July 15, 1943, President Roosevelt sent identical letters to the heads of various government departments, requesting that disagreements between various departments and agencies should not be publicly aired, but should be submitted to the President by appropriate heads of the conflicting agencies. He stated that he could not longer overlook violations of his instructions.

The President did not place restrictions upon the agencies or departments furnishing statements in response to congressional inquiries, but added, "if when you have a disagreement with another agency as to fact or policy, instead of submitting it to me or submitting it to the Director of War Mobilization for settlement under the terms of the order creating that office, you feel you should submit it to the press, I ask that when you release the statement for publication, you send to me a letter of resignation." The President added that if any subordinate of the various agencies or departments violated his instructions in this regard, he would expect the head of such department or agency to ask for his immediate resignation. The letter was sent to some fifty-five persons, including Cabinet members and McNutt.[51]

On April 29, 1943, the Office of Community War Services, generally known as the OCWS, was established within the Federal Security Agency by an executive order, Paul McNutt becoming its first administrator. It was the last of the three agencies established successively within the defense and war periods to develop and coordinate programs to meet emergency needs in the general field of health. The two previous ones were the Office of the Coordinator of Health, Welfare, and Related Defense Activities, and the Office of Defense Health and Welfare Services. The new Office of Community War Services superseded the latter. The OCWS was a coordinating agency working through and with other federal, state, and local agencies and national and private organizations and their local units.

Among the cooperating federal agencies were the Army, the Navy, the Office of Civilian Defense, the War Manpower Commission, the Federal Works Agency, the War Production

Board, the Federal Housing Authority, the Office of Defense Transportation, the Public Health Service, the Children's Bureau, the Office of Education, the War Food Administration, and the War Relocation Authority. The private organizations included the United Service Organizations, the American Red Cross, Community Chests and Councils, the American Social Hygiene Association, the National Recreational Association, the National Parent Teachers Association, and the Junior Leagues of America. It was the policy of the OCWS to use the services of established agencies to carry out OCWS functions, wherever there were existing agencies, and to establish operating programs only where no appropriate agencies existed. Two of its responsibilities were not within the scope of any other Federal agency—recreation and social protection. Charles P. Taft succeeded McNutt as Administrator in 1943, and Taft was later succeeded by Watson B. Miller, who served until the office was terminated at the end of the war.[52]

Just before McNutt relinquished his duties in connection with the Office of Community War Services, he wrote a pamphlet entitled "Citizens of Tomorrow," in which he gave a wartime challenge to community action. In the Foreword, he quoted from a message which President Abraham Lincoln gave to Congress on July 4, 1861, describing the reason for the Civil War:

"It is a struggle for maintaining in the world that form and substance of Government whose leading object is . . . to lift artificial weights from all shoulders; to clear the paths of laudable pursuits for all; to afford all an unfettered start and a fair chance in the race of life."

McNutt said:

"In war, as Lincoln well knew, the very intensity of the struggle may obscure what the nation is fighting for. The greater the need for concentrating on the battlefront, the greater the necessity of strengthening here at home all that justifies its sacrifices. The more war disrupts our lives, the more responsibility we have to those upon whom its burden falls most heavily. And these include not only men and women plunged into military service or uprooted from their homes to serve in war industry. They include also young people—the teen-age boys and girls who, especially in wartime, may find themselves stranded in a kind of home-front No-Man's Land—too old, in their own eyes, to tolerate the restraints of childhood; too young, in their elders' eyes, to have a part in the nation's war effort. . . . too many of them are being crippled in mind and heart—tragic casualties of wartime living.

"Yet these are the citizens of tomorrow. And tomorrow comes too soon. If they are unprepared, peace—when it is won—will be precarious. For the future is in their hands—not ours. What is in our hands . . . as parents and as citizens of today—is the obligation to see that, on the home front, this struggle does not fail of its purpose. Even more than in the war of which Lincoln wrote, that purpose is—'To afford all an unfettered start—a fair chance in the race of life.'"[53]

The main operating units of the OCWS were the Recreation and Social Protection Divisions. The Recreation Division had been established in January, 1941, to stimulate and promote recreation programs in communities adjacent to military posts and in communities affected by the needs of industrial war workers and their families. When the division and its functions were transferred to the Office of Defense Health and Welfare Services, it became a subordinate unit in the Division of Health and Welfare. On transfer to the OCWS, it again resumed divisional status. Working through a staff of field representatives, the Division advised and encouraged existing local and state recreation agencies to organize leisure-time activities for the armed forces and for civilians in war-congested areas. It certified, to the War Production Board, plans for recreation buildings that needed priorities for materials, and it collaborated with the Federal Works Agency in planning recreation buildings to be erected with federal funds. The Division's representatives aided communities in organizing local war recreation committees and helped them study their problems, appraise their recreational facilities, and organize local resources.

The Social Protection Division had been established in March, 1941, in the Office of the Coordinator of Health, Welfare, and Related Defense Activities, with McNutt as its head. It became a part of the ODHWS Division of Health and Welfare and, on transfer to the OCWS, it again became a division. The Division was responsible for organizing and conducting a national program to check the spread of venereal disease and to repress prostitution in defense areas. Its work was coordinated with the venereal disease control program of the Army, the Navy, and the United States Public Health Service through the Interdepartmental Committee on Venereal Disease control established by the Secretaries of War and Navy, and the Federal Security Administrator, McNutt.

The Day Care Division, known also as the Children's Care Division, was originally established as a section within the Health and Welfare Division of the Office of Defense Health and Welfare Services in July, 1942. It was responsible for promoting and coordinating Federal programs for the care of children of mothers employed in essential industries. It became a clearinghouse of information on the need for and the method of organization of child care services. Several other federal agencies were involved in the child care program, including the War Manpower Commission, the Federal Works Agency, and the Federal Security Agency. The Division was discontinued on June 30, 1943.

Closely associated with the OCWS and its predecessors were the Health and Medical Committee and the Committee on Physical Fitness. The former was set up on September 19,

1940, by the Council of National Defense to advise the Council on the health and welfare aspects of national defense and to coordinate health and medical activities affecting national defense. Its functions were later transferred to the Federal Security Agency and then to the Office of Defense Health and Welfare Services. In April, 1943, its functions were taken over by McNutt's Federal Security Agency. The Committee on Physical Fitness was established within the Federal Security Agency on April 29, 1943. Its function was to promote popular interest in the improvement of health and physical fitness as part of the war effort. The Committee was terminated on June 30, 1945.

Throughout the war, largely due to McNutt's administrative abilities, the various agencies with which he was connected were able to cooperate with one another without too much friction, and the purposes for which they were instituted were carried out most effectively. Federal, state, and local units worked together in an excellent spirit of cooperation. This was especially true in the field of community war services. Out of the wartime experiment in meeting community needs grew new concepts in the field of social services. Cooperative action was greatly expanded, among people as individuals and among public and private agencies. New techniques and methods of interrelationship among government agencies were explored. Many different groups of citizens within local communities and many agencies of government, federal, state and local, united in an interlocking effort to meet and solve problems affecting the lives of people.

When the Office of Community War Services ended its life on June 30, 1946, its director, Watson B. Miller, who was one of the successors to McNutt, praised the loyal and constructive service of the men and women who served on its staff. He said:

"There will be no monuments with names inscribed to mark the services of these workers. . . . There will be monuments to this joint effort, however, written across the length and breadth of the land—in new and improved schools, hospitals, community centers, health services, playgrounds, and swimming pools, stimulated by their counsel and services to communities; in day-care centers for children; in schools open for community use which once were closed when classes were over; in cities freed of the scourge of red-light districts and commercialized prostitution, and in better detention facilities for youth in trouble; in broad community planning and vastly increased expenditures for public recreation."

Miller praised McNutt, to whom the program owed much, for his vision and bold initiative.[54]

During the war, McNutt was relatively inactive in the political arena, although many people thought that his responsibilities in connection with the War Manpower Commission and other agencies placed him in an especially favorable position for a leading role in the elections of 1944. Shortly after President Roosevelt appointed him Manpower czar in 1942, Mark Thistlethwaite, writing in the Indianapolis *News*, wrote that some commentators "devoted quite as much space to his supposed 1944 ambitions as to his unprecedented and virtually dictatorial powers over the lives of his fellow Americans. That the Hoosier had been placed on a hot spot was assumed with a singular unanimity, but a diversity of opinion marked a wide discussion of the causes of his outstanding promotion and its effects on his political future."

Thistlethwaite stated that "some believe that no presidential candidate could survive for eighteen months the fires of wrath the czardom of manpower is certain to engender. Others, with less certainty, foresee the possibility of McNutt establishing his right to be President by his handling of the new job, admittedly one of the most difficult in connection with the war." He observed that "the speculation did not exclude political motives on the part of President Roosevelt," and raised the question "Had McNutt been designated as the heir apparent or consigned to the political fires of oblivion before the national convention?"

"Meanwhile," continued Thistlethwaite, "hats were off to McNutt as the victor in the behind-the-scenes struggle which has been dubbed the battle of Washington. Instead of being kicked upstairs into the Cabinet, as had been suggested, and then, as Secretary of the Interior, shunted into the war background, the Hoosier emerged on the front line of offense shoulder-to-shoulder with James F. Byrnes, Donald M. Nelson, Leon Henderson, . . . and Harold L. Ickes." The New York *Times* was quoted as having stated "The President has moved in the right direction" in commenting on the executive orders appointing McNutt and others. "Whether he has picked the ideal men remains to be seen. But our own view has been that the chief of manpower, because of the enormous powers he will exercise, ought to have been a figure wholly outside the field of active politics, and in no way vulnerable to the slightest suspicion of political ambition. We thought for this reason, that McNutt was not the right choice. We think now that he will be under handicaps that would not have existed for a man of different background," the New York *Times* concluded.

Thistlethwaite also quoted from the Baltimore *Sun*:

"McNutt now comes first, if not in the hearts of his countrymen, at least in their lives. . . . It has long been said of him that he would rather be President than right. Until recently it appeared that he would be neither. But now, it begins to appear that, pleasant or unpleasant as that prospect may be, he, after all, some day, may be both."

Apparently commentators still were undecided as to

exactly the fate toward which McNutt was headed, but all thought that he was on his way somewhere and going fast.[55]

As for McNutt himself, however, he seemed to have no further political ambitions after the 1940 election. He kept himself busy with his many war jobs, and remained quite aloof from active political involvement. He even parted company with three important Hoosiers who were in his 1940 presidential campaign. To be more accurate, perhaps, they had broken with McNutt.

These three men who had been most responsible for Mc-Nutt's defeat in 1940 were Oscar R. Ewing, Wayne Coy, and Fowler Harper. Ewing was the vice-chairman of the Democratic national committee. Coy had been secretary to McNutt when he was governor and his assistant in the Philippines. He was currently assistant director of the federal budget and an intimate friend of Roosevelt. Harper was a law professor at Indiana University when McNutt was dean of the law school. He later became vice-chairman of the Manpower Commission and then switched to the Bureau of Economic Warfare. These men did not like Frank McHale, who had been Mc-Nutt's political mentor, and the feeling was mutual.

According to Everett C. Watkins, writing in the Indianapolis *Star* on August 9, 1943, the break came during the 1940 Democratic National Convention when President Roosevelt had telephoned that he wanted Wallace as his running mate. Ewing, Coy, and Harper considered that it would be folly, under the circumstances, to promote McNutt for the nomination, and they recommended acquiescence to the President's wishes. McHale believed the convention would not accept Wallace, and that McNutt should not withdraw. But McNutt decided to be a good soldier and go along with his chief's request, rather than to throw the convention into chaos. By 1943, however, McNutt had come to the belief that

McHale was right and the other three were wrong. This conclusion was probably the basis for McNutt's decision to shun any further political candidacy.[56] He was not active in the 1944 campaign.

It had been quite obvious that the Roosevelt administration would have a tough time in renominating Vice President Wallace in 1944, and McHale still thought that McNutt would have a chance. He still believed him to be the outstanding Democrat in Indiana, and the one who had the organization behind him. Other state leaders thought otherwise, and were willing to go along with Wallace.

McHale demanded a roll call of the delegation, which voted overwhelmingly for McNutt, proving that McNutt was still popular in Indiana, at least. This seemed to satisfy Mc-Hale, and the Indiana delegation cast their votes solidly for Harry S Truman, the President's final choice. The McNutt supporters had realized that their candidate could get nowhere in the convention, but were anxious to make the move in his behalf. It really amounted to McNutt's political swan song.[57]

The War Manpower Commission was terminated at the end of the war. An executive order of September 19, 1945, transferred its functions and constituent agencies to the Department of Labor, with the exception of the Procurement and Assignment Service, which was transferred to the Federal Security Agency.[58] The following month, McNutt also resigned as head of the Federal Security Administration, to assume his second appointment as High Commissioner to the Philippine Islands.

Many of McNutt's colleagues and close associates in his various wartime posts extended to him their thanks for his cooperation and unselfish endeavors, and expressed their best wishes for the future. A farewell dinner was given in his honor on October 25, 1945, at the Hotel Carlton, Washington. It was attended by scores of his friends, including Watson B. Miller, who presented McNutt with testimonials of their esteem.

Miller said:

"Mr. High Commissioner, this is a completely spontaneous social parliament. That there are not hundreds of additional members of your truly fine organization here is entirely due to space and service limitations. So, some of us must be as happy as possible in this atmosphere of hail and farewell, and some of us must be regretful at not being able to be near you as you are about to go from us for awhile. You will want to hear from a few of your team captains who are, I am sure, certain to reflect the sentiments of all of us who are here and of all those who are a little distance away.

"Boss—and it would take a man of much less warmth and imagination to fail to detect what that word means between you and yours—the other night it was suggested to you that before very long we would all be working together again. If that time doesn't come, we shall paraphrase the 'Take It or Leave It' program and say 'You'll be sorry.' And if what *we* hope for does not come about, certainly all of us will be sorry."[59]

Warren F. Draper, Acting Surgeon General, spoke for the United States Public Health Service. He recalled three little incidents "which characterize the Governor for me." The first was McNutt's taking the oath of office as Federal Security Administrator in 1939 in the Surgeon General's office in the Public Health Service Building. "Never in my thirty-five years in the government service have I known a chief who was more scrupulous in protecting the integrity of the agencies under his control, nor more earnest, both through precept and example, in observing the spirit and intent of government laws and regulations," he said.

The second incident which Draper recalled was the visit of Doctor Parran and himself to the little office building of the National Institute of Health. On that occasion, McNutt had said:

"Let me know what you need. Give me sound supporting reasons and I'll stand behind you to the end."

"And that is the way it has always been," said Draper. "If there is anything more heartening and reassuring to the members of an operating agency than to have the positive knowledge that their chief will stand behind them with everything he's got, and carry their cause to the highest quarters if need be, I have yet to find out what it is."

The third incident was a "personal tribute that I shall always remember. In the midst of important meetings in Paris, the Governor took the time to come to my headquarters in the stables of the Palace of Versailles to give me a word of encouragement and cheer. When he came into our closely crowded office and greeted me joyously as 'Warren,' my stock went up by leaps and bounds. He was then gracious enough to receive the members of my staff and, best of all, to go to the room where our enlisted personnel of American WACS and British ATS were working, shake hands with each, and make a little speech which they will never forget as long as they live. That is an example of genuine friendship that means a lot down deep inside, and, Governor, that is the reason why your friends are here tonight with sorrow at having you leave, but wishing you all good things in the days ahead."[60]

Remarks were also made by Dr. Winifred Overholser, Superintendent of Saint Elizabeth's Hospital, Washington, D. C., who said:

"During the period of a little over five and a half years that the Hospital has been in the Federal Security Agency, it has consistently received from the Administrator and his assistants the most understanding, generous and strong support that any bureau could ever hope from a department head. Such an attitude calls forth from subordinates their fullest efforts; it is, indeed, the essential basis of loyalty. I, for one, know of very few indeed who can command the loyalty, the admiration, respect and affection that those whose privilege it has been to work with and for him feel for Governor McNutt. For these reasons we regret deeply losing him as Administrator, despite the knowledge that his successor will carry on his policies with energy and a warm human understanding.

"We rejoice, however, that Governor McNutt's extraordinary administrative and governmental abilities are to be utilized in a large and internationally important sphere as High Commissioner to the Philippines. It is, indeed, only a realization of the importance of the assignment that could reconcile us fully to the severance of ties that have bound us for these years.

"To you, Governor McNutt, the staff and the employees of Saint Elizabeth's Hospital express our deepest appreciation of your support and assistance, and our warmest wishes for your continued success in the high mission on which you are embarking."[61]

Another tribute was paid McNutt by P. B. Dunbar, Commissioner of the Food and Drug Administration. He said it was "not pleasant . . . to have to say good-bye . . . after our very happy association during five busy and fruitful years." But the Food and Drug Administration "shares the universal feeling that no man in the United States is better fitted to take up the very difficult task on which you are now embarking. No more convincing evidence could be offered of our national determination to deal sympathetically and helpfully with the gallant people of the Philippines than your selection as High Commissioner. . . . We in the Food and Drug Administration are sorry indeed to see you go. . . . We wish you Godspeed and the fullest measure of success in the vital work you are now taking over."[62]

Remarks were also made by A. J. Altmeyer, chairman of the Social Security Board. He quoted Lord Byron, who said:

"All partings should be sudden—otherwise they make an eternity of moments."

Yet, Altmeyer continued, "These occasions have a happy as well as a sad aspect because they enable us to say the things to a friend and associate which otherwise we, unfortunately, would never bring ourselves to say. Especially is this true in the case of a man who has been and is a great public figure. Many people come to look upon men in public life as they look upon public buildings—they assume such men can be talked about and criticized and castigated as if they were made of marble instead of flesh and blood.

"I think that has been true of the man we are honoring tonight. We all know how much unfair abuse and criticism he has been obliged to take. Because he has taken it without flinching, people have assumed he didn't have any feelings. We know differently. We also know that it was his very capacity for loyalty—loyalty to his commander-in-chief, to his associates, and to his subordinates—which made him shoulder blame which he might easily have shifted to the shoulders of others. . . .

"He has been a kind, considerate and, perhaps I should add, trustful boss. We can only hope we have deserved his trust. Our regret at his leaving us is assuaged by our realization that he is uniquely qualified to undertake the Herculean task of helping a brave people rebuild its entire national structure on the ruins caused by a cruel and treacherous enemy. Therefore, all that we can justifiably do is to say to our departing chief: Goodbye, good luck, and God bless you. Our love and affection go with you."[63]

Also praising McNutt was J. W. Studebaker, Commissioner of Education, in whose agency the Office of Education was located after it was transferred from the Department of the Interior in July, 1939. Studebaker expressed his appreciation for the many ways in which McNutt had been solicitous not merely of the official status of his subordinates but also of their personal welfare. He complimented McNutt on his prophetic vision before Pearl Harbor, and for his ability to realize important results. He said that McNutt had truly made of his organization a Federal Security Agency "Commonweatlth of Nations" rather than a Federal Security Agency "Empire." Studebaker concluded:

"As you go forth to the Far East to undertake the toughest job of your life, Governor, you have the best wishes and devoted friendship of all of us in the United States Office of Education."[64]

Mordecai W. Johnson, president of Howard University, was also called on to pay tribute to McNutt. As soon as McNutt had become aware that the work at Howard University was to be part of his responsibility, he said, McNutt visited the school and made the most thoughtful inquiries regarding their plans, progress, and hopes. He gave assurances of his support, and these assurances he kept. He supported the school's budget requests before the Bureau of the Budget and before Congress. Johnson said: "His spirit and good will toward us, has found a steady expression in the men and women of his staff. They have been friendly and helpful to the University; and more than once they have taken a spontaneous and strong initiative on our behalf.

"Governor McNutt has been entirely open and above board in all of his dealings with us. Whenever he has been called up by others to take any action with regard to our work, he has made us aware of the issue and has always consulted us before acting. Under his administration there has been no single instance when current political influences were projected into the internal life of the University. He has supported the inward integrity of our processes for the admission and graduation of students and for the appointment and retirement of personnel; and he has respected and protected the academic freedom of the teachers. It is not sufficient for me, therefore, to say that Governor McNutt commands our esteem. He has won our affection.

"When we think of ourselves and our work, we see him go away with the deepest reluctance. But when we think of our brothers in the Philippines, we join in sending him forth with our prayers. Governor McNutt, may God bless your work, and may He make His face to shine upon you also and upon your loved ones!"[65]

The Columbia Institution for the Deaf was represented at the dinner by its executive officer, Leonard Norstad. This school was the smallest child in McNutt's official family, yet it had received services out of all proportion to its size, and Norstad expressed his appreciation of all McNutt's efforts in its behalf.[66]

The final tribute of the occasion was expressed by the General Counsel of the Federal Security Agency, who said of McNutt:

"There are few men in the United States who have received as much public acclaim, support, respect and affection as you have."

He related that shortly after it became known that McNutt was to return to the Philippines, several members of the staff were discussing his leaving, and they spoke of the kind of boss he had been. One said how much he appreciated having responsibility delegated to him. Another stated how much it had meant to him to know that McNutt was always accessible for consultation and sound advice. A third spoke of the excellent work McNutt had done in "carrying the ball" for the Agency and for each member of the staff. A fourth expressed his gratification for the assurance of backing that everyone who worked with McNutt felt. And so the conversation went back and forth in praise of McNutt until one of the men summed it up by saying:

"He is the best G— D—— boss I ever had."

With that conclusion they all agreed, as did all the members of McNutt's staff.[67]

A poem —"To Governor McNutt" — written by Sidney Cohen, was read:

"Look around you Governor, and what do you see?
There's a tear on the face of the S. S. B.,
And a pain in the heart of the potentate
From the office that knows how to educate.
There's a sadness spread over Public Health,
Like the man who has lost his last bit of wealth.
And the boys who protect your Food and Drugs
In grief, are chewing their nails and rugs.
The large and the small will miss you much,
And regret the loss of your Hoosier touch.
In war you controlled the Nation's manpower,
In peace you built a security tower,
And now you return from whence you came,
To comfort the sick, impoverished and lame.
No doubt you know that the job is tough,
And your share will surely be more than enough
But think of what you may go through,
You're out of the fire—but into the stew.
Remember how McKellar would snort,
'. . . Give me this, or that, or some other report.'

[337]

But wait till you get to the Philippines
You'll need a battalion or two of marines,
To furnish MacArthur with detail and fact,
Or he's liable to say, '. . . I shall come back.'
No more House and Senate Committees,
Just satisfy Doug, Osmena, and Ickes,
You made your choice, you take your pick,
It's not too bad, getting used to it.
Courage, Governor, remember Bataan,
Go on out, do the best you can.
Our wishes and hopes are extended to you,
We're sure of success in whatever you do."[68]

McNutt was then presented with a scroll with ninety-three signatures affixed, together with the names of nine persons who participated in the program but who were unable to attend the dinner. The scroll was inscribed:

PAUL V. McNUTT
FEDERAL SECURITY ADMINISTRATOR
1939-1945

To "the Governor," who brought to the new-born Federal
Security Agency his vision of democracy in action
and his gifts for public administration —

To the leader, under whose guidance this Agency has
grown in breadth and stature and in devotion to the
cause of health, education, and security for the
American people —

To the public servant, who goes on now to postwar pioneering on the frontiers of the better world for which he
has ever striven —

To Paul V. McNutt, we members of the Federal Security
family, pay this tribute not only of respect but of
friendship, as we give him Godspeed.[69]

A year later on October 15, 1946, President Harry S Truman awarded McNutt the highly coveted *Medal for Merit* for his outstanding contributions during the war years. The citation accompanying the award stated:

"PAUL VORIES McNUTT, for exceptionally meritorious conduct in the performance of outstanding services to the United States. Mr. McNutt, as Federal Security Administrator, Director of the Office of Community War Services, and Chairman of the War Manpower Commission throughout the entire war period when maintenance of the Nation's civilian strength was imperative, performed a unique and vital service in coordinating and promoting essential home front services to safeguard the public health, to provide emergency health, education, recreation and other community services in hard-pressed war areas, and to meet the extraordinary demands of war industry by training workers for maximum efficiency, tapping new sources of manpower, and, through his leadership, obtaining the voluntary support of management and labor essential to maximum results in carrying out his programs for conserving the Nation's human resources and utilizing them in the best interests of the Nation's all-out war effort. By his broad grasp of these intricate and inter-related problems, by his skill in administration and in securing the Nationwide cooperation of diverse groups, by his unswerving devotion to the Nation's democratic principles even under the pressures of war, and by his far-sighted understanding of the necessity to maintain the essential fabric of American life, Mr. McNutt contributed to the successful outcome of the war, far beyond the demands of duty."

The citation was signed by President Harry S Truman.[70]

And so the curtain came down on another episode in the career of Paul V. McNutt. When the President pinned the Medal on the coat lapel of McNutt at an inner-sanctum ceremony at the White House, the Hoosier towered above the little man from Missouri. The scene recalled the fact that if President Roosevelt had accepted McNutt for the Vice Presidency in 1940, the man from Indiana might have been President instead of Truman. But such developments are the results of the shifting fates of history.

Notes for Chapter 7

1 Franklin D. Roosevelt to McNutt, August 3, 1940. Franklin D. Roosevelt Memorial Library, Hyde Park, New York, PPF 2836.

2 Roosevelt to McNutt, November 28, 1940. Roosevelt Library, PPF 2836.

3 *Hoosier Sentinel,* December 20, 1940.

4 Paul V. McNutt, *Special Problems in Our Health Defenses* (pamphlet). Reprint No. 2274 from *The Public Health Reports,* Vol. 56, No. 19, May 9, 1944, pp. 988-992.

5 Paul V. McNutt, *Health Agencies—Their Responsibilities and Their Opportunities During the Present Crisis* (pamphlet), Reprint No. 2376 from *The Public Health Reports,* Washington, 1942, Vol. 57, No. 19, May 8, 1942. pp. 685-691, p. 2.

6 *Ibid.* p. 3.

7 *Ibid.*

8 *Ibid.*

9 *Ibid.*

10 *Ibid.* p. 4.

11 *Ibid.* p. 5.

12 Donald D. Smith to Roosevelt, February 6, 1942. Roosevelt File OF 3700. Roosevelt Libary.

13 Roosevelt to Smith. Roosevelt Libary.

14 Frances Perkins. *The Roosevelt I Knew* (New York 1946), (viii-408 pp.) p 363.

15 *Ibid.* p. 370

16 *Ibid.* p. 373.

17 *On Active Service in Peace and War,* Henry L. Stimson and McGeorge Bundy (New York, 1948) (pp. xxii-698), p. 481.

18 *Ibid.* p. 374.

19 Roosevelt Library, File OF 3700, July 22, 1942.

20 Roosevelt Library, File OF 3700, October 8, 1942.

21 These statements are taken from an article which McNutt had prepared for the *Encyclopedia Americana.* A typed copy of the article is in the Lilly Library.

22 Fowler V. Harper, "The WMC Tackles the Manpower Problem," in *Industrial Manpower Controls,* 1942. Personnel Series Number 60, American Management Association, 330 West 42nd Street, New York, New York (pamphlet).

23 *Ibid.*

24 *Ibid.*

25 *Ibid.*

26 *Ibid.*

27 *Ibid.*

28 "Maritime Utilization of Manpower," a speech given by McNutt at the Winter Personnel Conference of the American Management Association, Palmer House, Chicago, February 10-13, 1943. Article in *Operating under Manpower Controls* (pamphlet), Personnel Series Number 64, American Management Association, New York.

29 *Ibid.*

30 *Ibid.*

31 *Ibid.*

32 *Ibid.*

33 *Ibid.*

34 Donald M. Nelson, *Arsenal of Democracy* (New York, 1946) (xviii-438) p. 307.

35 *Ibid.* p. 317.

36 James F. Byrnes, *All in One Lifetime,* (New York 1958, 432 pp), pp. 190-2.

37 *On Active Service in Peace and War,* p. 482.

38 Note from McNutt to Roosevelt, February 20, 1943. Roosevelt Library PPF 1820.

39 *On Active Service in Peace and War,* p. 482.

40 Bruce Catton, *The War Lords of Washington* (New York 1948, 303 pp), p. 223.

41 *All in One Lifetime,* pp. 206-7.

42 Catton, *The War Lords of Washington,* p. 223

43 *Ibid.* p. 238

44 *Ibid.* p. 278.

45 *All In One Lifetime.* p. 92.

46 Typed sheet: "Wanted: More Women Workers." by Paul V. McNutt for Fawcett Publications, 1943. Lilly Library.

47 Typed sheet: "Statement by Paul V. McNutt, for William A. Chambers, Indianapolis *Recorder,*" 1943. Lilly Library.

48 The Detroit *Free Press,* November 30, 1943.

49 "Draft Answer to Detroit *Free Press* Editorial," typed copy in Lilly Library. December 9, 1943.

50 Typed statement, March 3, 1944. Lilly Library.

51 Letter from President Roosevelt to Heads of Departments, July 15, 1943. Roosevelt Library, File OF 3700.

52 National Archives, typed material, "Introduction," *Preliminary Inventories,* Number 132, *Records of the Office of Community Services,* compiled by Estelle Rebec, The National Archives, National Archives and Record Service, General Services Administration, Washington: 1960.

53 Paul V. McNutt, *Citizens of Tomorrow: A Wartime Challenge to Community Action,* pamphlet, November, 1943. National Archives.

54 *Teamwork in Community Services, 1941-1946,* Washington, D. C. This is the final report of the agency.

55 Mark Thistlethwaite in Indianapolis *News,* December 2, 1942. Clipping in McNutt File, Indiana State Library.

56 Everett C. Watkins, Indianapolis *Star,* August 9, 1943. Clipping in McNutt File, Indiana State Library.

57 McHale to author.

58 Extensive material on the War Manpower Commission is found in the National Archives, Washington, D. C. Contains many items concerning McNutt.

59 Watson B. Miller to Paul V. McNutt, October 25, 1945. Mrs. Watson's scrapbook.

60 Warren F. Draper, Acting Surgeon General, to McNutt, October 25, 1945. Mrs. Watson's scrapbook.

61 Dr. Winifred Overholser, Supt. of St. Elizabeth's Hospital, Washington, D. C., to McNutt, October 25, 1945. Mrs. Watson's scrapbook.

62 P. B. Dunbar, Commissioner of Food and Drug Administration, to McNutt, October 25, 1945. Mrs. Watson's scrapbook.

63 A. J. Altmeyer, chairman, Social Security Board, to McNutt, October 25, 1945. Mrs. Watson's scrapbook.

64 J. W. Studebaker, U. S. Commissioner of Education. Mrs. Watson's scrapbook.

65 Mordecai W. Johnson, President of Howard University. Mrs. Watson's scrapbook.

66 Leonard Norstad, Executive Officer, Columbia Institution for the Deaf. Mrs. Watson's scrapbook.

67 General Counsel, Federal Security Agency, Mrs. Watson's scrapbook.

68 *Ibid.*

69 Mrs. Watson's scrapbook.

70 Typed copy, Lilly Library. There is a 240-page "A Short History of the Manpower Commission" prepared by the Dept. of Labor, draft only, June 1947, in Lilly Library.

CHAPTER VIII

A Nation is Born

With the ending of World War II, the United States quickly took steps to return to a peace-time economy. The War Manpower Commission was one of the first of the war-time agencies to be terminated. This was done by executive order on September 19, 1945. McNutt continued as head of the Federal Security Administration, but in October he resigned to accept the appointment from President Truman as High Commissioner of the Philippines for the second time.

These were very difficult days in the relations between the Philippines and the United States. The Islands had felt the full force of the war. They had been occupied by the enemy and their entire economy had been adversely affected. Many of the Filipinos had been disloyal during the occupation, and now there was the very difficult problem of reconciliation. The task of rehabilitation was enormous.

During the war, the armies fighting under General Douglas MacArthur had been unable to deal with the greatly superior force of the Japanese. On February 8, 1942, President Manuel Quezon proposed a plan for the neutralization of the Islands. He called for the immediate independence of the Philippines, instead of waiting until 1946, the year which had been agreed upon by the Tydings-McDuffy Act. Under Quezon's proposal, the forces of both Japan and the United States would be withdrawn from the archipelago. General MacArthur seemed to agree with Quezon's ideas, but President Roosevelt accepted the advice of General George C. Marshall and Secretary of War Henry L. Stimson that the Islands must be defended. There was the pledged word of the United States that the Islands would be defended until independence was granted in 1946[1]

At the time that the Japanese forces attacked the Philippines on December 7, 1941, Manuel Quezon was the President of the Commonwealth, and Sergio Osmena was the Vice President. Shortly thereafter, both men were brought to the United States along with members of the Commonwealth Cabinet, and the functions of the Philippine Government were carried on in Washington until the liberation. Quezon died in Washington in August, 1944, and Osmena assumed the presidency of the Commonwealth.

The American forces reentered Manila on February 3, 1945, and before the end of that month, General Douglas MacArthur had formally invested President Osmena with the full powers of a constitutional chief executive.[2] He served until April, 1946, when he was defeated in an election by Manuel Roxas, who became the last President of the Commonwealth and the first President of the Republic. Roxas died in office in April, 1948, and was succeeded by Elpidio Quirino.[3]

Throughout the war, the United States had never faltered in her determined effort to free the Filipinos from the Japanese invader. Secretary of the Interior Harold L. Ickes has summarized the American position:

"We had already proposed to give a loyal and fearless

people independence of the American variety, democracy in the American image. We envisaged in our minds the right, under the Filipino flag, of every citizen of that country to enjoy freedom and equal opportunity under the law in the first Christian republic in the Far East."[4]

As Secretary of the Interior, Ickes was charged with certain responsibilities with respect to the Philippine Islands. After the fall of Bataan, the powers of the American High Commissioner to the Philippines were transferred to him by a special mandate of President Roosevelt. He naturally shared President Osmena's happiness when America recaptured the Islands. General MacArthur immediately requested the return of Osmena to the Islands, but without an American High Commissioner.[5]

When the war ended, however, President Truman did not follow General MacArthur's advice, and McNutt's appointment followed.

The choice of McNutt for this post was a good one. He was well acquainted with the problems of the Far East, having served in this same capacity from 1937 to 1939. And he was popular in the Philippines, not only with the people but also with high government officials. All respected him for his integrity and candor, even though they did not always agree with him.

In some quarters, however, the appointment of McNutt came as a shock. President Sergio Osmena was especially disturbed by the selection, as he felt that it was a violation of a promise made by President Roosevelt at Warm Springs only a few days before his death, to the effect that independence would be effected no later than 1946, and Osmena was afraid this would mean delay. McNutt was familiar with Philippine affairs, but he was suspected of favoring a "re-examination" of the independence question—by which he meant a postponement of Philippine independence.[6]

Immediately McNutt was faced with a multitude of problems, not only those related to the results of the war, but also those in connection with the anticipated independence, which was scheduled to become effective July 4, 1946.

Under the Tydings-McDuffy Act, the conduct of foreign relations of the Philippines was entrusted solely to the United States Government. Yet considerable misunderstanding had developed in the public mind of the Filipinos. President Osmena had created the office of Commissioner of Foreign Affairs, but in a release dated December 19, 1945, High Commissioner McNutt pointed out that this did not in any sense transfer jurisdiction over foreign relations from the United States Government to the Commonwealth Government, but was merely intended to form a preparatory organization to set up the machinery for the conduct of foreign relations after the Philippines became independent.[7]

McNutt declared further that the Philippine Commissioner of Foreign Affairs was not authorized under law to conduct any transactions with foreign governments. It had only such authority, he said, "as the Philippine Commonwealth wishes to grant it for the study of foreign affairs problems and for the training of personnel to assume the functions when they are relinquished by the United States Government." The fact of Philippine representation in the United Nations Organization was at the invitation of the United States as the sovereign power, and constituted "ideological recognition of the forthcoming status of the Philippines as an independent nation and of the role of the Philippine people as allies in the war against the Axis."[8]

McNutt continued:

"By law and by international convention the conduct of foreign relations is reserved to the President of the United States and to his duly accredited representatives. . . . The only accredited representative of the President of the United States in the Philippines is the United States High Commissioner through whom all official contacts between foreign representatives in the Philippines and the sovereign power in the Philippines must be made. At higher levels these contacts must be made between the foreign government and the Department of State in Washington," McNutt concluded.[9]

During the next few months High Commissioner McNutt was busy handling the affairs connected with his office, especially matters concerned with the restoration of a peacetime economy and problems resulting from enemy occupation of the islands. On December 18, he left Manila for Tokyo for a series of conferences with American occupation officials and economic experts in Japan and China. In Tokyo he conferred with General Douglas MacArthur and with officials of Ambassador Edwin Pawley's Reparations Mission. He discussed with General MacArthur matters connected with Army operations in the Philippines, and the question of possible benefits for guerillas.[10]

The overwhelming problem in American-Philippine relations in the years immediately following the ending of the war revolved around the subject of independence and its probable results. All other matters were merely corollary to this central theme, although these economic decisions would determine the future of the Philippines. There was much concern not only in regard to the rehabilitation of the war-damaged land, but also the much more important question of trade relations with the United States. The fundamental issue involved was whether the Filipinos would continue to have highly preferential access to the American market for their exports, or be more nearly self-sufficient, with the power to sell their surplus products to other countries.

Writing in *Foreign Policy Reports*, October 1, 1945, Walter Wilgus declared:

"Viewed as a part of this country's general foreign policy, the independence program for the Philippines presents somewhat contradictory aspects. If we maintain that tariff preferences over a long period are essential to Philippine prosperity, but at the same time urge a world policy of nonpreferential agreements—in opposition, for example, to the British imperial preferences adopted in 1934—our position would be plainly inconsistent.[11]

"As the last four years may literally be called four years out of the life of the Philippine Commonwealth, the independence program could logically be deferred from 1946 to 1950, or even later, because of the new burden of war damage. But little Filipino or American sentiment for delay is manifest at present."[12]

Yet Jose C. Zulveta, Speaker of the Commonwealth House of Representatives, according to Wilgus, was "reported to be seeking a protectorate (*Christian Science Monitor*, July 21, 1945) and it has been rumored—although later denied—that General Manuel Roxas, President of the Senate, is inclined to favor Dominion status for the islands. Some American sources report that as many as 85 per cent of the Filipino people do not wish independence. (For example, Victor Ridder, *New York Journal of Commerce*, June 12-16, 1945)"[13]

Complete, immediate and absolute independence had been the demand of the leading politicians of the Islands for half a century, and the mass of the people "although not realizing the responsibility it entails, have been indoctrinated with its presumed desirability for the last forty years," wrote Wilgus. "While this sentiment has probably been weakened because of their unhappy experiences under the puppet government, which they were told represented 'independence,' a complete reversal seems unlikely, and a Filipino Presidential candidate who advocated anything short of independence would show unusual audacity."[14]

"It seems equally improbable," continued Wilgus, "that the question of independence will be reopened on the initiative of the United States." Yet he recalled that McNutt had suggested such a course in a quote from the New York *Times*, March 24, 1945: "If the Philippines step off into an uncharted sea, as some of their leaders seem to be advocating, the islands are surely destined for trouble"; but McNutt acknowledged that "we may have to let the Philippines take their freedom now and learn the hard way. It is more than possible that if they get their freedom now they may never again attain their pre-war economic stability and may destine themselves to a permanently lowered standard of living."[15]

In general, however, there appeared little disposition to debate the issue. The United States was definitely committed to the independence program, and any proposed change would hurt American prestige abroad. The Filipino leaders would not be expected to ask for any revised status. In the meantime, the internal policies of the Islands and their external relations increased in significance to the United States.

In order to clarify his own position on this matter, McNutt issued a statement from Tokyo on December 24, 1945:

"I have heard reports that most Filipinos do not desire independence. As far as I am concerned, those are only reports which have no official status. Officially the policy of the United States is crystal-clear. As requested by the Filipino people, through their leaders, we have promised to grant independence to the Philippines on July 4, 1946. We will carry out that pledge. For my part I shall do my best to make that grant possible and successful. All our efforts are being directed toward the establishment of a free and prosperous Philippine republic. Any move for any other status for the Philippines must come from the Filipino people themselves. The United States will not initiate such a move. Independence is not an issue today. Our problems deal with the preparation of the Philippines for independence. We must not lose sight of that goal."[16]

This statement did not clarify the issue, however, as the average Filipino had always associated McNutt with re-examination.[17]

McNutt's analysis of the situation seemed to prevail, regardless of the attitude of some who opposed independence in 1946. He said:

"Whatever sincere doubts as to the wisdom of independence may have been expressed in the past by some Filipinos and Americans there is no longer an independence issue today. The only issue is the tremendous task of rehabilitation and preparations for independence, on which all Filipinos and Americans should concentrate in order to make economic democracy possible."

He followed this up with reassuring statements in public speeches that the Philippines had won its spurs as an independent nation and that the United States would give every assistance to help them rise from the ravages of war. In January, 1946, in speaking to thousands of American soldiers in Manila, he paid tribute to Filipino loyalty and promised continued American help to the Philippines "based on their willingness to construct here a free land for free men, free of intolerance, free of repression, primarily devoted to Philippine interests, by accepting in full the obligations of the world community."[18]

In February, 1946, McNutt appeared before the House Appropriations Committee and gave some first-hand information as to the conditions in the Philippines: "The physical situation is indescribable," he said. "Manila is 85 per cent destroyed. It is a city of missing faces and missing places, and the same thing may be said for the rest of the islands, and for the other large communities of the islands. . . . They have suffered untold losses in materials, and they have suffered almost irreparable damage to their economy.

"The four things, of course, that the Philippines produce are sugar, hemp, tobacco, and cocoanut products. Those hardly exist as going industries. That is, that economy does not exist today. The result is that with their property destroyed, and their economy seriously injured, the Philippines face problems that would shake any people, and especially a people who are about to become an independent nation in the society of nations."[19]

The Indianapolis *Times* published an interesting article about McNutt during his flying visit to Washington. The author of the article, Donald D. Hoover, praised the High Commissioner for the important part he had played in the Far East policy of the United States. McNutt was characterized as a man "who is either liked intensely or disliked as heartily by his Hoosier associates . . . and many of them fail to grasp the job he has done on a national and international scale. This may be either because he has done them favors or denied them favors . . . or it may be because so often folks hate to see others get ahead, particularly if they appear at times to have 'grown too big for their britches.' McNutt's critics say he has done just that."[20]

Hoover saw a decided change in McNutt from the "ebullient glamour boy of even ten years ago." He thought he was "infinitely more serious and less full of conscious charm," and reflected by his seriousness "the contribution he has made in his present assignment and in his preceding posts as chairman of the War Manpower Commission, Social Security Administrator and other posts in President Roosevelt's inner circle. His friends . . . were impressed by the soberness of his approach, as well as pleased that he was an important international figure and making good at it."

As to McNutt's future, Hoover concluded with the observation that maybe McNutt had been "too busy to take care of his home fences, or perhaps he has no more political ambitions in Indiana . . . perhaps he will go to New York to a big law practice. Whatever he does, we should keep in mind that he has been a credit to Indiana."[21]

Manuel Roxas was elected the last President of the Commonwealth in April, 1946, in spite of certain charges that he had collaborated with the Japanese during the war.[22] He had formerly been secretary of finance in President Quezon's cabinet and chairman or member of various Philippine missions to the United States before the war. In 1940 he had favored a re-appraisal and re-examination of Philippine-American relations for the purpose of extending them beyond 1946, because of the war in the Far East. His views were understood to reflect those of President Quezon.[23] Yet following the war, he had become an ardent champion of the terms of the Tydings-McDuffy Act, and after his election as President of the Commonwealth, he devoted his efforts to paving the way toward independence for the Philippines.

During the Philippine presidential elections, the United States had not expressed a preference for either candidate. McNutt had adopted a hands-off policy, which had the approval of President Truman. McNutt had issued a matter-of-fact statement on February 26, 1946:

"We neither support, directly or indirectly, any candidate, nor do we look with disfavor, directly or indirectly, on any candidate. The United States Government will carry out its promised aid to the Philippine people regardless of whom they choose for their next president."[24]

Roxas took his Presidential oath of office on May 28, and delivered his inaugural speech before the ruins of the Legislative Building in Manila. The ceremony outshone the independence formalities five weeks later.[25]

Meanwhile, the fundamental features of American postwar policy in the Philippines were crystallizing. Congress finally adopted the basic legislation governing future trade relations between the United States and the Islands, together with a strong rehabilitation policy. After considerable deliberation, drafting and redrafting, Congress finally adopted the legislation and it was signed by President Truman. (Philippine Trade Act of 1946, and Philippine Rehabilitation Act of 1946, both approved on April 30, 1946)[26]

In order to implement this legislation and the future economic and political relations between the United States and the Philippines, President-elect Manuel A. Roxas and High Commissioner McNutt had flown to Washington early in May and conferred with President Truman. At a conference with the President, the men frankly discussed the manifold problems affecting Philippine-American relations. While in the United States, Roxas proposed that McNutt be named the first ambassador to the new Philippine Republic. "No other man could have done what he has done for us in the past six months," said Roxas.[27]

Roxas and McNutt undoubtedly reflected the thinking of the vast majority of the seventeen million Filipinos in regard to independence. "Six years of experience had proved the Commonwealth experiment serviceable and workable as an interim arrangement, for a youthful people attaining nationhood, but impracticable and unsatisfactory as a permanent form of government," wrote Francis B. Sayre, former High Commissioner. "It has spelled irritations and frustrations on both sides. It has meant in the last analysis division of power between two widely different peoples. Such an arrangement is unsatisfactory to both peoples and therefore lacks stability.

In the Philippines the hour has struck. Independence is the only practical way forward. Commitments have been made and expectations have been built upon the part of both peoples. There is no turning back now."[28]

As to the question of whether or not the Filipinos were ready for independence, Sayre said there was "only one way in which that question can be truly answered. That is through the actual experiment. Was the United States ready for independence in 1776? There were many people at that time who would have answered no. By actual experiment we proved that we were. In a strongly rooted independent Philippine nation America has a crucial stake. For over forty years we have been at work implanting in the Filipinos our ideas of individual liberty and the democratic way of life. Their success means our success in furthering American ideas and ideals throughout the strategic East."[29]

Sayre predicted that the greatest difficulty confronting the new Philippine government would be how to achieve economic independence. He said: "Although during the past forty years we were doing everything possible to prepare the Filipinos for political independence, the effect of our economic policy was to make them even more dependent upon the United States. . . . The building of the new Philippine economy will call for a high order of planning and statesmanship. . . . The solution of their economic problem will be a thorny and difficult task. It is not insoluble. American ingenuity and technical skill will be at the beck and call of the Filipinos to help in the solution. . . . Because the present economic dependence of the Filipinos upon the United States is largely of our own making and because it is to our own interest to build for future stability in the Pacific, the Filipino people must be given their independence under such conditions as will assure them sound economic foundations for their future. The American people will not be content with anything less.[30]

"The world has become a unity. Twentieth century conditions force either participation in world activities or else atrophy and extinction. The day of 'magnificent isolation' is past. The United States is compelled, irrespective of its desires, to play an active part in the Pacific and in the Far East or cease to be a great power. The peoples of the world today are interlocked economically, socially, politically. . . . People cannot sell without buying. Trade is a two-way process. . . . The days of imperialism are numbered. . . . The United States and the new Philippine government must work out some practical program for the winning of economic independence. The United States is morally bound to assist the Filipinos in finding a way to achieve independence without economic shipwreck."[31]

Sayre concluded:

"The eyes of the world, and particularly every people in Asia, are upon the Philippines. The measure of American influence for good in the Far East for years to come will depend largely upon the wisdom and the sincerity of American conduct in the Philippines. . . . In the months and the years ahead America has the chance to assist in writing a new chapter in human progress and freedom in the Far East. What is written will depend in large part upon the outcome of the Philippine adventure."[32]

McNutt himself had long been a strong advocate of a policy of re-examination of American commitment to the Philippines. He was viewed by many sections of Filipino public opinion as "one of the most prominent re-examinationists." The pressure of McNutt and other re-examinationists "had a profound influence on the Philippine legislation finally adopted by Congress" in April, 1946.[33]

As early as 1941, McNutt had advocated a re-examination

of Philippine-American relations. Writing in *The Annals of the American Academy of Political and Social Science* in May, 1941, he had declared:

"Recent developments in world affairs have given many Filipino leaders an object lesson and much food for thought. Many of them have come to realize that their complete independence on July 4, 1946, under the terms of the Tydings-McDuffy Act, however attractive from a spiritual viewpoint, may mean a mere trade of sovereignties. And if this becomes a reality, Japan militarists would act, so thinks the average Filipino, as they have acted in China and Manchuria. This would mean the establishment of a ruthless dictatorship aimed at the extermination of all freedom of thought and action. Philippine utilities, communications, mining, transport, and shipping would become operated by Japanese, for Japanese profit exclusively."

McNutt continued:

"The possible alternative to these possible developments clearly resolves itself into continued American union with the Philippines, military, economic, and political—not indissolubly so, but until such time as the Filipinos are capable of successfully manning their own inner defenses alone. Shorn of the Philippines and Guam, American sea power ebbs. To the United States, six thousand miles would mean the difference between a navy capable of fulfilling all its assigned functions, and one limited to coast defense work. . . . Withdrawal from the Philippines would very definitely once and for all time resolve our claims of freedom of the seas and freedom of the air."[34]

McNutt believed that "if we accept the only common-sense interpretation of trade between two countries—purchasing what you need, but have not, and selling what you have, but do not need—trade between the United States and the Philippines, as it has developed under free-trade provisions, can be shown to be wholly normal and mutually advantageous. . . . The United States wishes to solve the Philippine problem in fairness to all—we wish to solve it just as we wish to solve our own domestic problems. It can be solved. On the political side, our flag and sovereignty should remain, allowing to the Philippines every ounce of domestic autonomy they can absorb, holding in our hands foreign affairs, tariffs, immigration, currency, and public debt—scarcely more than marks of the necessary reservation of dominion. We must feel free, in case of any crisis, to help to preserve the democratic basis of the Philippine Government. On the economic side, we should from time to time give the Philippines the best trade deal without injuring our domestic producers. We must admit the possibility of competition. Our aim should be to assist with capital and men, with good will and such preferences as we can afford, the return to a complementary and reciprocal economy between the United States and the Philippines."

In conclusion McNutt said:

"Without too great a loss of time and with the cooperation of the leaders among the Filipinos, we should proceed to a realistic re-examination of the needs of these people and the long-range interests of ourselves. If this study should result in a policy of a permanent political and economic relationship with the Philippines, it must be because the Filipinos want it and because it is in line with our national objectives. America will not impose her sovereignty by force upon any people."[35]

This view was again expressed by McNutt in 1946, when, according to Abraham Chapman, the High Commissioner "was remarkably frank in explaining the essence of American economic policy in the Philippines in a statement he made at the hearings of the House Ways and Means Committee" in 1946. McNutt declared:

"In the Philippines the national economy was geared before the war entirely and completely to export trade. And 95 per cent of that export trade was with the United States. Except for rice and fish, which are locally consumed, 98 per cent of all other production in the Philippines, amounting to $266,000,000 in 1941, is produced for export. . . . And I might and should say here and now that we, the United States, managed it that way. We are responsible for the sole dependency of the Philippines on the American market. Our businessmen and our statesmen in past years allowed the Philippines to become a complete economic dependency on the United States to a greater degree than any single state of the Union is economically dependent on the rest of the United States."[36]

This statement was bitterly condemned in a pamphlet entitled "What Price Philippine Independence," by George Phillips, who called McNutt "a most zealous guardian and promoter of American imperialist interests in the Philippines." Phillips implied that this imperialist policy had made Roxas the president of the Philippines "by grace of American intervention in his behalf. . . . During the Japanese occupation he proved his ability to serve a foreign master well against the interests of the Filipino people. He was a leading member of the Japanese puppet government, holding key posts. That made him eminently suitable as the first choice candidate for American imperialism. . . . President Roosevelt's admonition to the effect that collaborators must be retired from positions of power was not heeded. McNutt was fully satisfied with the collaborationist control of the political life of the country and McNutt's office was in constant conflict with Osmena, the former president of the Philippines. . . . Filipinos now speak bitterly of the three Macs who run the Philippines—MacArthur, McNutt, and their Charlie McCarthy, Roxas."[37]

McNutt's public relations officer, Lieutenant Commander Julius C. Edelstein, was often seen with Roxas;[38] but McNutt himself, speaking about Roxas at the National Press Club in Washington, said he knew nothing about a report to the effect that evidence of alleged pro-Japanese collaboration had been found by the FBI against Roxas.[39] Edelstein was later designated by Roxas as his press relations officer until the day of his inauguration.[40]

Regardless of whether these charges were true or false, the Philippine Trade Act of 1946 was based on the principle of a prolonged period of free trade and continued the economic dependence of the Philippines on the United States for many years in the future. The policy marked a "departure by the Truman administration from the orientation of the Roosevelt administration against a prolonged period of free trade." There was considerable opposition to the act in the Philippines. During the elections there, Roxas kept his views to himself, but upon his arrival in the United States after his election as president, he praised the act as contributing to the good future relations between the United States and the Philippines.[41]

While the bill was being discussed in the Senate Committee on Territories and Insular Affairs, Senator Tydings, chairman, charged that the proponents of the bill were motivated by their opposition to Philippine independence. He raised the question:

"Will the Philippines be independent if they are forever hooked to our economy? If they get ingrained into our economic system we will hold the whip and they will not be independent, just as sure as you are born."[42]

Chapman claimed that it was not only with reference to this legislation that McNutt had aroused bitter criticism among the Filipinos as a foe of Philippine independence. "The practical policies of his office came into conflict with incumbent President Serge Osmena. The Democratic Alliance which grew out of the anti-Japanese resistance movement and which was the most articulate component of the coalition against President-elect Roxas, in the April 23rd elections, declared on March 5th:

'The Democratic Alliance has analyzed the points of controversy between the [Osmena] Administration and the High Commissioner. Fundamentally, the issue between the two is that of colonial liberation as against imperialism.' "[43]

Continuing, Chapman declared:

"Now the Administration is engaged in a controversy with the American High Commissioner over issues which are fundamental in that they affect the rehabilitation and reconstruction of this country and ultimately its independence and security. American insistence on the free trade program is emphasized by the fact that even compensation for war damage, provided for in the Philippine Rehabilitation Act of 1946, is made conditional upon the acceptance of the Free Trade Relations Act by the Philippine Government."[44]

In the meantime, significant events were leading toward the day of Philippine independence, although High Commissioner McNutt realized the difficulties which would follow. On January 20, 1946, in a radio address before a G. I. forum, he said: "Just as our interests in the Philippines will not end on July 4, neither by any means will our responsibilities."

And on January 22, in his report to President Truman, he said:

"It does not at this moment seem humanly possible for the Filipino people, ravaged and demoralized by the cruelest and most destructive of wars, politically split between loyalists and enemy collaborators, with several sizable well-armed dissident groups still at large, to cope with the coincidence of political independence and the tremendous economic demands of rehabilitation."[45]

Later, while speaking in Washington about the role of the United States in the Philippines after independence, McNutt asserted:

"As long as we wish to remain a power in the Far East, and as long as we wish to retain the friendship and respect of the eastern world, we must remain committed in the Philippines and must hold the friendship and confidence of that heroic people."[46]

Perhaps more than any other man, McNutt was cognizant of the tremendous problems which would face the Philippines after they had obtained their complete sovereignty. He realized that the process of adjustment to a more or less independent status would be a difficult one. After living under the domination of the United States for nearly half a century, there would naturally be some Filipinos who had developed an anti-American spirit, although most American citizens had come to regard our Philippine policy as generous and enlightened. But there was a considerable segment of Filipinos who believed that the United States was an imperialist nation bent on exploiting the Islands, and it was becoming increasingly apparent that the principle of United States good will toward the Philippines would only be proved by time, and not by words.[47]

By 1946 there had developed in the Islands increased American economic interests, resulting from the policy of close cooperation between American and Filipino leaders, and there was now the question of the extent that this economic policy would serve American interests as opposed to Filipino interests. During the Philippines national election in 1946, the Bell Trade Bill was seriously discussed. Known officially as the Philippine Trade Act of 1946, it provided for a complex commercial relationship over a period of twenty-eight years. This bill was opposed by many in the Islands as favoring primarily the sugar and cocoanut-oil companies, a big majority of which were owned by American vested interests. Paul V. McNutt was charged with being a tool of such interests.

McNutt himself had described his attitude toward the Bell bill, in a speech before the Philippine Bar Association.

He said he had never worked harder for anything in his life, and described his activity in the following words:

"We used every contact, every stratagem, every trading point we could through those long weeks of negotiations, deliberation, committee hearings, legislative drafting and re-drafting of that trade bill. We buttonholed senators and congressmen in their offices, at their homes, at social gatherings. . . . We had, perhaps, the most active and persistent lobby any bill has ever attracted. We met obstacles at every step, objections from many quarters. Many individuals and groups had different ideas on how best to accomplish the goals most of us were agreed upon. . . . We succeeded in neutralizing almost all the domestic sugar interests, which was a major accomplishment in itself. It took many hours of conferences and arguments, pleas and appeals to patriotism and citations of the economic facts of life."[48]

The absolute necessity for the passage of the Bell bill had been emphasized by McNutt before a Congressional hearing in Washington as early as February, 1946. He insisted that until the bill's passage, "things will be at a standstill; they are on a dead-center or, perhaps, I can best describe the situation by saying that things are in a state of suspended animation. They [the Filipinos] do not know where to turn or where to go or how to move. . . . Two things need to be done, one which will pay one-half of the damage bill . . . and the other which will define our trade relations for the next 28 years. If we do not do these things we are going to throw away 50 years of work out there. We are going to do what would amount to deserting some of the most loyal friends we ever had.[49]

"There is a broader aspect than that. The whole Far East is watching our experiment in the Philippines. If we do well in the Philippines we will maintain that friendship which has been engendered by our action in the Far East. . . . So I hope that we realize not only our responsibility but also our opportunities in the years that are ahead in the way in which we handle this situation. It is a delicate situation, and it calls for wisdom, and it calls for sympathetic understanding."[50]

Finally, according to a statement of the Philippine Lawyers' Guild, "Through their chief agent and spokesman in these Islands, High Commissioner Paul V. McNutt, American business interests succeeded in railroading the Bell Act through the United States Congress. This law, falsely labeled 'Reciprocal,' is so onerous that if carried into full effect, it will inevitably reduce the Philippine Republic to nothing better than its Jap-puppet predecessor."[51]

On June 15, President Truman nominated McNutt as the first Ambassador to the new Philippine Republic.[52] The United States Senate on June 21 unanimously confirmed the appointment. President Roxas was the first to welcome it. The White House announced, also, that McNutt would represent the United States at the independence ceremonies on July 4.[53] The Indianapolis *Times* editorialized that the appointment of McNutt was excellent, as he was the ideal man to represent our country to the Filipinos, and their country and its needs to the United States.[54]

Finally, on July 4, 1946, the new Philippine Republic was born. Under the terms of the Tydings-McDuffy Act, the President of the United States was authorized by proclamation "to withdraw and surrender all right of possession, supervision, jurisdiction, control, or sovereignty then existing and exercised by the United States in and over the territory and people of the Philippine Islands, including all military and other reservations of the Government of the United States in the Philippines (except such naval reservations and fueling stations as are reserved . . .), and, on behalf of the United States, shall recognize the independence of the Philippine Islands as a separate and self-governing nation and acknowledge the authority and control over the same of the government instituted by the people thereof under the constitution then in force."[55]

This proclamation of President Truman was released to the press by the White House on July 4:

"Whereas the United States of America by the Treaty of Peace with Spain of December 10, 1898, commonly known as The Treaty of Paris, and by the treaty with Spain of November 7, 1900, did acquire sovereignty over the Philippines, and by the convention of January 2, 1930, with Great Britain did delimit the boundary between the Philippine Archipelago and the State of Borneo; and

"Whereas the United States of America has consistently and faithfully during the past forty-eight years exercised jurisdiction and control over the Philippines and its people; and

"Whereas it has been the repeated declaration of the legislative and executive branches of the Government of the United States of America that full independence would be granted the Philippines as soon as the people of the Philippines were prepared to assume this obligation; and

"Whereas the people of the Philippines have clearly demonstrated their capacity for self-government; and

"Whereas the Act of Congress approved March 24, 1934, known as the Philippine Independence Act, directed that, on the 4th Day of July immediately following a ten-year transitional period leading to the independence of the Philippines, the President of the United States of America should by proclamation . . . recognize the independence of the Philippines;

"Now, therefore, I, Harry S Truman, President of the United States of America . . . do proclaim that, in accord with and subject to the reservations provided for in the applicable statutes of the United States,

"The United States of America hereby withdraws and surrenders all rights of possession, supervision, jurisdiction, control, or sovereignty . . . in and over the territory and people of the Philippines; and

"On behalf of the United States of America, I do hereby recognize the independence of the Philippines as a separate and self-governing nation and acknowledge the authority and control over the same of the government instituted by the people thereof, under the constitution now in force."[56]

This proclamation was read at the Luneta in Manila by the retiring High Commissioner (Ambassador-designate) Paul V. McNutt before thousands of assembled Filipino and world leaders from twenty-six countries, including some state officials, senators, and congressmen from the United States, as well as consuls and other foreign representatives, who had gathered together to witness the birth of the new republic. It was an historic occasion, hailed generally throughout the world as a tribute to America's enlightened policies toward dependent peoples. The ceremony was highlighted by the speeches of United States Senator Millard Tydings, who had come from Washington, General Douglas MacArthur, Supreme Commander of the Allied Forces, who had arrived from Tokyo, and High Commissioner Paul V. McNutt. President Truman, in a broadcast to the Philippine people, declared:

"This is a proud day for our two countries. . . . The United States has faith in the ability and in the determination of the Philippine people to solve the problems confronting their country."[57]

President Truman continued:

"The United States . . . will continue to assist the Philippines in every way possible. A formal compact is being dissolved. The compact of faith and understanding between the two peoples can never be dissolved. We recognize the fact and propose to do all within our power to make Philippine independence effective and meaningful. Our two countries will be closely bound together for many years to come. We of the United States feel that we are merely entering into a new partnership with the Philippines—a partnership of two free and sovereign nations working in harmony and understanding. The United States and its partner of the Pacific, the Philippine Republic, have already chartered a pattern of relationships for all the world to study. Together in the future, our two countries must prove the soundness and the wisdom of this great experiment in Pacific democracy."[58]

The President's message was carried on twenty-nine transmitters from the east and west coasts. It was heard in twenty-five countries of South America and Europe, as well as the Philippines, Netherlands East Indies, China, Japan, and India.[59]

Other voices heard included those of Frank Murphy, Associate Justice of the United States Supreme Court and former High Commissioner; Admiral Chester Nimitz; Trygve Lie, Secretary General of the United Nations; Carlos P. Romulo, former Resident Commissioner of the Philippine Commonwealth; General of the Army Dwight D. Eisenhower; and General Jonathan M. Wainwright.[60]

In Manila, President Roxas declared:

"American flags have been lowered from flagstaffs in this land—not in defeat, not in surrender, not by compulsion, but by voluntary act of the Sovereign American Nation. The flag which was first raised in conquest here has been hauled down in even greater glory. The Stars and Stripes will no longer fly over this land but in the hearts of 18,000,000 Filipinos, and in the eyes of many millions more in this part of the world, the American flag flies more triumphantly today than ever before in history."

Roxas concluded by declaring that the Philippines will be "a staging area for democracy in this part of the world."[61]

Ambassador McNutt said:

"In proclaiming the independence of the Philippines, we attach no reservations or exceptions. None is asked. None is needed. There will be proclaimed the full, complete and absolute independence of the Philippines. But those words, themselves, are relative to the new conditions we face in the world today. If by independence we mean non-dependence, there is no nation in the world which is independent today. All nations have yielded some of their independence, of their absolute independence, to the airplane, the radio and the atom bomb. There can be no absolute sovereignty, if by absolute sovereignty we mean freedom of action."

McNutt continued:

"America has a mighty stake in the Philippines. It is not an economic stake in the sense that we have an expectation of economic privilege in this land. As a nation the United States expects no profit from this pitifully devastated area. Our stake is our belief in democracy as a way of life. The Philippines are a democracy in our own pattern and design. We planned it that way. We made it that way. Now the chance is afforded us to set an independent and democratic republic on the high road to national success. Whatever effort is required on the part of the United States must not be spared."[62]

Acting Secretary of State Dean Acheson sent greetings to the people of the Philippines who, he said, had "worked diligently to prepare themselves for independence," and who had "responded eagerly to the efforts of the United States Government to transfer to them the institutions of self-government." Acheson stated that the Filipinos "have displayed a fealty to the principles of democratic government which materially aided them on the road to independence." Acheson warned, however, that "out of independence many new problems will develop for the Philippines." But he claimed the United States "would be falling short of its duty to its sister Republic if we were not to assist the Philippines in every way to meet these new problems." Acheson concluded:

"May there be born out of this new relationship between the American and Filipino peoples a spirit of friendship which will cause the two countries to work harmoniously together in promoting world peace and security."[63]

For some, however, the independence ceremonies seemed a little hollow. To the heartsick and the angry, "the historic day had none of the joy of 1935, nor any of the tense heroism of the second inaugural on Corregidor. It tried to pierce the fog of disbelief and weariness, and it only half succeeded," according to one observer.[64] Another writer commented:

"We gave the Philippines political freedom to enter the world family of nations, but did we give them internal political freedom? More important still, did we grant them economic freedom? Will the people of the Philippines find it necessary to fight for their civil rights, as did our ancestors, in order to give substance to the shell of freedom that we have bestowed?"[65]

July 4, 1946, was a day long to be remembered by the Filipinos and others who participated in the Independence Day ceremonies. Evidences of the havoc wrought by war were to be found everywhere. Manila had been practically destroyed. As far as the eye could see, there was nothing but rubble, destruction, and dust. When General Eisenhower had made an inspection trip there shortly before, he described the city as second only to Warsaw in devastation. Yet the Filipino leaders at that time were determined to keep their promises to the people, and the word "Independencia" was voiced throughout the Islands as the Millenium. So on July 4, independence became a reality, at least in name.

Despite the mood of the moment, it was an historic occasion. A grandstand had been erected on the Luneta, with a cream-and-gold reviewing stand pathetically designed to resemble the prow of a ship of state.[66] Honored dignitaries included Senator Tydings, General and Mrs. Douglas MacArthur, the High Commissioner of the Southeast Asian Territories, who had come from Singapore, and many Filipino officials with their wives, together with the then President of the Philippines, Manuel Roxas. The grandstand was filled with high government officials. Senora Roxas, Mrs. Mac-Arthur, Mrs. McNutt and daughter Louise sat together, all wearing dark glasses, not so much because of the light, but because they felt there might be tears. This wounded country was about to start on its way alone.[67]

When the speeches of praise and encouragement were finished, High Commissioner McNutt and President Roxas stepped forward, one to lower the American flag, and the other to raise the new flag of the Philippines. Both flags were on the same halyard, and as they passed midway, the sun, which had been hidden by clouds throughout the ceremony, shone forth brightly on both banners. It was probably the first time a flag had been brought down with gratitude and blessing as another brave emblem took its place. At that moment the High Commissioner had the privilege of saying "Today a nation is born."[68]

Notes for Chapter 8

[1] Eltinge E. Morrison, *Turmoil and Traditions: A Study of the Life and Times of Henry L. Stimson* (Riverside Press, Cambridge, 1960) XII-686. 549-550.

[2] Euphronic M. Alip, *Political and Cultural History of the Philippines, 1776-1947* (Fifth Revised Edition) Manila, 1947. Vol. II 273 pp. p. 238.

[3] "The Philippines Today" in *Background*, (pamphlet) U. S. Department of State, Office of Public Affairs, Nov., 1951.

[4] Introduction by Harold L. Ickes in Hernando J. Abaya, *Betrayal in the Philippines* (New York, 1946. A. A. Wynn, Inc.) 272 pp. p. 8.

[5] *Ibid.*

[6] David Bernstein, *The Philippine Story* (New York, 1947) XII-276 pp. p. 242.

[7] Press release dated Dec. 19, 1945. No place.

[8] *Ibid.*

[9] *Ibid.*

[10] Press release Dec. 18, 1945.

[11] Walter Wilgus, "Economic Outlook for the Philippines", *Foreign Policy Reports*, Oct. 1, 1945. Vol. XX1 - No. 14, p. 204.

[12] *Ibid.* p. 205.

13 *Ibid.*

14 *Ibid.*

15 *Ibid.*

16 Press release. Dec. 24, 1945.

17 Press release. Dec. 24, 1945.

18 McNutt at one time defended Roxas' activities, and insisted that he had known Roxas intimately, that he was both a gentleman, friend, and definitely not a collaborationist. "After all", said McNutt, "collaboration is a matter of the heart." Quoted in Abaya, p. 9.

19 Speech of McNutt before Congressional Committee on Appropriations, Feb. 28, 1946: U. S. High Commissioner to the Philippine Islands, 76th to 79th Congresses 1940-1946. One volume in National Archives.

20 Donald D. Hoover in Indianapolis *Times,* May 21, 1946.

21 *Ibid.*

22 Abaya, pp. 180-181.

23 Extension of Remarks of Hon. Ernest W. Gibson of Vermont in the U. S. Senate, Friday, Nov. 29, 1940 (legislative day of Tuesday, Nov. 19, 1940). *Appendix* to *Congressional Record,* Dec. 2, 1940. pp. 21236-39.

24 Abaya, p. 252.

25 Bernstein, p. 247.

26 Abraham Chapman, "American Policy in the Philippines" in *Far Eastern Survey,* June 5, 1946. Vol. XV, No. 11, pp. 164-169.

27 *Philippine Chronology, Jan. 1 to July 3, 1946,* by Filemon Poblador, Philippine Liberal Publishing Co., 40 Sta. Mesa, Manila. 155 pp. p. 91.

28 Francis B. Sayre, "Freedom Comes to the Philippines" in *The Atlantic Monthly,* March, 1945, pp. 82-88. Sayre had been High Commissioner from 1939 to 1942.

29 *Ibid.*

30 *Ibid.*

31 *Ibid.*

32 *Ibid.*

33 Chapman, pp. 164-169.

34 Paul V. McNutt, "The Philippines: Asset or Liability" in *The Annals of The American Academy of Political and Social Science,* May, 1941. Vol. 215. Phila., 1941. pp. 94-95.

35 *Ibid.,* pp. 98-99.

36 Chapman, pp. 164-169.

37 George Phillips, *What Price Philippine Independence?* pamphlet, New York, 1946. 32 pp.

38 Poblador, p. 2.

39 *Ibid.,* p. 46.

40 *Ibid.,* p. 99.

41 Chapman, pp. 164-169.

42 *Ibid.*

43 *Ibid.*

44 *Ibid.*

45 Poblador, p. 14.

46 *Ibid.,* p. 48. March 16.

47 See Shirley Jenkins, "Great Expectations in the Philippines", in *Far Eastern Survey,* Vol. XVI, No. 15, August 13, 1947.

48 Quoted in *Ibid.*

49 Speech of McNutt before a Congressional Appropriation Committee, Feb. 28, 1946, found in *U. S. High Commissioner to the Philippine Islands,* 76th to 79th Congresses, 1940-1946. One volume, National Archives.

50 *Ibid.*

51 Jenkins.

52 New York *Times,* June 15, 1946.

53 *Philippine Chronology,* p. 137.

54 Indianapolis *Times,* June 22, 1946. Editorial.

55 Taken from Hayden, *The Philippines: A Study in National Development,* p. 819.

56 "Independence of the Philippines" in *The Department of State Bulletin,* Vol. XV, no. 361, July 14, 1946. p. 66.

57 *The New Republic of the Philippines,* by Edward W. Mill, Department of State Publication 2662, Far Eastern Series 16 (reprinted from the Department of State *Bulletin* of Sept. 15, 1946). Mr. Mill was Acting Assistant Chief of Philippine Affairs, Office of Far Eastern Affairs, Dept. of State.

58 *Ibid.*

59 "Special Radio Program Celebrating Philippine Independence", *Department of State Bulletin,* July 14, 1946.

60 *Ibid.*

61 Mill.

62 Bernstein, p. 250.

63 Statement of Acting Secretary Acheson, *Department of State Bulletin,* July 14, 1946, released to press July 3.

64 Bernstein, p. 249.

65 Abaya, p. 7.

66 *Ibid.*

67 Mrs. Watson to author.

68 Letter from Mrs. Watson to author.

CHAPTER IX

"Giant Among the Peaks"

EPILOGUE

For nearly a year following independence, McNutt continued to render outstanding service as the first Ambassador to the Philippines. The young republic faced problems that seemed almost insurmountable, and it was due largely to his efforts that the new state was able to make progress toward rehabilitation. Chief of these problems were: How dependent should the Islands be on American economic support? What should be done about Filipino puppets of the Japanese? Should reform or repression be the watchword in dealing with the tensions generated by widespread poverty?[1] Free trade brought prosperity to the upper classes, but the rank and file realized little benefit. Francis B. Sayre, former High Commissioner, stated that "the bulk of the newly created income went to the Government, to landlords, and to urban areas, and served but little to ameliorate living conditions among the almost feudal peasantry and tenantry."[2]

Nevertheless, the United States was proud of its policy in the Philippines, and of the contributions which McNutt had made during his tenure there, in spite of some of the limitations imposed on the Filipinos by some of the clauses of the Bell Act and by extensive American military rights. In recognition of his efforts toward bettering Philippine-American relations during this period, McNutt was awarded the Philippine Distinguished Service Star.

On May 8, 1947, McNutt submitted to President Truman his resignation as ambassador to the Philippines. He gave "compelling personal reasons, of which you are aware," as his motive. In the letter he wrote:

"I am profoundly grateful for the opportunity which you have given me to serve our country and the Philippines as the last High Commissioner and as the first Ambassador. I have for the people of the Islands a great affection. I view their future with complete confidence, provided our Government lends the necessary financial support until the Philippine economy will support a proper governmental budget."[3]

President Truman accepted the resignation "with feelings of deep regret and an appreciation of the historic role you have played in connection with the granting of independence to the Philippines, and in the establishment of the new Republic of the Philippines. During your tenure of office you have not only witnessed the establishment of the new Republic, but have participated actively in the formation of the basic agreements now existing between the two countries with regard to trade relations, rehabilitation, military bases and military assistance. Your record of achievement, both as our last High Commissioner, and since your appointment as the first Ambassador to the Philippines, is one of which you can be justly proud. It entitles you to a particularly warm expression of the gratitude of your government. I am happy to know that you will still be available for consultation on matters pertaining to the Philippines. As you return to private life, you carry with you my best wishes for your health and happiness in the years to come."[4]

McNutt finally left the Philippines on March 22, 1947. He was given full military honors at Nichols Field. The Manila *Times,* in an editorial "Good Luck," commented:

"With the departure this morning of U. S. Ambassador Paul V. McNutt, a great personality passes, temporarily it is to be hoped, from the Philippine stage. Mr. McNutt's service in the Philippines has not travelled along a rose-bordered path of verdant lawn. He has had his problems, his conflicts, his share, and more, of criticism. But never, at any stage of that service, whether as the High Commissioner or the first Ambassador, have his sincerity, his singleness of purpose, and his courage ever been in question. . . . He has fought a good fight, and as he departs today the wish is paramount that he may have many more good fights before him."[5]

The Manila *Chronicle* praised the work of McNutt in the Philippines, and quoted from an article in the New York *Times* praising his accomplishments. "He leaves behind him as he relinquishes his post the real and well-merited affection of the Filipinos. . . . He has been a loyal and understanding friend. He leaves with most of the immediate questions of U. S.-Philippines relations settled or well on the way to settlement."[6]

After his retirement from the Philippines post, McNutt never again held a public office. He had been mentioned as a possible candidate for the United States Senate from Indiana, but this did not materialize. Early in 1948 some thought him a possible dark horse for the Presidency. He had established his legal residence in New York, and was expected to be a delegate to the Democratic National Convention in Philadelphia. When the New York reporters asked him if he would take second place on the ticket with Harry S Truman, he replied unequivocally but smilingly, "I've been taught by experience that the President is the one to pick his own running-mate, not the convention."[7]

Meanwhile, McNutt had established a lucrative law practice, with offices in New York, Washington, and other world capitals. But he remained a partner in his father's old law firm of McNutt, Hurt and Blue in Martinsville, Indiana, and his name was kept on the door of the Indianapolis Circle Tower law office of John E. Hurt, as counsel.[8] He was also engaged in world-wide business ventures, and was a consultant or trustee in many enterprises.[9]

Such strenuous activities over such a long period of time were destined to take their toll with even so vigorous a person as Paul V. McNutt. For several months, he was afflicted with a critical throat ailment which sapped his strength. In October, 1954, he underwent an operation in a New York hospital, and for a time he appeared to be convalescing satisfactorily. In order to speed his complete recovery, he and Mrs. McNutt left early the next year on a world cruise aboard the liner *Kungsholm*. As they approached the Philippines early in March, McNutt's condition grew worse, and they left the ship at Manila and flew to San Francisco, then by military transport to New York, where he died in his apartment on March 24, 1955.[10]

Tributes to McNutt were sent to his bereaved family from all over the world. They praised his honesty and integrity, his bold and forthright action in the dark days of the depression, and his great influence on state and national affairs.[11] He was called a "straight-shooter" by the press, which also commended him for his humor and sympathetic understanding.[12] He gained and kept the respect of newsmen. He never cried "misquote" when politically unfriendly articles appeared, nor did he ever display personal pique against his detractors. No reporter was barred from his conferences.[13] He was characterized as "a true gentlemen, first, last, and always."[14] One editorial said he was "not only a thinker; he was a leader of men,"[15] while another said, "Indiana can be proud that it sired this honored son."[16] References were made to McNutt's high accomplishment at home and abroad.[17] He was called "One of the most gifted men ever born in Indiana."[18] He was considered a true friend,[19] and "one of the great public servants of our time."[20] Other tributes conveyed similar sentiments.[21]

McNutt was buried in Arlington National Cemetery on March 28, on the side of a shaded hill in front of the home once occupied by General Robert E. Lee. Nearby was the grave of William Gibbs McAdoo. The funeral service in the small chapel at Fort Myer, adjacent to the cemetery, was attended by nearly two hundred persons coming from all walks of life to pay their last respects. Among them was General Carlos Romulo, a top figure for years in the Philippine Government, as well as a long-time personal friend of the McNutt family. Mrs. Perle Mesta, former ambassador to Luxembourg, was there. Supreme Court Justice Sherman Minton of Indiana was present; he and McNutt had been strong political allies and close personal friends for many years. Indiana's two Republican senators, Homer E. Capehart and William E. Jenner put aside their political allegiance and joined in paying their respects. Four Indiana congressmen, Winfield Denton of Evansville, Ray Madden of Gary, William G. Bray of Martinsville, and Charles B. Brownson of Indianapolis, also attended the rites. Others included Frank McHale, Frank McKinney, and former Indiana governor Henry F. Schricker, all political colleagues of McNutt.[22]

The brief service was characterized by military pomp, solemnity, and precision. The flag-draped bronze casket was borne on a black caisson drawn by six white horses. While the organ played softly, a uniformed chapel attendant lighted fourteen tapers in the sanctuary, and the stately beat of drums sounded outside. There was then the shouted order and the clatter of rifles as the blue-coated ceremonial honor guard of the historic Third Infantry Regiment Band played "Abide with Me." The casket was carried into the church where the Reverend William F. Adams, past department commander of the District of Columbia American Legion escorted the casket to the altar. Seaborn P. Collins, national commander of the American Legion, read the traditional funeral ritual of the organization. Dr. Herman B Wells, president of Indiana University, spoke briefly at the grave. The band played "Nearer My God to Thee," three volleys were fired, and taps was sounded. The flag draping the casket was given to Mrs. McNutt.

In his brief eulogy, President Wells said:

"After I received the sad news which is the occasion of our gathering today, I stood and looked for a time from my window out on the old central quadrangle of the campus where Paul McNutt achieved distinction as a student, professor, and dean. Through the ancient trees I could see Maxwell Hall where he began his teaching career and won the proud rank of professor which he dearly prized. Though separated from the campus by distance and decades, he never relinquished his position but remained Professor of Law at Indiana University, on leave of absence for service to the state, the nation, and the world.

"Viewed against the background of his early years, the vast panorama of his career can be seen in all of its dramatic outline, replete with struggle, triumph, and unselfish devotion to public duty. He has not left his power without witness, 'but has shown it by mighty proofs.' Even the listing of his achievements is impossible in the time allotted to me. Instead I shall mention two qualities which were dominant in his personality and character.

"The first is integrity. To this I can bear personal testimony. It was once my duty to present to him two possible courses of action in dealing with an important problem of government regulation. One was in the broad public interest, the other unquestionably served better his immediate personal and political fortunes. The proposed measure was technical, understood only by the specialists, but would establish a precedent of such importance that the opposition was willing to pay any price for its defeat. We met alone, only he and I to know the nature of his decision. As soon as he comprehended the significance of the issue, without a moment's hesitation he chose the course beneficial to the public. The measure was enacted in Indiana for the first time in any state. One by one other states followed and now it has been adopted by the entire nation. In Milton's phrase, he met the temptations of the day 'Godlike erect, with native honor clad.'

"The second quality I would mention is courage. He spoke often of the importance of courage in meeting life's problems. In his inaugural as Governor of Indiana during the dark days of 1933 when our society was in danger of disintegration, he said, 'It is possible to know the truth without fear, to meet a crisis with indomitable courage.'

"The poet sings,

> 'Courage—an independent spark from
> Heaven's bright throne,
>
> By which the soul stands raised;
> Triumphant, high, alone.'

"Throughout his life, clad in the armor of integrity, he was fearless in meeting his responsibilities.

"The great central range of the Colorado Rockies contains several important mountains—Cheyenne, Mount Almagre, Mount Arthur, and others. But dominating the scene on a clear day, four thousand feet higher than any of these, its snow-capped dome touching the blue of the skies, rises Pike's Peak.

"Some mountains, thrust higher in the beginning, formed of hard granite which resists the erosion of wind and snow, continue to loom above the others throughout the centuries.

"As it is with mountains, so it is with men. Some dominate

their scene even though they walk with giants. Such a man was Paul Vories McNutt.

"Born with a generous endowment of intellectual and physical strength, he eagerly bore more than his share of the day's work. Years of heavy burdens did not wear away his stature, and so today his life looms large upon our horizon, its high peak of achievement a source of lasting inspiration.

"Devoted husband and father, brilliant scholar, dedicated public servant, loyal friend, unforgettable leader of men, we hold him in grateful and affectionate memory."[23]

Notes for Chapter 9

[1] Lawrence K. Rosinger, "The Philippines - Problems of Independence" in *Foreign Policy Reports,* March 15, 1948 (New York, 1948). Vol. XXIV, No. 1, p. 82.

[2] Francis B. Sayre, "Freedom Comes to the Philippines," *Atlantic Monthly,* March, 1945. Quoted in *Ibid.*

[3] Letter to President Truman, May 8, 1947.

[4] Letter to McNutt from President Truman, May 22, 1947.

[5] Editorial in Manila *Times,* March 22, 1947.

[6] Editorial in Manila *Chronicle,* March 27, 1947.

[7] Quoted by Daniel M. Kidney in Indianapolis *Times,* March 28, 1948.

[8] *Ibid.* Also see Indianapolis *News,* March 25, 1955.

[9] *Ibid.,* New York *Times,* Nov. 16, 1948. See also Wayne Oliver in Indianapolis *Star,* July 30, 1950.

[10] Martinsville, Indiana, *Daily Reporter,* March 24, 1955. From Miss Louise McNutt's Scrapbook.

[11] Paul Feltus in Bloomington *Star-Courier,* March 24, 1955.

[12] Harold Feightner in Indianapolis *News,* March 24, 1955.

[13] *Ibid.*

[14] Mickey McCarty in Indianapolis *News,* March 24, 1955.

[15] Editorial in Indianapolis *News,* March 24, 1955.

[16] Editorial in Indianapolis *Star,* March 25, 1955.

[17] Editorial in Indianapolis *Times,* March 25, 1955.

[18] Fort Wayne, Indiana, *Journal Gazette,* March 25, 1955.

[19] Editorial in New York *Times,* March 25, 1955.

[20] *The Times,* London, March 25, 1955.

[21] Resolutions, found in McNutt Collection, Lilly Library: Board of Directors of the American International Assurance Co., Ltd. Hong Kong, March 26, 1955. Confederation of Filipino Veterans, Manila, April 12, 1955. American Legion, Department of the Philippines, Manila, April 16, 1955. Association of Life Insurance Counsel, Greenbriar, White Sulpher Springs. Annual Meeting of Members of United Service to China, Inc., held at China House, 125 East 65th Street, New York City, December 6, 1955. Mrs. Watson's Scrapbook.

[22] Indianapolis *News,* March 27, 1955. Miss McNutt's Scrapbook.

[23] *Ibid.*

March 12, 1947

Dear Governor:

We have been personal friends for many years.
I have long admired you as a public servant and as
a man. Your sterling qualities have been an inspiration to me. I know that we will continue to be
as long as both of us are on the scene, no matter
what position either of us may be holding.

As you leave the Philippines to retire, as you
say, from public life, it is difficult for me to
separate my personal feelings from my official regret
at your departure. As President of the Philippines,
I am deeply grieved that so great an Ambassador of
your country, who has so brilliantly served us, too,
should leave us.

I need not dwell on your historic contributions
to Philippine-American relations, nor even to the
success of the Philippine Republic. History will, I
am certain, assess those services at a premium. I
have no doubt that your name will stand at the highest
level among the great Americans who have served here.

I did not wish in this letter to write as the
President of the Philippines, but rather as your friend,
Manuel Roxas. The friendship we have shared during
the recent difficult days has made achievement a
challenge and accomplishment a joy. I have always
known that I could count on your sound and wise counsel
in our problems as one always can with a true friend.

When you were High Commissioner, you were more
than a representative of the sovereign power; during
your tenure as Ambassador you were much more than the
embodiment of the friendship of the United States.
You were also an ally and a colleague, working with me
toward the same ends -- the enduring freedom and welfare
of the Filipino people.

You and Mrs. McNutt and Louise have continued
and will always continue to occupy a dear and intimate
place in the hearts of my family.

This is not goodbye. We look forward to many
many years of continued intimacy and friendship wherever
our paths may lead us. I hope you will find the occasion
to come back with your family to visit us and to see the
fruits of your work here. We will meet again and often,
I hope. Whatever happens, our personal association will
endure.

With the affectionate regards of Mrs. Roxas and
myself and best wishes for your continued success in
whatever endeavors you undertake,

Very cordially,

Manuel Roxas

His Excellency Paul V. McNutt
United States Ambassador to the Philippines
M a n i l a

ACKNOWLEDGMENTS

Grateful acknowledgment is made to the publishers and individuals whose names are listed in the Bibliography, for permission to reprint material which is in copyright or of which they are the authorized publishers.

Extensive use was made of the Paul V. McNutt Collection in the Lilly Library at Indiana University. Mrs. Roy Garrett Watson kindly granted permission to use these papers. This Collection contains many letters and other materials, including extensive newspaper clippings. Mr. Robert R. McClarren, Director of the Indiana State Library, has made the large collection of newspaper files of the Library available. Special appreciation is also given to the National Archives in Washington, the New York Public Library, the Library of Congress, and the Franklin D. Roosevelt Library at Hyde Park, New York, for the use of their holdings.

No attempt has been made to list all the newspaper references. Credit is given for such sources in the footnotes.

BIBLIOGRAPHY

Printed Books

Abaya, Hernando, *Betrayal in the Philippines*, published by A. A Wyn, Inc., New York, New York, 1946

Alip, Euphonio Mills, *Political and Cultural History of the Philippines* (1762-1947), Alip and Sons, Inc., 1869 Azcarraga Street, Manila, P. I. Fifth Edition Revised, 1947

Barck, Oscar Theodore and Blake, Nelson, Manfred, *Since 1900*, Third Edition, Macmillan, 1949

Barnhart, John D. and Carmony, Donald F., *Indiana From Frontier to Industrial Commonwealth*, Lewis Publishing Company, Inc., New York, 1954. Two volumes.

Bernstein, David, *The Philippine Story*, Farrar, Strauss, New York, 1947

Byrnes, James Francis, *All in a Lifetime*, Harper and Row, New York, 1958

Farley, James A., *Jim Farley's Story, The Roosevelt Years*, New York, McGraw-Hill, 1948

Flynn, Edward Joseph, *You're the Boss*, Macmillan, New York, 1947

Flynn, John Thomas, *The Roosevelt Myth*, Devin-Adair, New York, 1948

Hayden, Joseph Ralston, *The Philippines: A Study in National Development*, Macmillan, New York, 1942

Morison, Eltinge Elmore, *Turmoil and Tradition: A Study of the Life and Times of Henry L. Stimson*, Houghton Mifflin, New York and Cambridge, 1960

Perkins, Frances, *The Roosevelt I Knew*, Doubleday, The Viking Press, Inc., New York, 1946

Poblador, Filemon, *Philippine Chronology, January 1 to July 3, 1946*, Philippine Liberal Publishing Co., Manila, P. I.

Rodriguez, Eulogio Balan, ed., *President Quezon, His Biographical Sketch*, '40 Pubs., Inc., 30 Dewey Blvd., Manila, P. I., 1940

Roosevelt, Eleanor, *This I Remember*, Harper & Row, New York, 1947

Sherwood, Robert Emmet, *Roosevelt and Hopkins: An Interpretation*, Harper and Row, New York, 1950

Stimson, Henry L. and Bundy, McGeorge, *On Active Service in Peace and War*, Harper and Row, New York, 1948

Timmons, Bascom N., *Garner of Texas: An Intimate History*, Harper and Row, New York, 1948

Periodicals

Alexander, Jack, "It Would Be Kind of Nice to Be President, Wouldn't It?" *Life*, Jan. 29, 1940

Chapman, Abraham, "American Policy in the Philippines," *Far Eastern Survey*, June 5, 1946

Friend, Joseph H., "Watch Paul McNutt," *Nation*, July 23, 1938

Jenkins, Shirley, "Great Expectations in the Philippines," *Far Eastern Survey*, Aug. 13, 1947

Johnston, Alva, "I Intend to be President," *Saturday Evening Post*, March 16, 1940

McNutt, Paul V., "The Philippines: Asset or Liability?" in *The Annals of the American Academy of Political and Social Science*, May, 1941

Pringle, Henry, "McNutt is Willing," *The Forum*, June, 1940

Rosinger, Lawrence K., "The Philippines—Problems of Independence" in *Foreign Policy Reports*, March 15, 1948

Sayre, Francis B., "Freedom Comes to the Philippines," *The Atlantic Monthly*, March, 1945

Wilgus, Walter, "Economic Outlook for the Philippines," *Foreign Policy Reports*, Oct. 1, 1945

Pamphlets

Harper, Fowler V., "The WMC Tackles the Manpower Problem" in *Industrial Manpower Controls*, 1942. Personnel Series Nos. 60 and 64, American Management Association, New York City

"Independence of the Philippines" *Department of State Bulletin* No. 367, July 19, 1946

BIBLIOGRAPHY

McNutt, Paul V., "Citizens of Tomorrow: A Wartime Challenge to Community Action," Nov., 1943. National Archives

----- "Health Agencies—Their Responsibilities and Their Opportunities During the Present Crisis." Reprint No. 2376 from the *Public Health Reports*, Washington, 1942

----- "Special Problems in Our Health Defenses" in *Public Health Reports*, May 9, 1941

Mill, Eward W., "The New Republic of the Philippines:," *Department of State Publication 2662*, Far Eastern Series 116, Sept. 15, 1946

Phillips, George, "What Price Philippine Independence?" New York, 1946

"The Philippines Today," U. S. Department of State, Office of Public Affairs, Nov., 1951, in *Background.*

INDEX

[389]